Harvard Business School

Research Colloquium

Contributors

Mary Lou Balbaky

Michael Beer

Paul R. Lawrence

George C. Lodge

Janice McCormick

D. Quinn Mills

Calvin Pava

Jeffrey A. Sonnenfeld

Bert Spector

Richard E. Walton

Shoshana Zuboff

Human
Resource
Management

HRM

Trends &
Challenges

Edited by
Richard E. Walton and
Paul R. Lawrence

HARVARD BUSINESS SCHOOL PRESS
BOSTON, MASSACHUSETTS

Harvard Business School Press, Boston 02163
Printed in the United States of America.

89 88 87 86 85   5 4 3 2 1

ISBN 0-87584-170-8

Library of Congress Cataloging in Publication Data
Main entry under title:
HRM, trends and challenges.

A collection of papers presented at the Human
Resource Futures Colloquium, 1984, sponsored by the
Harvard Business School.
Includes index.
1. Personnel management—Congresses. I. Walton,
Richard E.   II. Lawrence, Paul R.   III. Human Resource
Futures Colloquium (1984: Harvard Business School)
IV. Harvard University. Graduate School of Business
Administration.
HF5549.H66   1985   658.3   85-8485
ISBN 0-87584-170-8

Contents

Foreword

Founded in 1908, the Harvard University Graduate School of Business Administration celebrated its seventy-fifth anniversary in the academic year 1983–84. We chose to take this opportunity to involve our faculty in thinking seriously about the challenges and opportunities ahead in important fields of management research and teaching.

Field-based empirical research, within and across organizations, has always been fundamental to Harvard Business School's ability to meet its objectives of educating business managers and helping to improve the practice of management. In some respects, we are creating a distinctive model of research. We have often broken through the bounds of traditional disciplines and methodologies to borrow whatever tools and concepts were needed for a particular inquiry. In addition, we have been less concerned with testing existing theory than with generating new insights. And while we often find ourselves drawn to problems that are broad in scope, we strive for results that are operationally significant to managers.

Because Harvard Business School faculty members are committed to pursuing research on the way business actually *does* function, as well as theoretical explorations of how it perhaps *should* function, they can give students and practitioners a vital perspective on the real world of professional practice. Their continuing close contact with operating businesses keeps Harvard Business School faculty at the frontiers of management practice. Research conducted by the faculty often yields insights that are of considerable practical benefit to managers in both day-to-day operations and longer-range planning.

In sponsoring the colloquium series of 1983–84, we hoped to set the course for research development over the next decade, and in particular to encourage greater emphasis on multiperson, multiyear studies of major issues. The complexity of many issues confronting business today almost requires that academicians find more effective forms of collaboration in doing our research. The problems we study are often beyond the capacity of any individual researcher.

In addition to encouraging a reshaping of researcher's work habits, the conferences promised to help strengthen the ties between Harvard Business School and the outside academic and business leadership communities. The series comprised sixteen conferences held at the Harvard Business School campus, each lasting two to five days. Papers were presented by eighty members of the HBS faculty and an approximately equal number of practitioners and academics from other institutions. Altogether, some 450 academics and practitioners were involved as discussants and participants.

Some of these colloquia focused on current research topics, such as U.S. competitiveness in the world economy, productivity and technology, global competition, and world food policy. Others concentrated on establishing agendas for the coming decade's research and course development in a particular field. Clearly, these were not tasks to be attempted in isolation. Rather we wanted to work jointly with others in business, government, and the academic world who could contribute and would themselves gain from the undertaking. The papers presented in this volume have all benefited from the thoughtful discussion they received at the colloquium.

Beyond exploring research findings in particular areas, we hoped that these colloquia would sustain and enliven the continuing dialogue between students and practitioners of management. From that melding of perspectives, we have found, insights emerge that can revitalize the education of future managers and refine current professional practice. In that spirit of cooperative endeavor, I am proud to introduce this collection of essays.

John H. McArthur
Dean of the Faculty
Harvard Business School

Preface

How will human resources be organized and managed in United States businesses in the future? What dilemmas of policy and practice will management encounter? What steps can managers take to transform their human resource strategies? These are the broad questions addressed in the essays contained in this book.

The book is based on the research of a dozen faculty members of Harvard Business School and on the experiences of two dozen senior executives of companies with a record of leadership in human resource management. The Harvard faculty and business executives met in May 1984 to discuss the future of human resource management. That colloquium, entitled Human Resource Futures, celebrated the Harvard Business School's 75th anniversary; its activities are partially recorded in this volume.

In selecting the participants we applied criteria both for the type of company to be included and for the type of executive to participate. We sought companies that either had outstanding track records in managing human resources or were in the midst of a concerted effort to transform their human resource strategies. Even more important, we identified the top-level executives in these companies who were either the engineers of change or the architects of change, or both. We were successful in recruiting participants who met our criteria. In other respects, they were diverse; representing the high-tech and smokestack industries, manufacturing and service sectors, and growth and nongrowth companies. Nine of these companies were large U.S. corporations, and three were medium-sized. (See the Appendix for a list of participants and their companies.)

The faculty members had prepared preliminary versions of the papers included in this book. Summaries of these papers were distributed to participants as background reading. Articles by participating companies on some of their human resource practices were also distributed. The colloquium itself emphasized small-group exchanges about the direct experiences and observations of the participants. The key issues were identified and discussed in small groups and in plenary sessions. These discussions were wide-ranging, not confined to the topics addressed in the faculty papers, but they did offer insight into how the experiences of the participating executives related to the ideas of the faculty members.

The faculty submitted final versions of their papers after the colloquium. Thus, individual chapters take into account the colloquium discussion as well as prior research. In addition, a final integrative chapter in the book reviews the discussions by colloquium participants.

The book and the colloquium can best be understood as a part of a long-term effort to ensure that the Harvard Business School faculty provides leadership in human resource management. For decades, until the early 1970s, one could argue that the faculty at Harvard and behavioral scientists at many other schools espoused ideas about the management of people that were more advanced than those reflected in business practice. Harvard's pioneering Hawthorn Studies about the dysfunctional consequences of certain aspects of organizational structures, systems, and styles are illustrative. While some managers intuitively approached their tasks in ways that fully reflected what we in academia believed we knew about management and human motivation, they remained exceptions.

Relatively suddenly in the late 1960s and during the 1970s more and more managers began to innovate in the way they organized and managed work. Greenfield plants became the site of bold experiments that essentially turned conventional thinking on its head. The principles that guided the design of those new organizations were often the converse of those that had evolved in practice over the previous five decades. For example, the practice of progressive subdivision of labor was replaced by the idea of whole tasks; the fixation on individual accountability was replaced by a vision of collective accountability; the reliance on formal controls was subordinated to the development of shared goals, peer pressure, and self-control.

The striking success of many of these experiments eventually led to policies that called for corporatewide change in style, structures, and systems. Advanced practice had caught up with, and in many respects had surpassed, what we were teaching in professional schools of business about human resource management. American managers were no longer skeptical and resistant to the idea that they should change the way they managed the human side of enterprise. They were getting on with it.

In our executive programs and in our meetings with alumni, the administrators and the faculty of the school began to receive a strong message—give more priority to human resource management in your curriculum and play a more strategic role in improving practice in this area. In response, in 1980 the School introduced an entirely new course, Human Resource Management, into the first-year required MBA curriculum. Because this was in addition to the full course in Organization Behavior, the resulting curriculum committed 50 percent more time to the people-management courses than to any other general subject. A concerted development effort to produce teaching cases and notes has now brought our course offerings generally to the leading edge of practice, and in a few topical areas, beyond it.

In 1984 the time had come for us to take a second step, to make a determined effort to look down the road and try to identify a constructive approach to the future of human resource management and how to maange our way to that future. The colloquium has served that purpose. It has provided a way for us to assess the practice of leading companies and probe in depth the thinking of those who are committed to keeping these companies moving. It has stimulated current faculty research and pointed the way toward future research. It has given all the participants a vision of a possible human resource future. This volume is committed to sharing these benefits with a wider audience.

Acknowledgments

As editors of this volume, we have some conspicuous obligations to others. The authors of the various chapters have taken our editorial comments in grand spirit and have more than done their part in completing the book.

The executives who participated in the Human Resource Futures Colloquium in May 1984 gave generously of their time, ideas, and experience.

Two research assistants were very effective in their roles of helping to arrange for the colloquium: Jane Hodgetts, during the initial planning phase, and Cynthia Ingols, during the execution phase.

Our two secretaries, Betti Tiner and Rita Perloff, were great in handling the multitudes of specific items that are involved in such projects.

The Division of Research of the Harvard Business School has not only funded this endeavor but assisted the effort at all stages. We are especially grateful for the steady support of the director, E. Raymond Corey.

Richard E. Walton
Paul R. Lawrence

Human
Resource
Management
HRM Trends &
Challenges

Introduction

1
The Future of Human Resource Management: An Overview

Richard E. Walton

In the past ten years managers have reevaluated their approach to the management of human resources. We believe this reexamination and the changes it produces will continue to be management priorities throughout the next decade.

This chapter sets forth some broad hypotheses about the trends under way, identifies some areas in which the policy patterns are not yet fully apparent, and analyzes some factors critical to the effective management of change. It thus presents an integrative preview of the separate contributions to this volume.

THE GENERAL HYPOTHESIS: PROFOUND CHANGE TOWARD MUTUALITY

Today we are in the midst of a pattern of profound change in the way we think about and manage human resources in business. This change includes activities that have been given many names—quality of work life, employee involvement, sociotechnical systems, innovative work structures, and participative management. We believe the transformation occurring in human resource management (HRM) is broader than signaled by any of these terms. Each of the contributing authors has his or her own preferred term for talking about this emerging new pattern. For example, George C. Lodge has identified the essence of the future pattern as *consensualism*. I have coined

3

the term *high-commitment work system* and have proposed that high commitment is the essential ingredient in the future pattern of HRM. In discussions among us about this volume and at the colloquium, we collectively arrived at mutuality as the most dominant theme of the future policies that we envision. Hence, the hypothesis we set out to examine broadly is as follows: Senior managers in pace-setting firms in a wide assortment of industries have recently begun to revise their HRM policies to promote mutuality in the relations between managers and the managed, and between employees and employers. This trend will continue in the future and be manifest in all HRM policy areas, including employee influence mechanisms and labor relations (employee voice); compensation and benefit schemes (rewards); job design, work procedures, and management organization (work organization); and selection, development, and employment security (human resource flows).

Taken together, Chapter 2 (by Paul R. Lawrence) and Chapter 3 (by Richard E. Walton) set forth this hypothesis and the arguments and evidence supporting it. Lawrence establishes that there is such a thing as a coherent HRM system. He traces the evolution of human resource management through a succession of different HRM systems, each of which achieved dominance for a period of time until it was rendered obsolete, or at least partly obsolete, by changing economic, technical, and social forces.

The craft system, which featured the master, journeyman, and apprentice, gave way to the market system, which utilized unskilled laborers who were paid no more and who were given no more deference than current labor market conditions required. The next HRM pattern to emerge, the technical system, brought professional techniques to stabilize and systematize the work organization, pay scheme, employment practice, and management of adversarial labor relations. Then a new system developed in the new electronics industries, even while the technical system persisted in traditional industries. It is the career system, which features career ladders, long-term employment, and strong employee loyalty. The most recent development, the commitment system, is both a reaction to the technical system and an elaboration of the career system.

Lawrence develops the hypothesis that the policies of the market system manifested extremely little mutuality and that in each successive HRM system there was an increased ratio of mutuality to adversarialism. According to Lawrence, the emerging commitment system will bring us full circle in this respect— back to the high mutuality that existed earlier in the simple relationship between master, journeyman, and apprentice.

Walton's paper begins where Lawrence's ends—with the hypothesis that a new HRM strategy is emerging today. He reviews the dimensions of the emerging model, the commitment model, so called because it is consciously designed to elicit employee commitment. Its elements are a revised set of policies, each shaped to promote greater mutuality.

Reviewing current trends in practice, Walton finds that under the commitment strategy, jobs are defined more broadly, management is leaner and more flexible, ambitious and dynamic performance expectations replace minimum work standards, compensation systems place more emphasis on learning and collaboration, employees exercise more voice, union-management relations involve more joint problem solving and planning, and employment assurance becomes a high-priority policy issue.

STRATEGIC POLICY QUESTIONS

The broad direction of change can be discerned, as well as its implications in certain policy areas, such as broader job designs and increased employee participation. However, in a number of policy areas, the new patterns have not yet taken shape. Two such policy issues—employment assurance and economic sharing—are treated in a number of chapters.

Management is becoming convinced that employment assurance will promote commitment, but what level of assurance is feasible, given the economic uncertainties and advances in labor-saving technology? What forms should this assurance take? Lifetime employment for some categories of employees? Assurance regarding the steps that will be taken first in order to avoid or minimize layoffs? Assistance in out placement, and other steps that cushion the impact of redundancies?

Economic sharing is of increasing interest to managers who are trying to emphasize mutuality and promote high commitment. Profit sharing at the company level or gain sharing at the facility level are mechanisms for sharing both economic gains and sacrifices. More important, they can create a sense of equity. Whether or not a substantial trend develops toward economic sharing will depend on whether early efforts along these lines actually succeed in stimulating ideas and energy and in promoting a sense of equity. And success in that respect depends on how economic sharing schemes are managed symbolically and on whether or not other compensation issues reinforce or negate a sense of equity. For example, invidious comparisons between compensation for executives and pay at the shop-floor level can undermine other pay policies intended to promote a sense of equity.

The above policy issues—employment assurance and economic sharing—are being given considerable attention by management, labor unions, and academics. But in certain other policy areas like work technology and new patterns of union-management relations, the public discussion to date has been less developed. These two policy areas are the subject of Chapters 4 to 8.

Calvin Pava reviews the current and future applications of the microchip and provides an analytical framework for tracing the emergence of a new toolstock. According to Pava, an understanding of the potential impact of these new tools on the HRM system begins with recognition that microchips will make our tools more flexible, self-regulating, interconnected, and pervasive.

The introduction of these new tools "unfreezes" a number of constraints that have shaped existing HRM systems. Pava shows how the technology makes possible alternatives to the hierarchical structure; how it renders much less relevant the proximity of members in terms of space or time; and how the distinction between home and workplace can be blurred. These and many other factors are unfrozen, but managers must comprehend this opportunity in order to seize upon it and design the work organization and other HRM policies in line with its philosophy. Pava notes, for example, that technology can be configured to support mutuality in the form of team-based organization and self-supervision.

Whereas Pava reviews a broad array of implications of the new computer-based technology, Shoshana Zuboff analyzes in depth the implications of this technology for the nature of work and the experience of workers. Zuboff reports on an ethnographic study of three paper plants that employ advanced information technology. Her conclusions also draw upon her research and observations in other settings. Computer-based technology changes required work skills from hands-on to intellectual ones. These changes must be regarded as profound when viewed in a historical perspective, and they are experienced psychologically as significant by those whose prior work was based on traditional craft skills. A major policy question will be whether managers will choose to train people for the new technology by emphasizing active intellectual skills like hypothesis formulation and problem solving rather than routine operating skills. If they do, the new technology can lead to a blurring of the traditional divisive distinctions between workers and managers. The opposite possibility also exists, a point emphasized by Zuboff.

Janice McCormick analyzes the structure, processes, and outcome of collective bargaining in recent decades in the auto, steel, coal, and trucking industries. She identifies the dominant labor relations quid pro quo as one in which management gave priority to preserving its prerogatives but was willing to agree to relatively generous wage and benefit settlements. New sources of competition have made it impossible for the industries to continue this traditional pattern. In fact, wage concessions became a new pattern in three of these industries in the early 1980s. But these concessions, she concludes, do not begin to close the labor cost gap that would be one way to make the companies in these industries strong and jobs secure.

A structural pattern in three of these industries—national bargaining—promoted the earlier quid pro quo. She views adherence to national bargaining as an impediment to realistic concessionary bargaining. Such problem-oriented bargaining can best be tailored to economic realities and work-force priorities when it takes place at a local level.

McCormick concludes by examining the alternatives to national bargaining and by calling for the parties to develop a new quid pro quo, one that better serves the interests of all stakeholders in today's economic and social environment. She calls for a new concept of mutuality—one that will require cultural change affecting the parties and their relationships.

How prepared is the union to enter into the types of mutual relationships envisioned by McCormick? Bert Spector discusses recent trends toward mutuality. He analyzes the attributes of a trade union (contrasting them with those of a business organization), which act to limit movement toward the new pattern. What, for example, is the implication of the democratic political nature of trade unions for the management of change? He cites a number of ways it acts to inhibit union leaders from taking initiatives that they might regard as being in the interest of the institution and the membership. This has consequences for how rapidly we might expect a pattern of mutuality to develop or how widespread it will become in U.S. industrial relations.

The final chapter in this section, by Richard E. Walton, builds on the discussion of the preceding chapters. Walton sketches out what union-management mutuality might look like if it were pursued in one particular substantive area—new work technology. Like Pava and Zuboff, he foresees advanced information technology as working either in concert with or at cross-purposes with an HRM philosophy that seeks commitment. Walton shows how adversarial bargaining has led to patterns of introducing technology that are disadvantageous for workers and for management. The positive potential from joint problem solving and planning in this area, however, will not be achieved without a raised consciousness of the possibilities, more general institutional patterns of trust between union and management, and new methods for the development of work technology. Moreover, the movement from institutional adversarialism to mutuality in this area is not without risks for both parties.

MANAGING CHANGE IN HUMAN RESOURCE PRACTICES

What are we learning about the effective management of the change toward greater mutuality? Chapters 9 to 13 discuss this subject.

Michael Beer's and Bert Spector's in-depth study of several companies committed to human resource change found that these companies engaged in a comprehensive overhaul of policies. Change was not confined to a single policy area, such as compensation, employment security, work design, or employee participation. It involved all these and others. Wherever the review starts, it eventually leads to revision of other human resource policies as well. Some aspects of this change task are inherent in the nature of change itself. Because the change includes many policy areas, and because it involves revamping structures, processes, skills, and attitudes, it is complicated, requires time, and depends upon strong leadership.

Beer and Spector acknowledge the resistance and friction associated with change that requires altering basic attitudes, beliefs, and skills. They note that some inconsistency in management's behavior will always crop up during periods of radical change, and they explore the implications of these inconsistencies. They also analyze some techniques commonly employed in the change process—temporary structures and roles, education and training, succession planning, pilot projects and team-building, and statements of philosophy.

The chapter by D. Quinn Mills and Mary Lou Balbaky complements the in-depth studies of Beer and Spector. Mills and Balbaky surveyed executives in 224 large firms, mostly senior line executives, about their companies' HRM policies and practices. They found a noticeable fraction of firms taking HRM issues seriously and inferred that many of these companies are giving HRM matters increasing attention. Their study does point up, however, that American companies vary widely in accepting and applying current HRM ideas. The authors of other chapters have indicated that the types of progressive companies they cite are still a relatively small minority, and the Mills-Balbaky survey makes this point also.

Mills and Balbaky report in detail on the extent to which the companies surveyed engaged in planning in the HRM area. They identified five stages of HR planning, ranging from no planning, to HR planning separate from the long-range business plan, to HR plans integrated into the business plan. They analyze which characteristics correlate with the level of sophistication in planning, for instance, level of activity in trying to influence employee performance.

The Mills-Balbaky data also indicate the strength of current managerial interest in changing their own companies' cultures, the prevalence of formal programs to build morale, and the nature of managerial beliefs about the relationship of HRM to profits.

Training and education play an important role in the change process. Jeffrey A. Sonnenfeld identifies a broad set of questions about training and education. Business enterprises are already in the education and training business in a big way, and the prospects are for even greater investments. Shifts in product market, needed improvement in production processes, new regulatory changes, and new technology require adaptations that call for new knowledge and skills. These are in addition to the educational demands associated with revised HRM policies in terms of broader job design, increased participative decision making, and greater employment security. Sonnenfeld's analysis is highly critical of most efforts to provide the necessary education for business—both in-house efforts and academic programs. He concludes with some suggestions for ensuring that these activities are linked to the business strategy and to HRM philosophy and are managed effectively.

In Chapter 12, George C. Lodge takes as a point of departure that human resource policies and practices are changing—as Beer and Spector and Mills and Balbaky had reported. Even when these are planned and systematically implemented, Lodge asks, "Are these new policies understood in terms of their ideological implications?" He argues that the new policies reported in this volume imply a radically new ideology, emphasizing, for instance, communitarianism versus individualism. These ideological implications often have not yet been understood, leading in practice to ambivalence and inadvertence on the part of managers and union officials.

The final chapter, by Paul Lawrence, reports on the proceedings of the colloquium held in May 1984 at the Harvard Business School, sponsored by the School and organized by its HRM faculty. The participating executives, who represented twelve diverse companies, were most candid in sharing experiences and opinions with the faculty. A surprise for all was the amount of agreement among these practitioners on the nature of the HRM change, its importance, and its future prospects. This report from the front-line agents of HRM change provides an appropriate closure to this future-oriented volume.

Part One:
The General Hypothesis

2

The History of Human Resource Management in American Industry

Paul R. Lawrence

The management of human resources in American industry, responding to powerful external and internal forces, is in a state of significant change. For example, transformations in industrial tooling that result from the continuing development of the microprocessor are perceptibly affecting the deployment of personnel throughout industry. From the outside, intense international competition has exerted strong pressure on American labor rates, productivity levels, innovation, and product quality. Internally, a better-educated work force is bringing new values and expectations of increased involvement to the job. Among the responses to these forces have been newly broadened agendas for collective bargaining and new organizational arrangements aimed at increasing the flexibility and efficiency of factory and office production procedures. I believe that a review of the history of human resource management (HRM) in the United States can help us understand the future implications of these current developments and trends, and help us to evaluate possible pitfalls and opportunities.

Although traditionally relations between the managers and the managed in American industry have been adversarial, a solid foothold already exists for swinging the balance toward a mutuality of interests. A mutuality of interests in the size of the productive pie and adversarial interests in the distribution of the productive proceeds seem inevitable in the relationship between labor and management. History demonstrates that either

15

the mutual or the adversarial aspect of the employment relationship can be dominant. Which aspect is to be dominant at this critical stage in American industrial history? W. E. Deming, the quality engineer who has made such important contributions to Japan's industrial success, observes, "Eighty-five percent of the problem of low productivity in American business is a management problem, a problem of how to motivate employees."

As I have gone over the available literature, I have found no generally acknowledged framework for describing the development of HRM in the United States. However, there is evidence to suggest a useful chronology of five general HRM systems that for convenience can be called the craft, market, technical, career, and commitment systems.[1] Each system grew from specific technical, social, and economic preconditions, and each had certain human and economic consequences. If we examine the different ways in which each of these systems dealt with four basic HRM policy areas, we will be better able to appreciate the dynamics of past swings between adversarial and mutual relations and see the value of these historical facts in planning for the future. The four policy areas we will examine are ones that every organization must establish in one form or another: (1) work organization—the matching of people to assigned activities and decision responsibilities; (2) rewards—both the intrinsic rewards of recognition and the extrinsic monetary rewards; (3) flows—the policies and procedures for recruitment, training, promotion, discharge, and retirement; and (4) employee voice—policies providing for employee influence on their immediate work setting and on broader corporate affairs. *Table 2-1* summarizes this information.

THE CRAFT HRM SYSTEM

Americans' general familiarity with the lives of Ben Franklin and Paul Revere has probably given us all an anecdotal understanding of the craft system of human resource management, but rarely do we realize that it was the system that dominated American industrial life for nearly 200 years—up to the 1820s. The institutional context for much of the thinking that led to

Table 2-1
Summary of American HRM Systems

Policy Areas	Craft (dominant until 1820)	Market (dominant until WW I)	Technical (dominant until WW II)	Career (currently dominant)	Commitment (emerging)
Work organization	Master/journeyman/apprentice work team	Unskilled machine operators organized into work gangs by the foreman	Fine division of unskilled labor with machine pacing	Grouping of individual positions under a supervisor	Semi-autonomous work groups
Rewards	Rates set by individual contracts based on time	Pay by work performance (piece rate)	Hourly pay based on job evaluation	Salaries with multiple levels; raises by merit and seniority	Base salary with gain sharing

(continued)

Table 2-1 (continued)

Policy Areas	Craft (dominant until 1820)	Market (dominant until WW I)	Technical (dominant until WW II)	Career (currently dominant)	Commitment (emerging)
Flows	Multiyear mobility from apprentice to journeyman to master: lifetime system	In and out at open market rates; high turnover	Semi-long-term employment; layoff by seniority; exempt career barrier	Long-term employment; career-oriented; up through the ranks	Near lifetime employment; slow promotion; lateral and vertical movement
Employee voice	Direct consultation in traditional relations with power balance	Boss-worker direct relations; power unbalanced	Collective bargaining through union	Individual appeal system	Multilevel consultations with employee representatives
Balance of emphasis on adversarial and mutual interests	Mutual interests / Adversarial	Mutual interests / Adversarial	Mutual interests / Adversarial	Mutual interests / Adversarial	Mutual interests / Adversarial

the Declaration of Independence and the Constitution was, in fact, based on the philosophy and practices of the craft system; even today that system has implications for the industrial scene.

The production of industrial goods and services in colonial America was carried on for the most part in small workshops organized to supply, on a custom-order basis, the basic needs of the local market. The shop owner was typically a master craftsman—shoemaker, cabinetmaker, whatever—who was helped by a few apprentices and often a few journeymen, usually one or two of each. The roles of master and helpers were well understood and legitimated by tradition and law. When apprentices joined a given trade, they could reasonably expect to spend their lifetimes in it, hoping always to move from apprentice to journeyman to master, the customary career flow. The work was carried out in these small shops by a single team that shared the entire task, directed by the master. A master's right to dismiss journeymen and apprentices (the control, that is, of flows) was restricted by tradition and law. Tradition and law also governed the rewards of both apprentices and journeymen, for their contractual agreements with their master spelled out not only mutual rights and obligations but also wage rates. Disputes were usually handled directly in the shop, although a case could, of course, be taken to court. The "benevolent and protective" societies of the colonial period were associations of both journeymen and masters, the beginnings, as it were, of craft and trade unions. On rare occasions, "combinations" of journeymen expressed their employee voice by using the strike or the slowdown as a bargaining tool.

In response to the growth of cities and to technological advances, larger shops appeared in the colonial period. There one might find as many as twenty-five employees, with the work carried out by several teams, each under the leadership of a journeyman. The technology involved consisted almost entirely of hand tools and simple human-powered machines.

The craft system of human resource management was central to the early development of American industry. While evidence is limited, historians generally agree that the system, protected by law and community sanctions, was essentially harmonious. Skilled labor was relatively scarce. The exploitation of apprentices was rare. Wage rates for journeymen, while market-sensitive, were steadied by tradition and usually permitted a relatively good living standard. Turnover was low, and layoffs and strikes were infrequent. The long-term mutuality of interests that masters, journeymen, and apprentices perceived in their shared undertaking took precedence over the adversarial pulls of their relationship. The system provided a well-institutionalized balance of power between employer and employees. In the 1820s, however, this craft system quite quickly lost its dominance on the American industrial scene, and currently the system is used only in a limited number of small enterprises.

TRANSITION FROM CRAFT TO MARKET HRM SYSTEM

The eventual change from the craft system to the market system of human resource management was triggered largely by two developments. The first, the improvement of transportation and communication facilities, made possible the expeditious movement of manufactured goods from cities to outlying towns and from city to city. This expanded the competitive domain of many industries from local to regional. The second factor had an ironic twist. In the interest of their journeymen, masters tried to stabilize employment in slack times by producing goods to be inventoried for what we would now call retail or ready-made sales. In fact, the eventual sale of these goods in lots to independent merchants was the beginning of the wholesale trade. Since the master craftsmen were actually not equipped to handle the additional tasks associated with carrying large inventories—shipping between cities, extending credit, and predicting demand—the opportunity now arose for already established merchant-capitalists, particularly from shipping and real estate, to adapt their expertise in capital and market management to the realm of manufacturing. After 1800 these new merchant-capitalists began placing large orders with the owners of the workshops. The owners gradually became dependent on the wholesale orders, thereby giving the merchant-capitalists the power to press for lower prices, and by 1830 the latter dominated the industrial economy. With the new pressures, the employment relationship in the workshops changed dramatically as the craft system evolved into the market system of human resource management, which was to dominate American industry for nearly a century. Even today it characterizes the employment relationship for up to one-third of all employees in the United States.

The pressure on workshop owners for lower prices forced them to look for ways to cut labor costs. Early in the century the demand for both apprentices and journeymen had usually exceeded the supply. Immigration was low, and any surplus of workers had traditionally been quickly absorbed as frontier farm labor. The picture changed as immigration to the United States began its spectacular rise in the nineteenth century. Labor was no longer in short supply. Now, in order to survive, the hard-pressed workshop owner could—and did—change tactics. In Rayback's words, "They hired unskilled labor, women, and children; they pitted skilled against unskilled, increased exertion, and reduced wages."[2] These practices were frequent during prosperous times and overwhelmingly common during the many economic crises of the nineteenth century. In the early 1800s the first permanent unions, organized along craft lines by shoemakers, printers, cabinetmakers, carpenters, coopers, and tailors, were formed. Collective bargaining began, with strikes, picketing, and boycotting coming into use as bargaining tools. Employers fought back with lockouts, blacklists, strikebreakers, and even trade associations intended specifically to hold down wages and break up the labor combinations.

The effects of the depression and boom that had followed the War of 1812 became the prototypes for the effects that economic swings were to have on employment relationships. In 1819–20 unionization plummeted as large numbers of workers were laid off; only the shoemakers' union is known to have survived. As the economy strengthened during the 1820s, unions appeared in an ever-increasing number of crafts; strikes were frequent. In the resulting adversarial climate the unions turned to state legislatures for limited support, while employers turned more effectively to the courts in the so-called conspiracy cases. In the pivotal 1827 case brought against the tailors' union in Philadelphia the court ruled that although the tailors had the right to organize to raise wages, they did not have the right to use picketing, circulation of scab lists, and sympathy strikes to try to enforce their demands.[3] Union activity was slowed as a consequence of the conspiracy trials and was soon further jeopardized by the depression of 1828–31; few unions that had been active in the 1820s managed to survive. This cycle was to repeat itself again and again over the next century. With labor becoming more like a commodity responding to short-term fluctuations in supply and demand, an ongoing fight for survival developed, and employers and employees alternately took offensive and defensive postures. As early as the 1820s both sides had chosen their basic weaponry; only the scale and sophistication of the weapons were to change.

CHARACTERISTICS OF THE MARKET HRM SYSTEM

As the new market system became established, both skilled and unskilled labor were increasingly considered as variable costs, with hiring and firing a response to economic fluctuations. This flow system created a very high turnover rate. Without strong unions or legal recourse, each worker had to settle, as best he or she could, any disputes directly with their foreman. There were virtually no checks on the arbitrary power of the foreman to discharge a worker at will. Employee voice became but a whisper. As time passed, the team of crafts people working with the master gave way to a gang of unskilled workers working for the foreman or "pusher." This shift in work organization came with the change from small workshops to large factories, from hand tools to powered machines, and from craft jobs to highly specialized jobs with less skill content. The reward system essentially tied wages to the free market value of the work performed, as determined by comparing outside contracting prices with inside piece rates. These rates were subject to considerable variation based on the availability of replacement labor.

As the nineteenth century unfolded, the balance of power swung to the employers. The waves of immigration, which employers fostered, provided an ample labor surplus as limits were reached on the number of people the frontier could absorb.

Chronic unemployment then strengthened the employers' position. Even when the need arose for employers to seek help from the government and the courts, the ideology of the times favored them. Notwithstanding the workers' electoral advantage, the rationale of John Locke and Adam Smith, later reinforced by social Darwinism, effectively supported the status quo.

Intense conflict was pervasive throughout this period. Strikes went hand in hand with every major change in the economy, whether the shift was up or down. These sporadic public conflicts were paralleled on the factory floor by continuous covert conflicts between workers and foremen over working conditions and rates of output. To strengthen their position, workers tried to band together informally at work and occasionally to unionize formally. In fact, only among skilled craftspeople were unions able to survive, and even their numbers shrank until at the turn of the century only 6 percent of the labor force was unionized. During the last two decades of the nineteenth century the Knights of Labor made their unsuccessful bid to unionize all workers regardless of skill. The two great strikes toward the end of the century were lost by the unions at Carnegie Steel and at Pullman. After these defeats the workers' cause hit an all-time low. An intense adversarial relationship between labor and management prevailed, even though some employers were relatively generous to their workers, including, in fact, both Carnegie and Pullman. Investigators of the underlying reasons for the Pullman strike were surprised to learn that personal harassment by authoritarian and arbitrary foremen was cited as a complaint as often as wages and hours.[4]

Much was accomplished under the market system of human resource management in terms of creating industrial plant and infrastructure. The industry that was the pacesetter of the market system was textiles, and in our southern mills the system is still largely in place. It may come as a surprise to Americans to learn that a very similar market HRM system was introduced in Japan's pacesetting textile industry in the late nineteenth century, with very similar strengths and weaknesses. In both countries it was a highly productive system, central to bringing about the big decisive shift from an agrarian to an industrial society. No one can argue, however, that there was equity in the distribution of the resulting wealth. The cost of the market system, in terms of human suffering and conflict, was high.

TRANSITION TO THE TECHNICAL HRM SYSTEM

Although the HRM system that replaced the market system in America was basically technical, it began, in fact, in an attempt to address the problems of escalating conflict and hardship among the workers. During the wave of strikes in coal and steel at the turn of the century, certain writers, the "muckrakers," drew national attention to the appalling working conditions in both industries. Anxiety in the Establishment ran high over the ever-increasing strength of the Socialist party and the rapid rise of the Wobblies, the radical International Workers of the World. Violence became more frequent and more severe. A boatload of IWW supporters, for example, traveling from Seattle to Everett, Washington, in 1916 to support a lumber strike were met at the dock by armed vigilantes who opened fire. Thirty-six Wobblies and twenty-one vigilantes were killed or seriously injured.[5] The pendulum had clearly swung too far; key leaders in both labor and industry knew that some solution would have to be found. The establishment, in 1900, of the National Civic Federation was an important early step in this collaborative search. Money for expenses was supplied by J. P. Morgan, and William Gompers, the head of the American Federation of Labor joined industrial leaders like Mark Hanna in trying to settle their disputes around a conference table.[6]

Coincidental with this changing social climate were important technological and economic changes that contributed to pushing the new technical HRM system into place. A new wave of improvements in transportation (the intercontinental network for railroads and later trucks) and communications (the intercity telephone) made it possible for competition in many industries to expand from regional to national. The development of the electric motor allowed new factory layouts. Frederick Taylor's fresh ideas on how to use technical advances to increase productivity gave added impetus.

These various forces and ideas for change did not coalesce

into an actual system of human resource management until about 1914, when Henry Ford finally got his assembly line working well in his big Dearborn plant. Ford's genius was to combine a fine division of labor with the automatic pacing of the assembly line and high wages—his famous five dollars a day. Before this innovation the labor turnover at Ford had exceeded 400 percent per year and had hit 48 percent in the single month of December 1912.[7] With Ford's new approach to labor, turnover and unit costs dropped, volume increased, and profits soared. Widespread imitation of Ford came quickly. The technical HRM system had been established.

THE TECHNICAL HRM SYSTEM

The key feature of the technical system—its dependence on a fine division of labor and machine pacing—affected every aspect of a firm's management of labor: work organization, rewards, flows, and eventually employee voice. The foreman no longer needed to be a pusher; that role was built into the moving components of the machine (work organization). Once pace was determined, pay could be set at an hourly rate, so that employers could avoid piece-rate disputes and could even afford to be generous with workers who accepted the discipline of machine pacing. Improved wages reduced turnover, and the remaining turnover was less costly, since the fine division of labor permitted workers to acquire quickly the necessary knowledge and dexterity. As business fluctuated, employees were still laid off, primarily on the basis of foreman preference. Workers became relatively interchangeable. Jobs were essentially dead-end in terms of promotion. No feature of the developing technical system specifically addressed the problem of providing voice for employees. As we shall see, it was not until the mid-1930s, with the spread of industrial unions and collective bargaining, that that need was met.

At the end of World War I the unions launched a concerted drive to organize labor in the steel, automobile, rubber, machinery, chemical, and electrical industries—the leaders in adopting the technical HRM system. To fight the unions' efforts, management pushed the open-shop argument and publicized the "Red Scare" until eventually, often backed by state militia, they successfully blocked the drive to unionization. In the 1920s, for the first time in a century, an economic boom did not trigger an increase in union membership; in fact, in the decade following World War I, membership declined from 20 percent to 10 percent of all employees. The drive to unionization was further thwarted by the major effort of many employers to institute what went under the banner of "welfare capitalism." Most leading firms undertook extensive programs to improve the lot of both blue- and white-collar workers. Pride of place no longer went to the educational and recreational programs and the model company towns that had marked earlier attempts at reform. Company policies now included accident compensation, medical insurance, pension plans, stock purchases, profit sharing, and the beginnings of unemployment insurance. Sophisticated personnel departments were organized to develop and administer these plans. Although by contemporary standards the plans were limited, it is not surprising that the unions lost ground: management was offering significant rewards for labor not to organize.

In addition to sponsoring intraindustry programs, a large number of firms voluntarily adopted in the postwar years the employee representation plans, or company unions, that had been sponsored by the government during World War I. By the end of the 1920s, 1.5 million workers were covered. John D. Rockefeller, Jr., was a pacesetter for the movement. Workers in AT&T and its Western Electric subsidiary and in Rockefeller-owned mines were all covered. By the end of the decade Charles Schwab, the veteran head of Bethlehem Steel, declared, "Our primary job is to make steel, but it is being done under a system that must be justified. If this system does not enable men to live on an increasingly higher plane, if it does not allow them to fulfill other desires and reasonable wants, then it is natural that the system itself should fail."[8] Schwab, in fact, saw Bethlehem's employee representation plan as "an unobstructed channel in which unity of interest may be promoted."[9]

Schwab was not alone in his optimistic and philanthropic views. The economist Herbert Feis noted that many business leaders were foreseeing a future of "concord and plenty." Their optimistic view, Feis reported, was based "chiefly on the expectation of cooperation between workers and management. This cooperation is to show itself in the recognition of the workers' needs and desires."[10] Because these expectations were so widely held by both workers and management, the Great Depression proved particularly disillusioning and embittering. Often forgotten are the valiant, though futile, efforts that leading companies made in the first two years of the Depression to maintain wage levels and avoid layoffs. By October 1931, however, even the steel companies, faced with the ever-worsening economy, could no longer avoid cutting wages. As Schwab finally admitted, "None of us can escape the inexorable law of the balance sheet."[11] At the bottom of the Depression, one-third of the entire American labor force was unemployed. Vivid memories of the suffering and anger of those days fueled the drive that the CIO began at the first faint sign of economic recovery in the mid-1930s. All the major industries were quickly organized, and collective bargaining through independent unions became the established vehicle for expressing the employee voice in the technical system for managing human resources.

From the perspective of the 1980s, we can see that the technical HRM system had, from the first, two main strengths but, as time went by, three serious weaknesses. Its chief strength was making possible the production of large volumes of standardized goods at a low cost. In addition, even though adversarial relations with employers still predominated, the technical system reduced the level of conflict from the extremes of the market system. The institution of collective bargaining not only lowered the incidence of wasteful conflict but provided a more equitable distribution of wealth than had the market system.

The weaknesses in human resource management that are now so apparent in our smokestack industries took longer to show up. The technical system has many built-in rigidities that make it difficult to track changing market demands for more particularized and higher-quality products. As time has gone on, workers have come to question the attractiveness of bargaining high pay for boring jobs with no future. Furthermore, near-collusive industry-wide settlements frequently escalated labor costs, so that industries became extremely vulnerable to foreign competition. Finally, the resources and time consumed by continuing shop-floor disputes are no longer tolerable. Even though approximately one-third of the work force in the United States is still managed by some variation of the technical HRM system, this system has steadily waned as the career system has become dominant.

THE CAREER HRM SYSTEM

The career HRM system began in the fast-growing electronics industry because of a desire on the part of management to avoid unionization and to meet special needs for flexibility. The forces that led to its widespread use were, however, more basic. The career system was established in the post–World War II period, when American industry rapidly expanded into international markets. The technologies of jet airplanes, satellite communications, and computers facilitated the process. The resulting growth opened up unprecedented opportunities for career advancement in all American firms. These opportunities meshed with the career expectations of the increasing percentage of the work force with at least some college education. The bulk of the new jobs were of a white-collar or semiprofessional nature. Just as Ford and the auto industry were the pacesetters for the technical system, IBM and the computer industry took the lead in establishing the career system.

The hallmark of the career system is its flow policies. People are recruited for positions that are spelled out with explicit, detailed attention to duties and rights. Every position is linked to a career ladder, so that every worker has the opportunity for some upward mobility. Thus, the firm is in effect offering an employee not just a job but a career as well. Longer-term employment is encouraged, and layoffs are used only as a last resort. If layoffs are necessary, both seniority and merit are commonly taken into account in some orderly fashion.

Employees under the career system are typically on salary. A continuum of salary grades and subgrades is used, with explicit provisions for raises on the basis of both merit and seniority. Except for organizations in the public sector, employees are usually nonunion, but every worker's right to air individual grievances is nonetheless protected. All employees have the right to a second or even a third hearing on their own situation or in other company matters. Work is not organized in any distinctive way under the career system, but most commonly there are loosely structured groups of technically related positions, each group under a supervisor.

The career HRM system is notable for its capacity to create a single homogeneous work culture throughout a firm, thus avoiding the barrier between exempt and nonexempt employees that traditionally characterized the technical system. Adversarialism and its associated costs have been reduced. Flexibility has been increased. From the viewpoint of both the firm and the career-oriented employee needing flexibility, the career system is more advantageous than the technical system.

Major problems have not yet appeared in the career system of human resource management, but two related issues begin to cloud the horizon. The recent severe recession forced many firms organized in this way to lay off many professional and technical employees as well as blue-collar and clerical workers. Has this unusual situation created a vulnerability to unionization at a later time? The possibility seems real, since the typical mechanisms in this system for employee voice make no provision for collective representation. Employees are now aware that they have a joint stake in the rules by which layoffs are carried out and in some means of influencing this vital process. The continuing pressure of foreign competition, especially Japanese, on certain American industries raises another question: Does the career system, for all its advantages, sufficiently engage the minds and energies of all employees in the challenge of maintaining a position of international competitive leadership? To put it baldly, Is the American career HRM system good enough to beat the Japanese in the race for superiority in innovation and efficiency? A growing awareness of these questions about the career system as well as the widely acknowledged weaknesses in the still prevalent technical system are fueling a wave of experimentation with a fifth approach to human resource management. Using a concept introduced by Richard Walton, we can tentatively call the new approach the commitment system. This system will be explored in subsequent chapters and is outlined briefly here only to put it into its historical context.

EMERGENCE OF THE COMMITMENT HRM SYSTEM

The new approach draws upon a variety of experiences: earlier programs in American industry centering on job enlargement and enrichment; the British experience with sociotechnical planning; the quality-of-work-life approach; the Scanlon Plan and other gain-sharing programs; the European experience with work councils; and the Japanese model for human resource management, which makes use of enterprise unions, quality circles, and lifetime employment policies. The American firms now experimenting with the commitment approach include ones that are struggling with the inadequacies of the technical system: for example, General Motors, Ford, Cummins, Goodyear, Dana, Alcoa, and TRW. There are also firms conducting such experiments that have a strong history with the career system: Hewlett-Packard, Texas Instruments, Digital Equipment, Procter & Gamble, IBM, Exxon, and AT&T. Even service firms that still use a modern version of the market system with part-time employees, McDonald's for instance, are involving themselves in the new experiments. Clearly, any attempts to identify a definitive pattern in this new form of human resource management must be tentative. However, at this stage in its development, I see the commitment system's work organization and its arrangement for the expression of employee voice as pivotal to the emerging pattern.

New employee representation methods are being tested in joint union-management multilevel consultations at GM and Ford. A somewhat similar approach is being tried by AT&T with the Communication Workers of America. In their non-union plants Polaroid and Cummins are learning from multilevel consultation. But we must look overseas to see the most fully developed voice arrangements as a key part of the commitment system. It is ironic that the United States and its allies, perhaps as a war reparations penalty, forced Japanese and German industries after the war to adopt multilevel employee representation schemes. In Japan, without many unions, they forced the creation of independent, enterprise-bounded unions in large organizations. In Germany they mandated multilevel consultation primarily with existing unions. When I teach in Harvard's international management program, I find it still always comes as a shock to participant managers from the United States, Great Britain, and France to hear their German and Japanese counterparts calmly agree that they could not imagine running their businesses effectively without the help of shop-level joint consultations. It is no coincidence that our strongest foreign competition comes from those countries where workers are well-known for their high level of commitment and involvement in the tasks of their enterprises. Japan's very low strike rate is even surpassed by Germany's. It is primarily on this evidence that I anticipate the emerging commitment system will, in all likelihood, contain some form of an extensive multilevel, broad-agenda employee representation scheme. Only some such scheme will be able to handle the intensive information exchange that is essential to sustain the necessary level of mutual understanding and trust.

The second distinctive element in the evolving commitment system is its prototypical work organization, the semiautonomous work group. Japan, without using this term, has of course made extensive use of this work organization. In Germany its use is less extensive, but the nation's traditional master-apprentice (craft) system creates somewhat similar work groups in many industries. The use of these groups is being tried out in a growing number of American firms in many industries, using many technologies, in all parts of the country. There is more experimentation to be done to achieve high performance consistently, but even now most of the new arrangements are clearly outperforming the methods they are replacing. As we get further along the learning curve, our capacity to employ them successfully in a variety of different circumstances should improve.

The flow policies in the commitment system are evolving, and their eventual form is more difficult to anticipate. There are some strong reasons, given our continuing experience with recessions and structural unemployment, for management to be wary of its ability to deliver on lifetime employment promises.

Yet some form of job security may well be essential to achieve the level of mutuality and involvement that competitive challenges call for. We will probably see a slower promotion process and more lateral moves, as in Japan. It will be a "one-culture" system that deemphasizes the symbolic distinctions between levels of the hierarchy and eliminates the nonexempt/exempt barrier to upward mobility.

The type of rewards that will be associated with the commitment system are also still subject to a good deal of experimentation. A number of American firms that are moving toward the commitment system are postponing revisions of their reward system until after they have made more progress in the other policy areas. This seems to be a viable strategy as long as managers recognize that change in reward arrangements must eventually be addressed. If the commitment system delivers on its anticipated improvement in efficiency and innovation, some form of gain sharing must eventually be undertaken to sustain the essential sense of equity.

It is, of course, too early to make any definitive and balanced assessment of the commitment system of human resource management. However, I believe it is emerging as a distinct system with all of the interrelated elements of policy we saw in its four predecessors on the American scene. Whether it will become the dominant system is hard to say. There are powerful economic, technical, and social forces working to push it forward. On the other hand, it is hard to leave familiar methods and adopt new ways of thinking and doing. Many American managers have grave concerns about the commitment system. Will the many varieties of American workers respond to the challenge of involvement? I, for one, saw reason twenty years ago to doubt that urbanized workers with a deeply entrenched blue-collar family tradition could or would respond.[12] More recent evidence to the contrary has changed my mind, but the question still remains for many thoughtful people. Another concern is how to handle job security given the commendable concern for avoiding promises that may not be possible to honor. Finally, there are concerns in the voice area. Will the necessary consultations consume too much time and money? Will they result in bad decisions regarding the long-range health of the enterprise? Will they diminish the power of managers and thereby make their jobs less attractive? Will American managers, given the culture, be able to work effectively in the commitment system? Can we successfully retrain managers accustomed to other systems, and at what cost? Furthermore, does the commitment system work to best advantage only under a limited set of market and technical conditions? If so, what are they? Is it viable to use the commitment system in one part of a diversified business when other HRM systems are used in other parts, or must a business choose to go across the board to make it really work? These are all very important and legitimate questions that will be addressed in later chapters.

CONCLUSION

Our review of the five HRM systems will help set the stage for addressing the many critical questions arising in this time of rapid change. We have seen that American industry has functioned under some distinctively different HRM systems. We have seen that economic, technical, and social conditions drove the change from one dominant system to the next. Economic and technical forces combined in opening up an expanded arena for competition that pushed managers to search for a more effective HRM system. Industry moved to the market system as competition shifted from local to regional, and toward the technical system as competition primarily became national. The move of American firms into overseas markets, and now the wave of foreign competition into the United States, has served to fuel the transition to the career and the commitment systems.

Meanwhile, the forces of immigration and higher education were the key social elements in bringing about HRM change. We have seen that, while the adversarial issues around the equities of wealth distribution and work loads have tended to dominate the employment relationship, this is not inevitable. Mutual interests in better performance dominated in the early craft system and do so currently in the career system. The prospect is that mutuality will be even more prominent in the commitment system. In this regard, one important observation can be made: It seems that mutual interests are more likely to dominate the management-employee relationship when there exists some well understood, institutionalized method for resolving the inevitable adversarial aspects of employment—a method that embodies a reasonable balance of power between employee and institutional representatives.

We have also seen that each new system has historically emerged without totally displacing the earlier ones. There are still large numbers of people working under the market and technical systems. History indicates that newer systems, even if they come to dominate the employment scene, do not by any means totally displace earlier systems. It seems true, however, that firms that led the way into each new system, such as Ford and IBM, did experience a significant competitive advantage.

3

Toward a Strategy of Eliciting Employee Commitment Based on Policies of Mutuality

Richard E. Walton

A broad consensus has emerged that U.S. managers generally have come to rely upon poor models for managing their work forces and to expect and accept much less from workers than is potentially available. Managers have failed to motivate the workers and to use and develop their latent capacities.[1] In the case of organized labor, U.S. trade unions must share with management the responsibility for failing to achieve a partnership that will serve the interests of all stakeholders in the enterprise.

American managers have themselves been in the forefront of the critics, recognizing that their management solutions were not working. They have also led in developing alternatives. Journalists have helped raise our consciousness of the deficiencies, and academics have helped shape new approaches. But the search for a new work-force management model has been carried on in large part by managers themselves, sometimes joined by trade union officials.

This chapter builds directly on the historical analysis by Paul Lawrence in Chapter 2, which traced a succession of HRM systems. We both call the emerging HRM system a *commitment model*. Its elements are all attuned to eliciting commitment. I will call the most prevalent approach that is being replaced the

This chapter is adapted from a paper presented to an earlier colloquium at the Harvard Business School, Colloquium on Technology and Productivity, March 27–29, 1984.

35

control model, because the common denominator among the systems being replaced, especially the market and technical systems, is the emphasis on imposing control.

The control and the commitment models are radically different from each other in conception and operation. The strategy of eliciting employee commitment requires that management overhaul a large number of human resource policy areas. The common theme in the revision of these policies is increased mutuality between workers and managers and between employees and employers. Thus, the new management strategy involves policies that promote mutuality in order to elicit employee commitment, which in turn can generate increased economic effectiveness and human development.

THE EMERGING HRM MODEL AND THE ONE IT REPLACES

Recognizing that the new model is still evolving, we can nevertheless sketch its broad outlines. We will describe illustrative applications and contrast the characteristics of the emerging model with those of the prevailing one. Finally, we will identify a transitional model. *Table 3-1* summarizes the features of the traditional control model, the new commitment model, and a transitional model.

ILLUSTRATIVE DEVELOPMENTS

The most dramatic evidence of U.S. management's interest in developing new HRM models appeared in the new plants built during the 1970s. These included the plants of General Foods at Topeka, Kansas; General Motors at Brookhaven, Mississippi; Cummins Engine at Jamestown, New York; and Procter & Gamble at Lima, Ohio. The following description of one of these plants illustrates the innovative greenfield plants started up during the 1970s and early 1980s:

> The work force of the new plant is organized into teams responsible for segments of the work flow. They are delegated many self-supervisory responsibilities. They make internal work assignments, make production trade-off decisions, diagnose and

Table 3-1
Work-Force Management Models

Policy Areas	Traditional Control Model	Transitional Model	New Commitment Model
Job design principles	Individual attention limited to performing individual job	Scope of individual responsibility extended to upgrading system performance via participative problem-solving groups in QWL, EI, and quality-circle programs.	Individual responsibility extended to upgrading system performance
	Job design deskills and fragments work and separates doing and thinking	No change in traditional job design or accountability	Job design enhances content of work, emphasizes whole task, and combines doing and thinking
	Accountability focused on individual		Frequent use of teams as basic accountable unit
	Fixed job definition		Flexible definition of duties, contingent on changing conditions
Performance expectations	Measured standards define minimum performance. Stability seen as desirable		Emphasis placed on higher, "stretch objectives," which tend to be dynamic and oriented to the marketplace

(continued)

Table 3-1 (*continued*)

Policy Areas	Traditional Control Model	Transitional Model	New Commitment Model
Management organization: structure, systems, and style	Structure tends to be layered, with top-down controls	No basic changes in approaches to structure, control, or authority	Flat organization structure with mutual influence systems
	Coordination and control rely on rules and procedures		Coordination and control based more on shared goals, values, and traditions
	More emphasis on prerogatives and positional authority		Management emphasis on problem solving and relevant information and expertise
	Status symbols distributed to reinforce hierarchy	A few visible symbols change	Minimum status differentials to deemphasize inherent hierarchy
Compensation policies	Variable pay where feasible to provide individual incentive	Typically no basic changes in compensation concepts	Variable rewards to create equity and to reinforce group achievements: gain sharing, profit sharing
	Individual pay geared to job evaluation		Individual pay linked to skills, mastery
	In-downturn, cuts concentrated on hourly payroll	Equality of sacrifice among employee groups	Equality of sacrifice

(*continued*)

Table 3-1 (*continued*)

Policy Areas	Traditional Control Model	Transitional Model	New Commitment Model
Employment assurance	Employees regarded as variable costs	Assurance that participation will not result in loss of job Extra effort to avoid layoffs	Assurance that participation will not result in job loss High commitment to avoid or assist in reemployment Priority for training and retaining existing work force
Employee voice policies	Employee input allowed on relatively narrow agenda. Attendant risks emphasized. Methods include open door policy, attitude surveys, grievance procedures, and collective bargaining in some organizations Business information distributed on strictly defined "need-to-know" basis	Addition of limited ad hoc consultation mechanisms. No change in corporate governance Additional sharing of information	Employee participation encouraged on wide range of issues. Attendant benefits emphasized. New concepts of corporate governance Business data shared widely

(continued)

Table 3-1 (*continued*)

Policy Areas	Traditional Control Model	Transitional Model	New Commitment Model
Labor-management relations	Adversarial labor relations. Emphasis on interest conflict	Thawing of adversarial attitudes. Joint sponsorship of QWL or EI. Emphasis on common fate	Mutuality in labor relations. Joint planning and problem solving on expanded agenda Unions, management, and workers redefine their respective roles
Management philosophy	Management's philosophy emphasizes management prerogatives and obligations to shareowners	Ad hoc shifts in stated priorities	Management's philosophy acknowledges multiple stakeholders—owners, employees, customers, and public

solve production problems, and select personnel replacements to their team. Support functions such as quality control and maintenance are integrated into team responsibilities. Team members are paid for acquisition of additional skills, not for doing a particular job. Common parking lots and cafeterias and other symbols deemphasize status. Employees do not punch the time clock. Supervisors are expected to be facilitative, exercising progressively less direction and control as team capacities develop. Employees exercise voice over a wide range of conditions that affect them. Finally, and critically important, the organization is characterized by very high expectations about task performance and about people treatment.[2]

During the early 1970s new plants with this kind of design were all nonunion. By the end of the decade similar designs were developed jointly by General Motors and the United Auto Workers. A leading example is the Cadillac plant in Livonia, Michigan.

Sometimes inspired by the achievement of these new plants and sometimes driven by a breakdown in functioning in their own plants, managers of existing facilities also began to revise their approach to managing. The dramatic turnaround of General Motors' assembly plant in Tarrytown, New York, stimulated other union-management efforts in this spirit. The typical pattern of these efforts is as follows:

Local management and local union officials enter into a dialogue about the nature of their common interests and the barriers to communication and problem solving. When the parties have passed a threshold of mutual trust, they agree to jointly sponsor quality of work life (QWL) or employee-involvement (EI) activities. They establish a joint structure to guide these activities, which typically involve workers in joint problem solving of production and people difficulties that arise in their work areas. Training in participative problem solving for workers, supervisors, and union officials supports the change. Often the training is conducted by trainers drawn from both union and management ranks. Worker participation is voluntary. Assurances are given that production improvement will not result in layoffs. Often individuals or labor-management centers serve as joint consultants to the companies and unions in facilitating this process.[3]

These joint ventures typically have been initiated and sustained by efforts of local managers and union officials. One major exception is the joint effort between the Communications Workers of America (CWA) and American Telephone and Telegraph Company (AT&T) to promote QWL throughout the Bell System, which has been led by CWA President Glenn Watts and AT&T Vice President Rex Reed. Another exception is the UAW-Ford employee involvement program, which was launched and energized centrally by Don Ephlin of the UAW and Pete Pestillo of Ford. The earlier UAW-GM effort also had national champions in Irv Bluestone and Steve Fuller, but the change strategy relied primarily on stimulation and education of local leaders rather than on central direction. While a growing number of officials at the national levels of unions, such as Sam Camans of the Steelworkers, are now supporting union involvement in QWL activities, they remain a minority in 1983.[4]

In some instances the combination of the QWL spirit and threatening competition has prompted the parties to break new ground in union-management relations. Ford-UAW offers the most striking example:

> In 1982 the Ford Motor Company and the UAW agreed to wage restraints, profit sharing, limitations on plant closing and outsourcing, and experimental approaches to job security. The parties also agreed to a joint venture in retraining and new joint problem-solving forums. UAW's Don Ephlin was given an opportunity to meet periodically with the board of directors of the Ford Motor Company. More important than the specific outcomes of the negotiation was the spirit in which the parties chose to cast them. The parties signaled that they were entering into a new partnership based on joint initiative and a strong sense of the mutuality of their interests. The statements of the parties clearly indicated that they were less concerned with preserving prerogatives than with finding solutions to joint problems.[5]

Most concession bargains between companies and unions, including the GM-UAW negotiations that followed, have not sent out such strong signals about the dawning of a new era of mutuality in labor relations. However, these negotiations have often moved the parties along the path of emphasizing their common fate and relinquishing some prerogatives or principles previously held sacred. In the nonunion sphere the spirit of the Ford-UAW agreement was matched by the workers of Delta Airlines, who showed their loyalty to the company and their support for management by collecting monies to help fund the acquisition of a new plane.

A more recent development that appears to be gaining momentum since the late 1970s is management restructuring. Changes at the plant floor have redefined the management task, and the minimal management structures incorporated in many new plant designs have proven effective. Consider the following illustrative example of management restructuring:

> After evidence of increased self-management and problem-solving capabilities of the work force, and with the stimulus of the division manager, a plant task force developed a phased plan to be implemented over three years. The plan was to remove two levels of the plant hierarchy, increase substantially supervisory spans of control, integrate the quality, process development, and production activities at a lower level of the organization, structurally combine the production and maintenance organizations (except for some specialized maintenance functions), and open up new career path possibilities for managers and professionals. The plan was implemented on schedule. These changes achieved increased responsiveness, improved effectiveness, and better management development. Although decreased salaried personnel costs were not the primary motivation, they were a welcome benefit.[6]

This pattern of restructuring to increase responsiveness is not confined to manufacturing organizations. Sales organizations and staff departments such as purchasing, materials management, and engineering have also eliminated managerial layers that were passing along information without adding value.

Finally, the movement that began in the plant is now finding expression at the corporate level. In many companies that have had some local successes of the types just described, top management has begun to chart the organizational renewal of the entire company.[7] Cummins Engine Company, for example, has drawn up a statement of its ambitious intentions in this respect. Cummins's new management principles are intended to "achieve the most productive organization possible." These include an unprecedented effort to inform employees about the business; leadership that encourages participation by *everyone*; and jobs that involve greater responsibility and more flexibility. Cummins's statement spells out the implications of these and other principles for the role of the supervisor (less control, more facilitation); for union-management relations (more joint sponsorship); and for staff organization (smaller size as others grow in capacities to do multiple tasks).

Similarly, the founders of certain new companies, working with a clean slate, have chosen to adopt a bold, ambitious, and comprehensive HRM model. When Don Burr left Texas International Airlines to found People Express with a group of his colleagues, he was committed to creating an organization that would be extraordinarily effective in developing and utilizing its people. The following is a description of their initial human resource policies:

> People Express featured a minimal hierarchy of three levels and positions with exceptionally broad scope. Every full-time employee was a "manager." Flight managers were pilots who also performed other tasks such as dispatching and safety checks. Maintenance managers were technicians who oversaw maintenance of P.E.'s airplanes, which was subcontracted to the maintenance departments of other airlines; they also performed various other staff jobs. Customer service managers performed all passenger-related tasks, such as security clearance, boarding, flight attending, ticketing, and food service.
>
> Everyone, including the officers, was expected to be "cross-utilized" and to rotate among functions, in order to increase their understanding of the business and to promote their own personal development. The work force was organized into three- or four-person work groups as an alternative to larger groups with supervisors. Teams and the individuals within them were expected to be self-supervising and to collaborate with others. Performance reviews were based on peer feedback gathered by the person under review.
>
> Salaries at the first level were very competitive. Those at the two higher levels were more modest. However, base salary for all employees was supplemented by a very ambitious set of policies for tying employees' financial stake to the company's: two forms of profit sharing and stock ownership. All employees, as a condition of employment, were required to buy, at a greatly discounted price, shares of P.E. stock. In addition P.E. awarded stock option bonuses.
>
> There was a plan providing for broad-based participation in the governance of the corporation.
>
> Finally, the recruitment, selection, and training were all de-

signed to produce a work force that would work effectively under the above management strategy.[8]

It is too early to judge the effectiveness of the People Express policies and practices, indeed even their workability. A case study reporting on the first year of operation described some striking achievements that could be attributed to certain organizational policies.[9] But in some other areas, such as the governance structure and the cross-movement policy, implementation had not yet occurred because of the demands of growth and the strain from heavy work loads. The experience of People Express is cited here as illustrative of the visions of a growing fraction of those who are fortunate enough to have a chance to found a new company today.

THE CONTROL MODEL

The traditional model for managing the work force was refined and institutionalized over the first half of this century.

Job Design Principles In this model job design is based on subdividing work into small tasks, clearly fixing job responsibilities, and holding individuals accountable for specific job requirements. Planning work is separated from implementation activities.

Performance Expectations These are expressed as standards that define minimum acceptable performance. Both standards and job definitions are based on the least-common-denominator concept in terms of the worker skills and motivations they assume.

Management Organization Managerial roles and departmentalization also follow the same spirit of specialization and top-down control and coordination. Management prerogatives and positional authority are emphasized, and status symbols are allocated in ways that reinforce the hierarchy. Inevitably, layering develops and is justified by control considerations.

Compensation Policies Worker compensation in the traditional model is based on a fair day's pay for a fair day's work. Because job requirements are carefully prescribed, they can be systematically evaluated and priced. Fairness in compensation is assured by comparing jobs. When jobs are deskilled, these jobs lead, justifiably, to a lowering of the fair day's pay. Where feasible, pay is varied to provide individual incentives for meeting performance expectations.

Employment Assurance In practice, the degree of employment security offered by companies has varied widely, even when other elements of the work-force management model are similar. Strong employment assurance is sometimes given, reflecting the values of the founders or a belief by management that this policy is of strategic importance in avoiding unionization. However, the basic logic of the traditional HRM model is that labor is and should be managed as a variable cost.

Employee Voice Policies In the traditional model there is generally little policy definition with regard to employee voice, unless the work force is unionized, in which case damage control strategies predominate. If the work force is not unionized, management relies on an open-door policy and on devices such as attitude surveys to learn about employees' concerns. If the work force is unionized, then management is forced to bargain terms of employment and to establish an appeal mechanism for resolving disputes under the contract. Labor relations specialists are expected to handle these activities as separately as possible from line management's task of managing work.

Labor-Management Relations Labor relations strategy follows naturally from the other policies, which emphasize interest conflict between employees and employers and between managers and the managed. Adversarial relations are often an accepted corollary of the traditional HRM model.

Management Philosophy The management philosophy associated with the traditional model emphasizes property as a source of management prerogatives and management's exclusive obligations to the shareowners. Employee claims, when enforced by bargaining power, are treated as constraints.

The common theme of the many elements of the traditional model is to establish order, exercise control, and achieve efficiency in the application of the work force. The model's antecedents include the bureaucratic organizations of the military and church. But it is Frederick W. Taylor who deserves credit for developing and promoting the industrial model. Because it was consistent with the prevailing ideologies of U.S. management and because it worked satisfactorily for many decades, the model was internalized by successive waves of managers. It has been reinforced by the policies of the U.S. labor movement, which has emphasized jurisdictional boundaries and insisted upon sharp distinctions between the managed and managers.[10]

Two developments have prompted the current movement away from the control model. First, as workers' expectations changed over time, the control measures often led to employee alienation, which in turn undermined both control and efficiency. The old model began to break down because it too severely violated current expectations. This development had been forecast by organizational psychologists a decade or two earlier,[11] but it did not manifest itself in a way that compelled management rethinking until the late 1960s and early 1970s.

Intensified competition was a second force toward change. The control model can operate satisfactorily with moderate to moderately low employee commitment. The system of policies and practices is designed to produce reliable if not outstanding performance. Beginning in the mid-1970s, it became increasingly apparent to many managers that this "satisficing" solution was not sufficient. New foreign competition in several industries set significantly higher standards of excellence. The heightening of domestic competition also placed satisficing organizations at risk. High-performance organizations require high-commitment work systems. More highly committed work forces required a radically different management model.

THE COMMITMENT MODEL

Over the past fifteen years a new mode of work-force management has emerged.[12] This commitment model can be found in the design of new plants and of newly founded companies such as People Express and Transtech, a subsidiary of AT&T. Hewlett-Packard, Digital Equipment Corporation, and many other high technology companies also represent variations of the high-commitment model.

Job Design Policies In the new model jobs are designed to be broader and to combine planning and implementation activities.[13] Individual responsibilities often are contingent upon changing conditions and extend in any event to upgrading the system. Teams, rather than individuals, often are the unit accountable for performance, thus promoting mutuality at the level of task management.

Performance Expectations These are set relatively high; they are "stretch objectives" rather than definitions of minimum performance. These expectations are dynamic, emphasizing continuous improvement, and often are oriented to the marketplace. (The control model's static standards, in contrast, are based on measurement of the work itself.)

Management Organization The management system tends to be flat, to rely upon shared goals for control and lateral coordination, to base influence on expertise and information rather than on position, and to minimize status differences. These systems promote mutual respect.

Compensation Policies More emphasis is placed on reinforcing group achievements. Acknowledging the broader and more contingent nature of job definitions, and therefore the expanded scope for individual contributions, pay is geared less to the logic of job evaluation and more to skill or other proxies for contribution. In some cases, mutual rewards—gain sharing, stock ownership, or profit sharing—are a cornerstone of the commitment model. In others, there is nothing of this sort. No clear pattern of policies has yet emerged.

Employment Assurance Employment assurance is recognized as an important element of the new model, fostering a spirit of mutual commitment. Companies may go to great lengths to avoid unemployment or to assist in reemployment. Existing employees may be given high priority in training and retraining as old jobs are eliminated and new ones created. However, here again, no dominant pattern of policies has emerged.

Employee Voice Policies Increased employee voice, yielding greater mutual influence, is a central feature of the new management model. If the work force is not unionized, management provides a variety of mechanisms for giving more employees more voice on more issues. This includes more assurances of due process. In unionized settings both the representative systems and the mechanisms for direct participation are elaborated to provide greater employee consultation. At the same time, a more systematic effort is made to inform the work force about the business conditions affecting the workplace.

Labor-Management Relations The relation between union and management is by definition not an issue for many of the organizations that have pioneered the high-commitment model, because their work forces have never been unionized. It is however, an important question for corporations with unionized work forces that are committed to evolving toward a new model, such as Dana, GM, Ford, Goodyear, and AT&T, to mention a few. The new model requires that union-management relations become less adversarial. Just how far the unions and companies are prepared to go toward broadening the agenda for joint problem solving and planning remains a major question and one of the problematic aspects of the new model, as we will discuss later.

Management Philosophy The philosophy that supports the new commitment model typically is inspiring or compelling in its content and is usually embodied in a published statement. The legitimate claims of multiple stakeholders—employees, customers, and the public, as well as owners—are usually acknowledged. The fulfillment of many employee needs is taken as a goal rather than merely as a means to other ends.

The common thread of the policies of mutuality is first to elicit employee commitment and then to expect effectiveness and efficiency to follow as second-order consequences. The theory is that these policies can both generate high commitment and provide ways to translate that commitment into enhanced performance. In the absence of the requisite high commitment, the work-force management systems based on these policies are distinctly more vulnerable than control models.[14] If broader and more contingent jobs, more general supervision, and more dynamic performance expectations are to be effective, there must be trust between levels of organization. Without mutual trust, management is forced to reinstitute controls to ensure acceptable performance.

THE TRANSITIONAL MODEL

While some new organizational units have adopted a comprehensive version of the commitment model, the transformation from control to commitment that occurs in established organizations usually involves a more limited set of changes. Usually only certain elements of the work-force management model are affected. We refer to this typical cluster of changes as a transitional model. It appears to represent a sufficient degree of change to modify expectations, to make credible the leaders' stated intentions to move toward a more comprehensive commitment model, and to support and reinforce the initial changes in behavior. The transitional model can achieve a temporary equilibrium, but only if there is evidence of movement toward the more comprehensive commitment strategy.

The cornerstone of the transitional model is the widespread involvement of employees in problem-solving groups. Such groups are sometimes called quality circles. These groups expand the individual's responsibilities from performing the immediate job to upgrading the larger performance system. In unionized organizations the precondition for this type of employee involvement is union-management dialogue leading to a jointly sponsored program. In any event, this type of employee involvement must be supported by additional training, a shift in management style, and additional communication. Participation is voluntary. Often managers develop ad hoc mechanisms for consulting employees about changes that affect them. Assurances are given that productivity improvements will not result directly in layoffs, and extra effort is made to avoid, defer, or minimize layoffs that result from technological change or decreased volumes. When layoffs or compensation concessions are necessary, they conform to the principle of equality of sacrifice and involve all employee groups, not just the hourly work force. Some visible changes are also made to deemphasize status differences.

Several elements of the work-force management model typically are not affected in the first major movement that creates the transitional model. The basic design of jobs, the compensation system, and the management structure and systems ordinarily remain unchanged. Over time, these elements are examined and modified in ways that will support the commitment strategy.

POTENTIAL BENEFITS FROM THE COMMITMENT STRATEGY

Those who advocate the commitment model believe it is superior in several respects to the control model. Properly implemented, it is more competitive—in terms of quality, cost effectiveness, and adaptiveness to change, including technological change. It provides more satisfying work and a more humane work environment. It accords more legitimacy to the management of the enterprise. In short, it does well in balancing and integrating the contemporary interests of the many stakeholders of the enterprise.

Is the superior potential from commitment universally available? Or do different task technologies offer different potential advantages from the commitment strategy? Theory indicates the latter.[15] Practice requires a more complicated assessment.

Both theory and practice confirm that some work technologies are better suited than others to an ambitious version of the commitment model, that is, those technologies that inherently require intricate team work, problem solving, learning, and self-monitoring. These conditions characterized many of the organizations that pioneered the high-commitment strategy—a fertilizer plant in Norway, a refinery in the United Kingdom, a paper mill in Pennsylvania, a food-processing plant in Kansas. All were continuous-process technologies. Capital-intensive and raw-material–intensive, all provided high economic leverage to any improvements in human skills and attitudes. All were capable of providing a high level of intrinsic job challenge.

Is the converse true? Is an extreme version of the control model appropriate when the work can be completely prescribed, where it will remain static over time, and where the tasks are inherently individualized? These conditions may be met literally in the case of prisoners breaking rocks with sledgehammers in a prison yard. Mass production, epitomized by the assembly line, also was thought to illustrate these conditions, but this view is changing. In fact, U.S. management's interest in moving from control to commitment has been as strong in assembly-line units as in other task technologies.

Although the assembly-line task has seemed to emphasize reliable productivity, some managers have reconceived the tasks of the work force in larger system terms and in more dynamic terms. Many elements of the assembly task do not change, but a role in process problem solving and methods improvement are added.

While the commitment model may yield greater absolute economic benefits and more impressive job satisfaction and human development in certain continuous-process technologies, the incremental economic benefits and human gains in assembly lines may be equally important to the survival and prosperity of companies applying the commitment strategy to their operations of this type.

What are the costs and benefits of the commitment approach? When the model has been implemented effectively and succeeds in eliciting high commitment, management reports the following types of benefits: higher in-plant quality, lower warranty costs, lower waste, higher machine utilization, increased total capacity with the same plant and equipment, fewer operating and support personnel, lower turnover and absenteeism, and faster start-up of new equipment. To achieve these gains, managers have had to invest extra effort, develop new skills and relationships, cope with higher levels of ambiguity and uncertainty, and experience the pain and discomfort associated with changing habits and attitudes. Some managerial skills have become obsolete, and some managerial careers have been casualties of change.

When union officials have entered into joint sponsorship of QWL and similar programs, they report improved product quality; reduced absenteeism and turnover; reduction in discharges, disciplinary layoffs, and grievance load; reelection of union officials who are proponents of QWL; increased dignity; and enhanced financial rewards.[16] Their basic motivations for entering into joint sponsorship include increased job security for the work force and the advantages to the union that come from influencing this transformation rather than standing apart from it. Like their counterparts in management, union officials have had to make the investments and experience the difficulties associated with changing attitudes and skills.

For the worker, the quid pro quo includes greater autonomy and more influence in return for accepting more responsibility; more social support in return for operating in more interdependent modes; and more opportunity for development and self-esteem in return for accepting greater uncertainty, including the possibility of failure.

Research generally supports the hypothesis of a net advantage in moving toward the commitment strategy.[17] That is, the average effectiveness of these units appears to be higher than the average of more conventionally organized but otherwise comparable units. Poorly conceived or badly implemented commitment-oriented systems are undoubtedly less effective than the better-managed conventional ones.

PROBLEMS AND PROGRESS IN THE TRANSFORMATION PROCESS

What type of errors have companies made as they search for conceptually sound and implementable versions of the commitment model? What are the most problematic aspects of the new model? And what factors and forces are determining the rate of transformation in U.S. industry?

ERRORS EN ROUTE TO A NEW MODEL

Overreaching In most management policy areas the appropriate
direction of change is clear, but the amount of change must be
determined through a process of initial judgment, experience,
and subsequent adjustment. For example, we envision jobs that
are broader in scope, that incorporate planning as well as doing.
But how broad? We are seeking optimal, not maximum breadth.

The optimum in terms of job scope, delegated self-supervision, voice, and other elements depends in part upon the degree
of choice provided participants. In the initial redesign or in new
organizational start-ups individual participants may have had
a personal influence on the design of the more ambitious version of the commitment model. Such involvement typically helps
create a higher resolve to make the new model work. Those
who join the organization later may not feel the same high
resolve, as employees may not in organizations where the commitment model is initially implemented without the involvement of the work force.

In most cases of ambitious designs of a new organization,
whether a single plant or a new enterprise, the planners initially
overreach with respect to one or more elements of the model.
In one plant planners assigned an unduly large role to peer
influence on decisions about pay adjustments. In another plant
they underplayed the role of first-line supervisors as a link in
the chain of accountability. In still another plant they over-
emphasized learning of multiple skills and flexibility at the expense of depth of mastery in critical operations. In a new financial
services company the initial structural design called for un-
manageably large spans of control. In the People Express case
the planners overestimated by a wide margin the amount of
personnel flexibility and therefore individual job movement
that would be feasible. These design errors, by themselves, are
not fatal to the development of a high-commitment work system. Some balance between pragmatism and conceptual purity
is necessary, however, and the organization must be especially
competent in monitoring and adjusting elements of its work-
force management strategy.

Tokenism A common error in the transformation from a control-based to a commitment-based strategy is to make only token changes. To be effective, modifications to the existing model must reach critical mass. The coordinated set of changes that we have identified as the transitional model suggests the rough magnitude of change required.

Over several decades U.S. management has made a series of attempts to modify the control model, but only on the margin. Management experimented with a succession of technique-oriented changes: job enrichment, sensitivity training, management by objectives, group brainstorming, and so on. In the past decade quality-circle programs often have been implemented in this same spirit. If quality circles or any other technique is implemented without corresponding changes in other areas of the work-force management model, or without a genuine change in management philosophy, positive effects will be limited and will decay rapidly.

Implementation Deficiencies Implementation failures are perhaps the most common form of error in moving toward a commitment model. In participative systems, for example, it is very important to define the boundaries of participation skillfully, so that one fully taps the creative energy of subordinates but does not generate unrealistic expectations. Easier said than done. Similarly, effective groups must develop peer-influence mechanisms but must also internalize restraints and standards of due process to temper the power of the group vis-à-vis the individual. Considerable conceptual clarity and skill are needed in shaping the norms of the organization.

PROBLEMATIC ASPECTS OF THE COMMITMENT MODEL

Continued development and definition are required in all elements of the model. In several areas the search is for an optimum that will remain a moving target. This applies to broadening job design, to streamlining management structure and systems, and to the narrowing of status differences. In five areas of this work-force management model more basic difficulties are apparent.

Employment Assurance It is difficult if not impossible to create high commitment on the part of employees unless there is some reciprocal employment commitment to them. Why should employees strive to produce changes that may cost them or their fellow employees their jobs? Many observers see the lifetime employment guarantees extended to some segments of a corporation's work force as a cornerstone of the successful Japanese management system. Many U.S. managers in heavy manufacturing have become more interested in employment assurance because they would fit the new work-force management model. At the same time, however, current economic realities make employment assurance a less available policy alternative. Similarly, many high-technology companies that pioneered high-commitment work systems and have emphasized employment security are now forced to rethink this aspect of the model.

What will emerge from this dilemma? Will the policy of mutuality provide lifetime assurances for the few, most senior employees? Or will mutuality be signaled if the company makes special efforts to avoid layoffs, thus clarifying that while the employment commitment for employees is not absolute, it is high priority—significantly higher priority than under the control model? Will the company accept greater responsibility for out placement of redundant employees? I expect that the model will combine the last two options. In any event, the commitment model is likely to incorporate a new level of effort to retrain existing employees to move from eliminated jobs to newly created jobs.

Compensation If the work-force management model is based on higher performance expectations and succeeds in both utilizing and developing employee capacities, it would be appropriate and just for employees to receive more generous financial rewards. Never has it been more appropriate in this sense to increase real wages and never has it been less feasible. This condition exists today because in the United States not only has the work force been underutilized but also the wage rates have risen to levels that render many industries noncompetitive internationally. In certain industries, for instance, trucking and airlines, new sources of domestic competition have placed companies that maintain the prevailing wage rates at a significant disadvantage.

Wage freezes, pay cuts, and concession bargaining create handicaps to commitment that must be overcome by other aspects of the work-force management model. Moreover, it is difficult to develop new compensation concepts at a time when the overall level of compensation cannot be raised, and it may even be necessary to reduce pay in order to survive and to save jobs.

Even if overall levels of compensation were not a problem, it would not be obvious what type of compensation policies would best reinforce the commitment model.

New organizations search for alternatives to pay structures based on traditional job evaluation, the mainstay of the control model. Traditional wage structures involve dozens of job-classification levels, with each job closely analyzed and differentially priced. For trade unions rigid job demarcations have been a basis for limiting supervisors' latitude in directing the work force; they also help to protect jobs. For the individual worker these carefully drawn and enforced demarcations give a sense of job ownership and accommodate his or her territorial instincts. Thus, within the spirit of the control model, job evaluation has served the interests of all stakeholders.

However, the job-evaluation structures tend to become counterproductive in the context of the commitment model, which emphasizes broader individual responsibilities, an orientation to end results rather than to minutely prescribed job input, and flexible, multiskilled workers.

New organizations pursuing the commitment model frequently base their pay structure on the employees' skill levels. Skill-based pay structures have long been in place in the engineering profession and skilled crafts but have not been applied to many other employee groups. The extreme version of this system is to pay all job entrants at the same rate initially and to move individuals to a progression of higher rates as they master additional skills and become more knowledgeable about the total work process and better able to take on assignments throughout the system. The motivational rationale for this system is that individuals will be reinforced for developing their capacities, for attending to the needs of the larger work process, and for accepting the uncertainty associated with changing assignments in response to business requirements. In designing the system an economic analysis must ensure that the advantages resulting from the redundancies in skills generated, the positive motivational effects, and the work-force flexibility will more than offset the higher average wage that results when the system matures and a larger percentage of the work force becomes highly skilled.

This economic advantage is more readily assured in capital-intensive or raw-material-intensive businesses, where the total payroll is a relatively small percentage of the cost of goods. But even when there is a good conceptual fit between skill-based pay and the rest of the work-force management model, and the design of the structure is economically justified, many implementation difficulties remain to be solved: how to measure skill mastery and adhere to common standards in pay progression decisions, how to allocate opportunities for employees to learn new skills, how to ensure an optimal amount of breadth and flexibility versus depth and stability, how to handle the potential demotivating effects of topping out in a system in which the individual previously has been repeatedly reinforced for growth.

In existing plants a traditional wage-classification structure cannot be converted overnight to a skill-based structure because of the vested interests of those who occupy the more highly rated classifications. However, it is sometimes possible to progressively reduce the number of job classifications, to build more contingent duties and requirements for flexibility into certain key jobs, and to adjust the pay for those jobs accordingly. This is a common approach to moving beyond the transitional model.

Many organizations reaching for the commitment model adopt some form of gain sharing. Conceptually, profit sharing and group productivity bonuses both fit with a work system that emphasizes collaboration, coordination based on shared goals and values, and ambitious standards of performance. Profit sharing is an available option in many situations and contributes to a general sense of equity, but its positive effect on commitment often is relatively modest. The most widely recognized form of gain sharing is the Scanlon Plan, which shares with workers any gains in productivity, measured by improvements in the ratio of payroll to the sales value of production. Such group bonus schemes may have potential merit in a wide range of situations, but what is conceptually appropriate cannot always be operationalized. For example, at the plant level, often one simply cannot devise a formula for sharing productivity gains that is readily understood, adequately responsive to employees' efforts, and appropriately independent of factors beyond their control. Organizational units that are stand-alone businesses, are smaller, employ mature technologies, and participate in relatively stable markets are more likely to be able to devise a satisfactory gain-sharing scheme.

Role of the Supervisor The commitment model implies a new set of role requirements for first-line supervisors: They should facilitate rather than direct the work force, impart rather than merely practice their technical and administrative expertise, and promote the development of self-managing capabilities of individual workers or work teams. In short, supervisors should delegate many of their traditional functions. This role prescription is regarded as essential to support other commitment elements, especially meaningful jobs, lean and flexible management, and effective employee voice. However, supervision has proven to be one of the more problematic aspects of the commitment model.[18] Difficulties are encountered both in implementation and in basic conception.

Some of the implementation shortfalls of early projects are gradually being remedied: failure to train, support, and reinforce first-line supervisors for their team development task; and failure to recognize the supervisors' own needs for voice, dignity, and fulfillment while directing them to attend to the same needs in the work force.

Conceptual dilemmas are signaled by the titles often used in newly founded organizations, for instance, team advisers or team consultants rather than supervisor or team manager. Taken literally, these titles signal that, unlike their superiors, advisers and consultants are not in the chain of accountability. In practice, however, team advisers are expected to be directive if necessary and to reassume functions delegated to the work force if they are not being performed. It is not surprising that the team advisers find this role exceedingly difficult. In many cases management has confused the style that supervisors are expected to use with the basic responsibilities they are expected to assume. The ideal style is advisory, but the responsibilities are to achieve certain human and economic outcomes. Interestingly, this ambiguity in titles has not extended to other management roles, such as plant manager, which are nevertheless expected, in the commitment model, to be performed in a participative and advisory style. I expect that with experience management will gradually regard the issue of delegation between the first-line supervisor and workers as similar to the delegation between other levels of the organization, that is, one delegates what subordinates are ready and able to perform. Then titles will not attempt to signal otherwise.

Other difficulties with the supervisory roles are even less tractable. The role in a commitment strategy requires relatively sophisticated interpersonal skills and some conceptual abilities that are not uniformly present among existing supervisors. Some supervisors are not able to adapt to the new role.

Some companies have tried to provide the quality of talent required by the newly defined role by using it as an entry point to management for college graduates. This may work where the work force already has acquired the necessary technical expertise. However, it blocks a route of advancement for the blue-collar work force and sharpens the dividing line between management and the work force, thus weakening the thrust of other commitment practices. Moreover, unless the company is growing rapidly enough to open up higher-level positions for those college-educated supervisors, it is likely to find them increasingly impatient with shift work and other work conditions associated with first-line supervision.

Where the new supervisory roles are filled from the ranks, even supervisors who become effective face dilemmas. If they successfully develop the teams they supervise and delegate their functions, what new responsibilities are delegated to them so that their own capabilities are fully utilized? Do their capabilities match other managerial work that could be transferred? If fewer and fewer supervisors are required as they broaden their span of responsibility from one to several teams, then what promotional opportunities exist for those who are no longer required?

The search continues for a viable and satisfying role for the first-line supervisor in the commitment model.

Union-Management Relations Many companies that are trying to move away from the control approach deal with unions. Often these companies have unions in most of their plants (the older ones), while a few newer plants are not unionized.

Some managers aspire to decertify their existing unions or render them ineffective. They expect other policy elements of the commitment strategy to strengthen employees' tie to the company and weaken those to the union. They hope that employees no longer will see the need for a third-party organization to represent them. With this set of hopes and expectations, they attempt to change the other policy elements with as little involvement by the union as possible. The obvious risk is that the union will perceive the threat and find ways to block both the policy changes and the attitudinal changes in the work force that management seeks. I do not expect this particular management strategy to be successful.

Other managers have decided to actively promote more cooperative relations with their existing unions. They have concluded that they could not successfully transform their workforce management strategy without the active support of their unions. General Motors, Ford Motor Company, and AT&T offer well-publicized examples of this management approach. The unions in these instances and many others often have responded cautiously but also positively, for their own reasons. As indicated earlier, they may value the prospect of increasing the involvement of the work force; they may see this involvement as instrumental to improving competitiveness and preserving jobs. In addition, they may see in it the opportunity to expand the union-management agenda and therefore their own influence.

These developments have presented both unions and management with new challenges and dilemmas.[19] These issues are explored in depth in later chapters in this volume. It will take the better part of a decade for these labor-management issues to be worked out in a large enough segment of industry to establish a new prevailing pattern.

Work Technology Policy The application of computer-based technology has profound implications for the evolution of human resource management. This technology can be designed and implemented to reinforce either the control model or the commitment model. To date, the directional effects have been variable and mostly unplanned. My assessment of the potential leverage that can be gained from treating technology policy as a manageable element of a human resource strategy, along with the difficulties which must be overcome, is set forth in Chapter 8.

RATE OF TRANSFORMATION

How rapidly is the transformation described here occurring? To my knowledge, no studies have yet attempted to quantify the rate of change. It is not clear what operational indices one would use to chart this cultural change, inasmuch as the early stages of a shift in approach can be reflected by changes in any of several policy areas—job design, management restructuring, or participation. Moreover, the same phenomenon—for instance, the establishment of quality circles—may reflect a basic shift toward commitment in one organization but be merely a gimmick within the control model in another organization.

Since we lack more systematic data, let me note some trends that I find indicative of the pace of change. In 1970 only a few plants in the United States were systematically revising their HRM approach. It was possible for those of us interested in this phenomenon to learn about most of these cases. By 1975 hundreds of plants were involved. I have learned in subsequent years of major projects that were under way in 1975, of which I was not then aware. By 1980, I estimate, thousands of plants were undertaking the comprehensive type of change that was limited to a few in 1970.

Within each of a number of companies I have observed over the past decade, the number of active plants grew from a few in the early 1970s to a dozen or dozens in the early 1980s.

These companies include Owens-Illinois, Procter & Gamble, TRW, Goodyear, Butler Manufacturing, and Cummins Engine.

The source of initiatives within companies has shifted upward, and the change process is no longer experimental but rather a matter of policy. In the early 1970s experimental projects were generally initiated and sponsored by plant managers. Later the projects tended to receive more support from division-level management. In the early 1980s company presidents and chief executive officers are increasingly structuring policy to promote companywide change.

Many of the managers who were associated with this type of innovative change at the plant level in the early or mid-1970s are in senior management positions today. Transformation of work-force management remains one of their principal means for achieving enterprise effectiveness.

We have been referring primarily to the blue-collar work forces. Where clerical operations resemble factory operations, the shift from control to commitment is conceptually analogous to the blue-collar transformation. However, the rate of change in these clerical operations has been slower, in part because the control model has not produced such overt employee disaffection and in part because management has been slower to recognize the importance of quality and productivity improvement in offices.

There has been more change in the model for managing the blue-collar work force than in the model for managing professional employees, partly because it is more readily apparent how to reform blue-collar (and clerical) operations. In a sense, the blue-collar reforms are a move in the direction of the model already idealized in managing professional work forces. Apart from improvements in implementation and some marginal changes, for instance, in consultation, no major conceptually different options are being considered for the management of professionals.

Paul Lawrence has shown that the prevailing HRM systems have evolved over a long period, and it would not be surprising if several decades were required for the evolution and establishment of the commitment model. A more rapid transformation is to be encouraged, however.

There can be no doubt that industries facing increased competitive pressure have been most active in moving toward the commitment model. But within any industry the leading edge companies are not necessarily those facing the greatest competitive threat. AT&T and the CWA were dealing from strength when they undertook their joint sponsorship of QWL in 1980. Similarly, Goodyear enjoys a leadership position among tire makers, but it has been the most aggressive and systematic in drastically revising its work-force management model. While greater competition increases the general sense that change is required, those who lead in the change process will not necessarily be those who feel the threats most sharply.

What differentiates the early changers from the followers? Executive leadership? Yes. A prior management philosophy that emphasizes people and therefore makes high commitment a more credible policy objective? Absolutely! General managerial competence in implementation? Certainly. Visionary and secure union leadership? Indeed.

SUMMARY AND CONCLUSIONS

A new work-force management model is emerging in the United States that should be well suited to the requirements of a postindustrial society and that promises to support the restructuring and renewal of traditional American industries. The new HRM model is composed of policies that promote mutuality—mutual goals, mutual influence, mutual respect, mutual rewards, mutual responsibility. The theory is that policies of mutuality will elicit commitment, which in turn will yield both better economic performance and greater human development.

In some policy areas the new pattern has clarified itself, but in others major questions remain to be addressed: For example, what level of employment assurance is desirable and feasible? What forms will such assurance take? What compensation policies will reinforce the other elements of the commitment model, that is, what is the relative emphasis on individual pay-for-performance features and group sharing of productivity gains? What will characterize the role of first-line supervision and, more broadly, middle management? How far will unions and managements go in replacing adversarial bargaining and unilateral management action with mutual problem solving and planning? Will new computer-based work technology be shaped to promote the new work-force management model, or will it continue to be treated as an exogenous variable?

Despite uncertainty about some of its elements, the commitment model has been increasingly adopted. Newly founded enterprises and new plants continue to design ambitious versions of the new model. With increasing frequency, the top managements of major corporations are articulating visions of the future that contemplate a transformation of practices in existing organizational units. As a company converts its existing management systems, it often reaches a temporary equilibrium in a transitional model that contains only some of the elements of the commitment model but that represents a significant step toward the comprehensive version of that model.

Only a small fraction of U.S. workplaces today are managed by the comprehensive commitment model, but the rate of transformation continues to accelerate. Moreover, the trend toward the commitment strategy is extensive, affecting a large number of plants and a growing number of offices in a very diverse set of industries. Economic necessity is fueling the transformation, while other factors are shaping and pacing it—individual leadership in management and labor, philosophical choices, organizational competence in managing change, and cumulative learning from change itself.

Part Two:
Strategic Policy Questions

4
Managing New Information Technology: Design or Default?

Calvin Pava

Managing new information technology has resembled waiting for Godot. Twenty-five years have passed since urgent warnings were first voiced about the dire consequences of automation, but since that time there have been few catastrophes. This has led executives to become skeptical about the need to manage new information technology in any special way. Yet recent installations of highly advanced systems indicate that significant alterations in human resource management (HRM) will be needed as such technologies proliferate. At this point, managers will confront a new domain of responsibility. Change will occur whether or not this responsibility is exercised. The fact is that organizations will be modified, by design or default.

This chapter analyzes how the adoption of advanced information technology unfreezes key elements of human resource management, and it suggests what managers can do about it. These factors include hierarchy, professionalization, proximity in time and space, relation between home and work, competitive advantage, experience of doing work, labor as a commodity, and reliance on outside services. A pervasive thaw like this coincides with the shift in HRM addressed by this book. Managers at many leading companies have already begun to explore new patterns of human resource management; advanced information technology will hasten this unfreezing and yield greater potential advantage.

My thanks to Dick Walton and Paul Lawrence of Harvard Business School, Kathy Herald of the Exxon Corporation, and Diane Gherson of the Management Analysis Center for their invaluable comments and suggestions.

The chapter begins with two brief case examples to show how information technology goes awry when deployed without suitable organizational modifications. Second is an examination of novel features that distinguish advanced information technology from previous generations of equipment. These novel features involve the temporary suspension of constraints that favor traditional methods of human resource management. It is suggested that this unfreezing poses a new competitive challenge that specialists, by themselves, are ill-prepared to solve. This challenge is to harness advanced information technology by designing suitable modifications to the organization of an enterprise. Finally, a set of actions are proposed for managers who seek to deploy effectively advanced information technology with methods that yield collaborative change yet avoid the quagmire of participation for its own sake.

THE RISKS OF DEFAULT

It may seem extreme to propose any new management role with respect to advanced information technology. Prior generations of automated equipment have been installed without overwhelming disruption to industrial economies. To call for a new approach may seem excessive, particularly given the false alarms that have characterized the literature on automation.

But I believe that with advanced information technology it has become risky for an enterprise to leave its HRM systems unchanged. Old habits seem natural, and continue, despite the addition of vastly different equipment. A mismatch can result between organization and technology that leads to diminished performance. The following two examples taken from companies that installed advanced systems illustrate the need to redesign the organization of an enterprise.

MULTISTATION COMPUTER-AIDED DESIGN

A multistation integrated computer-aided design (CAD) system was installed at a large industrial manufacturer. It replaced a less sophisticated stand-alone system. The system's multistation architecture allowed cross-departmental integration and greater rationalization of product design. Materials specialists, located in the manufacturing function away from engineering, were able to prohibit specific supplier's parts from entering an engineer's design. Using their CAD workstations, the materials specialists could preset the system's software to reject specific options if they were entered later at an engineer's workstation.

The system was heralded as a major advance, providing a way to keep engineers from developing unproduceable designs. The engineering function saw it differently. To them the new CAD systems unduly restricted their professional discretion. They maintained that the greater power of the materials specialists would undermine product innovation. This would place the firm's strategy of obtaining high margins for technologically advanced products in jeopardy while diminishing the firm's attractiveness to a tightening supply of bright engineers.

In this case, management opted to default their organizational prerogatives, failing to alter the process of product design so that it would better capitalize on the new CAD system. This oversight created a mismatch between the social and technical aspects of the firm's product-design process that actually decreased performance. The resulting contention decayed into an arbitrary power struggle. Better ways to organize design work around the CAD system may someday be demonstrated by an astute competitor.

DISTRIBUTED DISTRIBUTION SYSTEM

A national distributor replaced its internal order-processing computer with an advanced distributed system. It provided each major customer with terminals for direct order processing. Based on more powerful hardware and software, the system was further advanced than prior generations of timesharing equipment; it allowed customers to obtain shipment dates immediately and ran software that was easy for customers to use without special training. Data entry by the customer allowed quicker determination of product availability and faster order entry. Less frequent sales' visits were needed to provide this higher level of service, so the growing company anticipated hiring fewer salespersons than before. Major accounts praised the system. It performed reliably and incurred few operational problems.

However, orders for the distributor's new, more profitable products declined. This drop threatened to curtail the distributor's competitive position. A mismatch had developed with the advanced computer system; the sales force was not modified to take advantage of it. The staffing pattern had become leaner, but the actual work of a salesperson had gone unmodified. Under the new computer system with the role of sales unchanged, customers experienced less need to adopt new products.

Both these examples involve advanced information technology that superseded previous equipment. In each instance unforeseen difficulties arose because the organization was not modified to better match a new capital stock, despite prior experience with earlier generations of computer systems. Such difficulties will proliferate as advanced information technology changes the nature of work everywhere.

WHAT IS DIFFERENT ABOUT ADVANCED INFORMATION SYSTEMS?

Three new features distinguish advanced information technology from prior generations of computing equipment—pervasiveness, heightened functionality, and greater interconnectedness. This section examines advanced information technology, showing how it is beginning to revolutionize the tools used in every kind of enterprise. After years of false alarms Godot is arriving. Such technology is unlike previous generations of automatic equipment, and the skepticism about dramatic change that has been engendered by the dire warnings concerning automation is fast becoming unwarranted.

PERVASIVENESS

Recent technological advances make information processing a pervasive capability that will become a part of every tool. This ubiquity is due to microelectronics. Unlike large, expensive,

Figure 4-1
Improving Semiconductor Cost/Performance

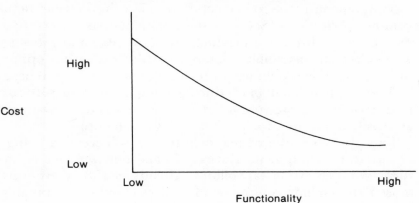

stand-alone computers, microchips are not confined to any single device. With their low cost, miniature size, and dependability, microchips lend themselves to diverse applications in forms of equipment that previously contained no information-processing capabilities. The range of potential applications is vast, including appliances, office machinery, robotic equipment, control systems, instruments, weapons, games, and motor vehicles.

Since its inception the technology used in microelectronics has improved steadily. For instance, the cost of memory chips has declined from $0.05 per bit in 1971 to below $0.003 per bit in 1975, and $0.0001 per bit in the mid-1980s.[1] Continued advances in microelectronics are likely through the 1980s, because the physical limits of semiconductor materials have not yet been reached.[2] A uniform trend of price and performance improvement will continue through the 1990s, fostering wider application of microchip technology (see *Figure 4-1*).

As price drops and capability rises, competition pulls companies to employ microelectronics, allowing novel features that improve product positioning.[3] Microchips endow current products with new capabilities while also making totally new products attainable. Furthermore, competitive cost advantages can be obtained through replacing inflexible mechanical assemblies with reprogrammable plug-in circuitry. This substitution requires that even common manufactured goods incorporate micro-electronics with information-processing abilities.

Simultaneously the cost structure of microchips pushes high-volume applications.[4] Software development costs, necessary to incorporate chips into a product, are substantial and growing, while electronic assembly operations afford numerous opportunities for scale economies with volume component purchases and capital investment in production equipment. Also, software is amenable to large-volume savings; once written, programs are easily duplicated for placement into many units.

This push and pull of microelectronics will create a deluge of innovative equipment. Devices old and new will take on information-processing capabilities. Already in 1982 there were more than 5 billion computers of all sizes in existence, ranging from microprocessors to large mainframe computers. By the mid-1980s the number of electronic functions incorporated into everyday products will be at least 100 times greater than in the late 1970s.[5]

Hence, the real information revolution is only beginning. It did not arrive with the computer. Instead, it will develop as microelectronics technology becomes ubiquitous. The computer age depends less on computers as discrete products than on computers included as part of every device. This pervasiveness distinguishes advanced information technology from prior generations of equipment that were used for more confined applications.

HEIGHTENED FUNCTIONALITY

One endowment that microchips impart to equipment is heightened functionality. With a capacity to process information any device can be made more flexible and self-regulating. For example, consider microelectronics applied to industrial machinery. Tools can switch among jobs easily by loading different software into the same equipment (flexibility), and the same machinery can monitor critical properties and adjust settings appropriately without human intervention (self-regulation).

Greater interconnectedness is another capacity that will pertain to every tool equipped with microchips. Wherever they are used, microchips require translating machine activity into digital (binary) code. These impulses can be transmitted, allowing microelectronic-based devices to "talk" with each other. For instance, "smart" machine tools can be linked to form integrated clusters, allowing mutual adjustment in equipment settings and materials flow. In addition to making devices more interactive with each other, microelectronics will soon permit more sophisticated interaction with the people who use the new devices. Speech generation, voice recognition, and artificial intelligence capabilities enrich the interface between people and machines, not simply among machines themselves. "Smart" devices will therefore not proliferate in isolation. Often they will be linked together into extended networks that compound their already heightened functionality.

No single device fully conveys the richness of this evolution. Yet the progression involved can be well illustrated by one example—the typewriter. Microchips have changed the typewriter radically. In 1965 magnetic card typewriters were introduced, making repetitive typing easier. The first screen-based word processor came onto the market in 1974, allowing revisions to be made on a video display before printing copies on paper. By 1976 programmable word processors were being sold that made it easy to improve equipment with software revisions. In the late 1970s word processors gave way to less expensive personal computers and multifunction workstations that were dispersed widely and could do more than just process text; and these units shrank to briefcase-sized portable units and "smart" telephones. Meanwhile, voice-date communication began to take hold, via local and long-distance networks, allowing integrated systems where different workstations could exchange information electronically. Also, this time marked the appearance of far easier software, made possible by greater hardware capability; and early products containing artificially intelligent software emerged. This rapid development is summarized in

Figures 4-2(a) and *4-2(b)* in terms of different levels of equipment capability.

Like any instance of a single application, the example of office systems presents a restricted scenario. A corresponding evolution is beginning to unfold everywhere as developments in computing technologies accelerate. Soon every device wil become more animate and interconnected in a similar way. Society's entire population of equipment will come alive; isolated, passive devices will be exceptions to the rule. Earlier false alarms regarding automation have eased the sense of urgency about dealing with this shift. Extrapolating from the lack of prior disruptions, one could conveniently minimize the magnitude of this change. But the greater pervasiveness, functionality, and interconnectedness of advanced information technology will unlock constraints shaping the form and function of every enterprise. Existing systems of human resource management will be hard pressed to keep pace with this transition.

WHAT BECOMES UNFROZEN?

Pervasive alterations affecting the entire population of tools will, at least temporarily, suspend many constants that shape the organization and human resource policies of an enterprise. As many factors become destabilized, established strategic barriers and traditional organizational patterns become unfrozen; their previous outcomes are no longer assured. In this era of technological transition, an enterprise can better obtain favorable results when these discontinuities are explicitly acknowledged and deliberately managed. This section identifies eight factors that will become unsettled as a more functional and interconnected tool stock is deployed.

HIERARCHY

To classical management theory, the key attribute of any organization is hierarchy: a vertically stratified pyramid of organizational roles in which higher roles have control over lower ones. The organization is centralized, with clear chains of command that do not cross.[6] Ideally, no major initiative can proceed

Figure 4-2(a)
Typewriter-Technology Evolution

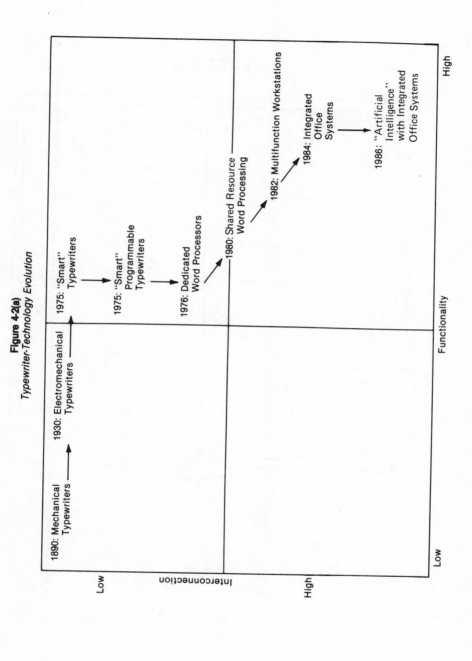

Figure 4-2(b)
Toolstock Evolution

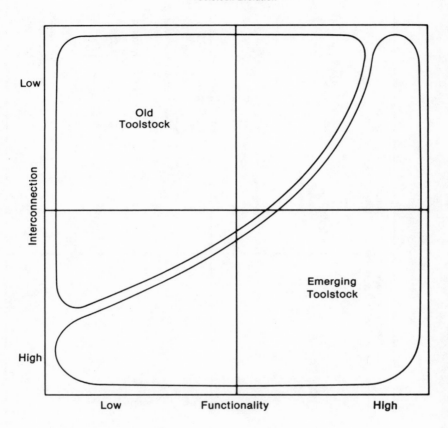

without approval from the appropriate higher levels. Finally, all chains of command lead to ultimate authority, the top general manager, who is supposed to make the most essential decisions for the enterprise.

The concept of hierarchy is intuitively appealing. It has long been a basis for organizing work. Mumford and Weber trace hierarchical arrangements back to Egyptian and Mesopotamian bureaucracies.[7] Clear unitary chains of command ensure that local choices add up to a greater good. However, the concept of hierarchy takes much for granted. At least two major assumptions must hold true if this approach is to work.

First, the environment of an enterprise must be relatively tranquil. Rapid or widespread change puts new demands on all levels, thereby diminishing the time available for seeking and securing approval of lower-level decisions. Ironically, the more the environment changes, the greater is the need for higher and lower units to confer. Yet today organizations face an increasingly turbulent environment. Consequently, the hierarchical arrangements used to organize activity are no longer adequate. As the president of a leading personal computer company put it, "Pyramid-like organizations are good for just one thing, talking to God." The vertical stratification of roles need not be eliminated completely, but new work configurations are needed at least to supplement this structure.

The dissemination of new information technology undermines the other condition essential to reliance on hierarchical organization: exclusive access to an overview of the whole enterprise. Advanced technology shifts the distribution of information in an enterprise and enlarges the capacity of numerous locations to process it. Point-to-point data flow permits wide circulation and tabulation of information. Analytic capabilities also become more widely available as greater on-site computing power enables many small units to undertake complex information processing. Once there is dispersed capability to process information, developing an overview is possible in more than one location. Central management organs lose their exclusive prerogative, and hierarchical command loses its raison d'être.

New information technology drives down the transaction costs of time, money, and inconvenience that have traditionally been the price of gaining an overview from which to monitor a situation.[8] Given appropriate organization and computing resources, dispersed units can work together to take coordinated action in reference to their overall situation without edicts from a higher central authority. At first, the greatest pressure will be on middle managers, who can be "caught in the middle" if their traditional role remains unchanged, as networks of more functional equipment dissolve their monopoly over the summary of data.

There is, of course, no guarantee that dispersed information processing will benefit the conduct of an enterprise. A multiplicity of information sources and the proliferation of available overviews may heighten existing conflicts if data are used as ammunition when units clash. Under these circumstances, a profusion of numeric tables and fancy graphs may actually hinder effective decision making. But for a while at least, traditional reliance upon hierarchy will unfreeze. With a new stock of tools it becomes more attainable and advantageous to refreeze in a different configuration, one that might involve less hierarchical stratification.

PROFESSIONALIZATION

Besides hierarchy, professionalization is another common way to organize group effort.[9] With professional training, individuals learn standard skills and procedures that they can bring to collective endeavors. This allows professionals to work competently without extensive supervision and regardless of their unfamiliarity with clients or other professionals on the same assignment. In addition, a professional standing has functioned as a passport to elevated status. Professional knowledge is a limited resource. If it is in short supply, professionals can expect handsome rewards, both salary and privileges, for delivering their expertise. Only some professions gain official recognition, like physicians and lawyers, but every occupational group that holds collective control over a base of knowledge or expertise, like circuit engineers or airline pilots, constitutes a profession.[10]

Professional training will always be a means of standardizing skills and procedures, yet new information technology may eliminate a large degree of the exclusivity that some professions trade on. Microelectronic-based equipment often performs a higher proportion of the routine assessments rendered earlier by professionals. Software with growing ability, so-called artificial intelligence, to exercise some degree of inferential choice (for example, production scheduling or portfolio management) will further challenge the preeminence of many professions.

Cooptation is a possibility: Professionals might try to develop microelectronic-based tools that augment their own professional judgment instead of replacing it. Another possibility is conflict: Threatened professionals may actively resist the introduction of microelectronic-based equipment that would loosen their exclusive hold over a body of skills and practices. This battle, of course, would be waged under acceptable political banners like "quality services" and "better care with a human touch," but the fundamental struggle would be over preserving a concentration of skill and status.

Deprofessionalization clearly runs against the grain, for in the 1970s and 1980s almost every type of worker has claimed professional status. The 1970s were the "me decade," which gave expression to the desire for autonomy, recognition, enrichment, and uniqueness. If the introduction of sophisticated devices begins to blur current lines of professional differentiation, then new means of stratification will be sought. The struggle by professionals to restore their relative advantage over other groups may often be bitter.[11] Attempts by newly empowered practitioners to designate themselves as a fresh professional category (like, "knowledge engineers" in artifical intelligence) will further complicate struggles to reallocate privilege.

PROXIMITY IN TIME AND SPACE

Working the same hours and occupying the same premises is traditionally a mechanism for people doing related tasks to harmonize their efforts. Advanced information technology will lessen the importance of time and space as constraints on the coordination of work as many devices gain unprecedented capacities for telecommunications and data transmission.[12] Some are synchronous and richly interactive, like teleconferencing and cellular radio telephones. Others, like computer-based telephone messaging and high-speed facsimile equipment, provide asynchronous ties that are less interactive but still support coordination among people working at different times and places.

Time and space constraints on the coordination of work go hand in hand with hierarchical organizations. As these limitations are overcome, one can abandon status ascription based on position in a hierarchy as well as the physical constraints favoring a traditional configuration of human resources.

Consider engineering project management. Traditionally, engineering teams working on the same project are gathered at the same place. If this is not possible, the project is usually divided into relatively self-contained segments, with coordination among these segments remaining problematic. New communication devices permit an alternative. For example, teleconferencing is now used to link dispersed engineering units that are jointly designing a new product. Both travel time and idle time diminish, a reduction that translates into direct cost savings. In addition, problem solving becomes more sophisticated. It is impossible to anticipate before meetings which issues may prove important, but teleconferences provide quick access to on-site engineers who are directly involved with issues to be settled. These consultations were often not feasible prior to this technology.

Time and space constraints are easing not only for high-technology firms. A growing contingent of major companies is developing teleconferencing systems for geographically dispersed managers. Other firms are installing telephone and computer messaging systems that allow information to flow quickly and flexibly without common location in time or space.

Of course, shared workplace and hours will continue to be important. New information technology merely expands the degree of choice. Even so, failure to make use of sophisticated communication systems that permit novel patterns of organization will discourage innovative choices. Perhaps the most substantial obstacle to freeing work from time and space limits is not technological but social. Use of advanced telecommunications means less face-to-face contact, upon which goodwill, complementary objectives, and matching styles of getting work done depend. Without these social-psychological prerequisites, it is very difficult for people to coordinate their efforts, especially with highly discretionary tasks.

Flexibility in work sites and timetables is feasible only if the people in an enterprise are disposed, by virtue of organization norms and problem-solving protocols, to use new devices for better work coordination.[13] Accordingly, these more subtle social coordination mechanisms are receiving closer attention in the form of organizational culture.[14]

RELATION BETWEEN HOME AND WORK

The new technology may profoundly affect the traditional boundary between home and work. Toffler described "telecommuters," people who work at home and link up to the office using computer networks.[15] This is now becoming more frequent for work that includes word processing, software development, and electronic mail.[16] Even some top executives now work at home through computer links accessible at any telephone jack.

The flexibility afforded by new information technology will put home life on a more equal footing with work life. Greater flexibility over scheduling and completing work activities may prove especially beneficial in families with child-care responsibilities.

New equipment allows automated bookkeeping, mass mailing, word processing, job costing, database analysis, telephone answering, and typesetting to be done in the home at relatively low cost. Assorted studies suggest that perhaps 35 to 50 percent of jobs in both factories and offices could be done at home.[17] The availability of powerful office functions in small-scale formats encourages the creation of facilities, based inside or near the home, that offer services in the open market.

Flexible work schedules and the possibility of working at home may alter the traditional patterns of family and community. Job sharing and new family-care patterns become feasible; community ties may grow stronger; and alternative leisure pursuits may develop. Corresponding shifts may occur in the distribution of traditionally cosmopolitan attractions like cultural events or nightlife. Patterns of housing and transportation also are likely to change. The "workplace" is unlikely to disappear, but its function and location in everyday life will be open to redefinition.

COMPETITIVE ADVANTAGE

Technological capabilities subtly influence the way in which an enterprise defines and achieves success. As new information technology proliferates, the traditional grounds for competitive advantage will alter. Because the precise nature of this shift will vary by industry, only the most general trends can be suggested in advance. Specific opportunities or disadvantages require in-depth analysis.[18]

One key competitive advantage is the learning (or experience) curve effect. Learning-curve advantages are realized when unit costs decline as a function of cumulative experience.[19] Many small improvements throughout an operation add up to more efficient methods, highly functional equipment, better layout, improved product design, and more sophisticated quality standards. Together, such improvements spur overall learning-curve effects for a particular industry.

Learning-curve effects are not equally potent for every industry or every niche. They seem most important in businesses requiring high labor content and intricate operations. While learning-curve advantages are usually associated with manufacturing operations, they are also important in service operations, where many tasks can be performed more efficiently as employees gain experience.

New equipment may change both the magnitude of experience-curve effects and the way in which they are produced. Formerly manual operations will increasingly be controlled by intelligent equipment. Therefore, operators need not be so greatly involved in every step of an information-processing operation, and traditional learning-curve effects may diminish. On the other hand, with a greater proportion of operations regulated by equipment, there is time for employees to add value at a more comprehensive level of work involving system redesign and the management of external forces. New learning-curve advantages may accrue in the domain of tertiary production work, such as improving systems performance (e.g., developing new applications for reprogrammable equipment) or better management of relations between work units and their environment (e.g., expanded services). This shift in the locus of the value added by human resources has already been observed at certain pilot installations of advanced information systems.[20]

Channels for product distribution and service represent a second competitive factor that information technologies will unfreeze in virtually every industry. Opportunities to provide better service, often with greater self-service, will multiply; capital investments will intensify; and existing roles will be opened for redefinition.

The installation of automatic teller machines (ATMs) in banks provides a case in point. ATMs give greater customer convenience by allowing greater freedom as to where and when banking services are obtained. Banks that utilize this new technology can reposition themselves in consumer banking markets. A shift in labor distribution and cost structure also occurs. With ATMs, the consumer contributes a larger proportion of self-service, punching keys to accomplish the bank's data entry. Banks pay less for platform personnel and large branch facilities as ATMs supplant teller-based services, but the capital investment in computer technology rises (a shift that carries its own HRM implications for banking institutions). Further alterations of banking distribution will be induced by a combination of regulatory change (e.g., nationwide banking in the United States) and technological advance (e.g., home banking using home computers).

Banking thus illustrates the generic changes that accelerate when information technology is applied to market channels. Capital investment supplants the conventional patterns in the deployment of labor and equipment. Greater convenience becomes possible, with customers providing a higher level of self-service. Traditional customer-liaison roles, like bank platform tellers, require extensive redesign and reassignment. Competitive advantage is sustained with continued data accuracy, ongoing systems redesign, new forms of customer assistance, and reliable maintenance.

Experience curves and market channels are two examples of the ways advanced information technology will transform strategic options for every business. The magnitude of this discontinuity is analogous to development of roads and automobiles, providing an altogether new medium for competition, but it will become established far more quickly.

THE EXPERIENCE OF DOING WORK

A more intelligent toolstock is likely to alter the experience of doing work.[21] The prevailing view is that a new information age will dawn, based on an information economy and populated by information workers. The information economy is the rapidly growing sector that produces information-processing machines or runs data through them. The information worker is the new breed of laborer who will manipulate information. Some employees will continue to serve as management and staff professionals, but the preponderance of information workers will tend processing devices at screens, consoles, and switching panels. They will be designated by quasiprofessional titles such as systems operator, knowledge engineer, or administrative associate. As portrayed in many industry advertisements, information workers will be stylishly clean-cut, motivated, content, and alert employees.

The imagery used in advertisements suggests an equivalence to the industrial revolution. Supposedly information work will become automated, much as physical labor has been. The turmoil occasioned by the mechanization of physical work is forgotten. Vestiges of the attendant social damage are also forgotten. Meanwhile, the diffusion of microelectronic-based tools beyond office settings promises to change the form and content of work for many others besides clerical information workers. A tranquil and well-ordered transition is not inevitable. It may not even be desirable. The increasing sophistication of the entire toolstock threatens to degrade the very experience of work, perhaps with far-reaching deleterious consequences.

The classic view of technology is that capital should replace labor. There are humanitarian aspects to this notion, for machines can eliminate human drudgery. There is also economic justification: Automatic equipment can seemingly eliminate human error. Yet sophisticated automatic equipment can push the technological imperative too far. Equipment that is both highly self-regulating and highly interconnected can easily make work too abstract and intangible. Information manipulated by people running sophisticated devices can become many steps removed from the events they ostensibly control. Under these conditions, equipment seals off users from tangible reality and encourages them to become passive, docile, and complacent. They do no more than monitor unintelligible data entry. Contact with people or tangible events may be replaced by interface with equipment (a computer terminal or a control panel). The user is rarely in a position to understand or test the assumptions and limitations that are inherent in the software program and database being employed; blind acquiescence to computer-driven equipment is already evident in the unthinking legitimacy often ascribed to any computer-printed analysis.

Work has always been an important crucible for development and sustenance of character; one product of work is people.[22] Workplace activity not only contributes to individual psychological development but also shapes the kinds of initiatives people are likely to take as members of society. Intelligent equipment can overfunction, engendering passivity in the workplace and beyond. Technology that invites people to abdicate discretion blunts their critical judgment, undermines their courage, and diminishes their contributions to society at large. The irony is that so-called knowledge work may actually discourage intelligence among the population doing it.

LABOR AS A COMMODITY

A new stock of more functional tools is likely to alter the prevailing notions about the nature of labor and the fair exchange between employer and employee. In the traditional view, labor—especially the work of hourly employees—is a uniform, incremental commodity, procured in discrete units of contributed time (for example, hours at work) with some minimum level of compliance to performance standards. This view assumes that there is a strong, direct correlation between the number of hours worked and the amount of output—hence the age-old inclination to tighten the screws periodically if higher performance is necessary, for instance with overtime or additional temporary workers.

When "smart" equipment is linked together, number of hours worked is less directly correlated with success. To a large degree, operational details are continuously regulated by machine; thus, there is a decline in the marginal benefit of occasionally increased labor. Instead, self-regulated equipment requires the operator to be constantly diligent and alert while on the job, with an anticipatory stance toward potential opportunities and difficulties.

Advanced systems make it less possible to compensate by a burst of conscientiousness for chronically inadequate maintenance, inaccurate data entry, poor levels of service, or other lapses. Systems with automatic self-adjustment may actually increase an enterprise's vulnerability to error. With higher integration, systems can amplify operator mistakes by instantly transmitting a single error through numerous subsystems before it can be detected and corrected. For instance, an integrated accounts-payable system can allow one improper keystroke to produce errors throughout a host of related data records. Automatic self-adjustment and greater interdependence thus diminish the value gained by managing labor as a discrete input.[23]

Accordingly, advanced technology nullifies the traditional definition of labor as an incremental commodity that can be obtained in discrete quantums of time and quality. With more functional equipment, the worker bolsters output less directly and less intermittently than before. Use of such technology demands continual, rather than periodic, diligence and an anticipatory stance that draws on a higher level of abstract thinking than required in the past. Ironically, this kind of effort requires broad-based competence and judgment that are at odds with the tendency of designers to oversimplify tasks with new technology.[24]

Implicit in this shift is a new definition of productivity at variance with most management literature. With mechanical or premechanized equipment, a ratio of output to hours of labor input furnished a reasonable yardstick for measuring productivity. But this concept breaks down with a more functional and interconnected stock of tools, as hours of compliance no longer yield acceptable performance. Productivity becomes an outcome less tightly coupled to easily quantified input. To the dismay of those with a "hard-nosed" temperament, no uniform formula exists to replace the former one. Instead, productivity becomes situationally determined. Hours of employee input ceases to be the pivotal factor. Employee value added is no longer equivalent to hours of work. With advanced information technology, employees add value through a variety of contributions—such as preventive maintenance, quick response to problems, and systems redesign.

The strict demarcation between white- and blue-collar employees seems bound to diminish. With more highly functional and integrated systems in both office and factory, high performance is obtained by getting all workers to take on values and prerogatives till now expected only from exempt management personnel. An alternative basis of allegiance and reward therefore seems necessary in the exchange relationship between employer and employee. Relevant options being explored by major firms, which are discussed in other chapters of this book, include gain sharing, participative supervision, pay for learning, substantial employee equity participation, and group-based organizational structures.

ORGANIZATIONAL ARCHITECTURE

The new technology of any era makes new forms of organization possible. For example, it is difficult to imagine large multinational corporations without telephones and jet travel. It is likely that advanced information technology will similarly alter organizational architecture; as a multitude of factors are suspended, a new template of organization may arise. The size and form of enterprises in which human resources are deployed may thereby change.

Equipment with greater functionality and interconnectedness will increase the power and flexibility of small discrete units, internal or external, while lowering the costs of coordinating work between them. Cellular patterns of organization become more powerful, with small units temporarily linking on the basis of explicit contracts. This provides an alternative to monolithic organizations composed of large units that are guided by administrative directives.

Inside companies, this cellular pattern takes hold as a lower utilization of central services. Today, for instance, the adoption of personal computers is lowering reliance on central services like research libraries, graphics departments, typesetting shops, and data processing sections.

Between companies, a cellular format is demonstrated by greater reliance on outside suppliers for critical elements of a product or service. This redistribution of "make versus buy" is propelled by the accelerating fragmentation and change of markets resulting from economic, demographic, and technological instabilities. Competitive advantage will be accrued through flexibility, quickness, and tailoring products or services to offer high value in very specific markets. To gain these advantages, a firm may find it necessary to buy services from the open market instead of taking time to produce expertise internally or to absorb it via acquisition. Even longtime proponents of self-reliance, like IBM, have recently found it beneficial to rely on external suppliers for key product ingredients.

Advanced information technology can fortify the capacity of every firm to operate in liaison with other companies. Point-to-point data transmission will allow different companies' equipment to function as if they were located at the same facility, while "smart" equipment makes possible flexible operation without high cost.[25]

Many new systems have recently appeared that illustrate this combination of flexibility and low cost. For example, advanced computer-aided engineering systems can electronically transmit a new custom circuit design to an independent foundry company for quick fabrication; a clerical support bureau can service many different companies remotely, with documents for each firm instantly transmitted to its own computer, video display, or printer; a multicompany production operation can be optimally scheduled via the data network between suppliers and machinery ("just in time" inventory is one example of the shift involving greater reliance on a higher degree of coupling between firms); numerous service firms, like banks, travel companies, and municipalities, could share access to a special automated transaction network owned by an independent company that provides sidewalk computer stations (like advanced ATMs) across the country. As these examples suggest, greater functionality and interconnection in equipment everywhere will make coordination between companies more practical, while an era of rapid market change makes it necessary.

Employees may also find benefits in working for a smaller enterprise. Recession in the early 1980s showed that working for a large company might be detrimental to employment security; the multiplicity of potential clients available in the external market might provide greater redundancy of work assignments during lean times. Compensation structures may also be more attractive in smaller businesses; they find it easier to establish gain sharing or equity participation. The barriers to initiating these small but capable enterprises may drop; capitalization requirements diminish as the price of powerful technology falls. Finally, the psychological tax imposed by membership in a large enterprise in the form of social conformity may be lower; faceless electronic transactions do not require all workers to belong to the same clan. Thus, it may be that employees as well as companies will reinterpret the distinction between "make" and "buy."

Market contracts may routinely supplant employment contracts as a primary means of organizing large undertakings. Firms will hire a greater proportion of temporary agency workers, contract employees, and subcontractors to achieve their objectives. Eventually, these choices may add up to a different kind of organizational architecture for the 1990s—a multinode enterprise.[26] A multinode enterprise is a network of firms that link together conditionally for a specified endeavor in which many firms play essential roles. More than one multinode can function in a single industry, and one firm can participate in many. The kinds of linkage and mechanisms of control can vary, including purchase agreements, joint ventures, limited partnerships, equity participation, marketing agreements, and information shared in public or private.

Organizations involved in a multinode enterprise would fall into one of three categories: (1) a core group of a few strong firms that lead the multinode, (2) a group of prime firms that become essential to the effort undertaken by the core firm, (3) a tertiary group of firms that follow core and primes and are less essential and more vulnerable. In a multinode, competitive success involves gaining centrality by moving from periphery to core while bumping other firms.

The multinode architecture is not totally new. U.S. auto producers and aerospace programs often assume this pattern, as do Japanese zaibatsu combines. But the multinode is distinguished by its vague distribution of responsibility among many units for important strategic contributions, its patchwork of linkage and control mechanisms, its extensive reciprocity of innovation, its high instability of member firms, and its multiplicity of capital sources. With advanced technology, such multifirm ensembles become operationally more integrated while retaining their differentiation and required expertise.

America's Silicon Valley is a vivid prototype of a geographically centered multinode, where most firms are small, turnover is high, and most companies are short-lived.[27] Numerous Silicon Valley firms temporarily link or correlate their efforts to develop new products at a rapid pace, and many depend on their connection with a few large core enterprises.

General Motors' recent development of Buick City may indicate a variation of the multinode architecture in a more mature industry. Buick City is a multifirm industrial zone where GM (the core enterprise) and its suppliers plan to locate facilities. The intent is to achieve better coordination, higher quality, and lower inventory levels. Advanced information technology may help this array of related firms coordinate their work.

A multinode organization is not flawless. It gives rise to many difficulties, particularly in the realm of human resource management. The multinode raises important questions in contracting, remuneration, pooling risk, and basis of allegiance. For example, it poses new dilemmas about the distribution of risk when business activity declines. An imbalance of protection against downturns can develop if a core enterprise is always cushioned by cutbacks in prime or tertiary firms. A more balanced allocation of this risk may become a priority human resource issue—if core firms strive to attain leaner staffing, more people would be employed by tertiary firms. The question of government's role in dispersing this risk would also arise.

Despite potential drawbacks, the prospects for multinode organization are promising, especially considering the capabilities gained if advanced information technology is effectively employed. Thoughtful use of this technology with a careful reappraisal of make/buy boundaries can serve as a first step to this new form of large-scale organization through which human resources are deployed.

Hierarchy, professionalization, proximity, relation of home and work, competitive advantage, the experience of doing work, the nature of labor as a commodity, the associated definition of productivity, and organization architecture represent the broad spectrum of human resource factors that become unfrozen with advanced information technology. Refreezing will eventually occur as different arrangements take hold; the ultimate effects of advanced information technology depend on the exercise of choice during the interim. Here is a temporary window of opportunity. Companies that grasp the nature of these choices and methods will find expanded opportunities to renovate and become more competitive.

THE HUMAN RESOURCE CHALLENGE

Since so many aspects of human resource management become unfrozen with advanced information technology, the purchase and installation of new equipment is not automatically beneficial.[28] There is a distinction between equipment functionality and tangible user benefits. One device may offer more memory, faster processing speed, and better-quality display than another. These attributes belong to the machinery itself and to the relative efficiency of the technology around which it is built. *Figure 4-3* illustrates the challenge of translating technical functionality into operational benefits.

To gain concrete advantages from these technical capabilities, specific operations must be changed. In most cases, this translation of enhanced technical functionality into substantive ben-

Figure 4-3
*Translating Technical Functionality
into Tangible Advantages*

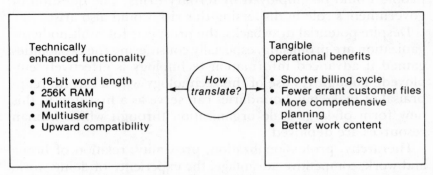

efits requires both learning and changing by the user organization. To alter human resource management in parallel with advanced technology, four specific kinds of learning and change are involved:

1. *Operator skills.* New knowledge and skills are required to make the new equipment function.
2. *Procedural enhancements.* Often the work of nonoperators must change to accommodate the new technology; the most common adaptation is change in administrative procedures.
3. *Structural factors.* Changes in a unit's organizational structure—distribution of responsibility, information flow, coordination of roles, incentives, and compensation—are necessary to the effective use of new equipment.
4. *Cultural fabric.* Tangible user benefits may be realizable only with profound changes in the basic principles of a collective enterprise, such as status differentiation, human resource management philosophies, definition of mission, and key basis of competitive advantage.

It is becoming more complex to translate functionality into benefits. The more sophisticated the equipment, the more learning and change will be required in order to realize benefits (*Figure 4-4*). As greater functionality and interconnectedness unfreeze structural and cultural factors, an enterprise must undertake higher levels of learning and change.

Figure 4-4
*Correlation between Equipment Functionality
and Types of Learning*

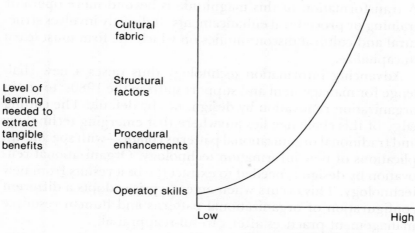

This challenge is exemplified by architectural firms that use advanced computer-aided design (CAD). CAD equipment brings with it more than a need to train operators and alter procedures; many structural and cultural factors must also change if the system is to be cost-effective. As the work flow becomes quicker, the associates must coordinate their efforts more intensely; and as they begin to do their own drawings and filing electronically, support staff roles must change as well. Standards of work and methods of supervision must reflect these shifts. Also, new sources of professional self-image and self-esteem need to evolve and gain legitimacy. Even the scope of the firm's business definition may change as the system's great capacity allows new business lines to be pursued (selling excess CAD capacity to other firms, offering traffic flow and urban design services, internally producing plumbing and wiring diagrams to supplant outside vendors, and so on).

This sweeping transformation rises from the greater technical functionality delivered by the advanced CAD system. CAD equipment is much more capable than prior graphics or word processors. Programs, data, and workstations are more highly integrated than for stand-alone systems. But the opportunities created by these powers are secured only if the firm purchasing the CAD makes the requisite organizational and cultural changes. A transformation of this magnitude is beyond mere operator training or procedural enhancements. It directly involves structural and cultural discontinuities on which the firm must learn to capitalize.

Advancing information technology thus raises a new challenge for management and support staffs in the 1980s: to attain organization renovation by design, not by default. The cutting edge of this challenge lies anywhere that emerging technology and traditional organizational patterns collide—with specific applications of new information technology. Organizational renovation by design is needed to extract the best results from new technology. This occurs when an enterprise adopts a different configuration of organizational patterns and human resource management practices after careful reappraisal.

The technocratic vision of efficiency improvement is misguided in this respect. It presumes that the work of an enterprise is determined by technology alone minus its pattern of organization; that capital substituted for labor brings maximum efficiency at every installation. This was never so and is increasingly less so as microelectronics bring higher functionality and interconnection to equipment everywhere. Organizational circumstances, involving structural factors and cultural fabric, must become a key element in the success of new equipment.

WHAT MANAGERS CAN DO

To mobilize organizational learning and change, managers can engage in six important leadership activities.

1. REDEFINING MANAGEMENT RESPONSIBILITIES

Final approval power over budgets and plans is no longer sufficient to provide leadership for the installation of new technology. Managers must reconceptualize their role to include being the champion of organizational change. This begins with the acknowledgment that the issues are not merely technical.[29]

Required is an insistence that greater raw functionality must be harnessed to new strategic capabilities and different patterns of human resource management. Familiarity with the intricacies of new technologies is not required.

2. SETTING FORTH A GENERAL POLICY

Managers should formulate a policy that leads others to renovate their organizations as new technology is deployed. A simple policy statement is required, consistent with the strategy, ethos, and style of an enterprise. This policy should not be overly specific, but it should raise organizational renewal as a legitimate element of deploying new technology. Articulating a general policy gives others a lens through which to reinterpret the situation posed by a specific information system. Propositions can be woven into the policy that suggest a new direction for enterprise to develop as advanced information technology is deployed.

For example, when a large engineering group installed a very sophisticated computer-aided design (CAD) system, management's involvement did not stop with their budget approval. Senior executives proclaimed the new CAD system a means of "shortening the product design cycle." This interpretation presented the new system as part of a broader organizational change that was vital to their business strategy.

Establishing a general policy for advanced information technology is more than a one-shot affair. Long after its declaration, managers must continually revive it as a priority; a general policy becomes easily misplaced without management's continuing affirmation to keep it operative. Such leadership activity is critical with the deployment of advanced information technology, and it can occur in numerous ways. For instance, at system review meetings, managers can pose questions that reassert their policy as a basis for making decisions. Or managers can draw on their policy statement to formulate measures for evaluating a new system.

Executives at the company attempting to shorten its product design cycle were urged by an outside consultant to invest this extra effort. After initial formulation of their policy, top managers circulated throughout the firm to broadcast it clearly. Later, they raised the policy objective at system development meetings when critical choices were pending ("What will this do to help shorten the design cycle?"). This recurring emphasis led people to explore numerous organizational changes separate from the new CAD system. As the system became operational, the company's senior managers focused attention on their general policy by making it part of assessment (tracking the length of design projects as they were run with the system).

3. SUPPORTING AND STRUCTURING DECENTRALIZED INITIATIVES

Managers cannot produce organizational change by edict. Design of specific changes must proceed on a departmental or unit basis, preferably in advance of equipment selection and installation. The users who are targeted for this equipment have access to the detailed knowledge needed to modify their organization, and they must take part in the value choices associated with the introduction of new devices if these preferences are to become operative. Thus, managers should inspire and support local initiatives to redesign organizations. At first, education may be necessary to develop greater understanding. Special resources like support staff, dedicated review time, technical support, and consulting services may be needed to sustain redesign projects. Eventually, these efforts must be organized to avoid waste and confusion, with clear objectives, explicit review procedures, and specified resources. Throughout, management must persevere while taking care that everyday actions sensibly correspond with the decentralized program's basic values.[30]

4. PROMOTING ORGANIZATIONAL DESIGN

To set priorities and to provide resources is not enough. Managers must also disseminate a procedure that explicitly addresses organization and technology together; a *design method* is needed that indicates how to plan and enact renovation. It will involve four elements.[31] First, It must promote a few basic concepts that enable people to appreciate how their work and its organization can be redesigned by choice. Second, the method must guide data collection and analysis about how work is currently organized and accomplished. Third, the method should generate a tentative outline of new alternatives. Finally, the method should include basic guidelines for the process of enacting design and change. With these elements, a design method provides an orderly agenda for action, so that units can develop an improved fit between their organization and new technology.

A design method is essential. It provides tangible and consistent guidelines for action without excessive detail. Management will recommend a specific design methodology, but units can apply the proposed approach in their own way. New policies remain empty slogans if not bolstered by a design method that can guide specific renovation projects. To allow organizational renovation, it is vital that the design method encompass both the social and technical aspects of a unit. Field-proven methods have recently been summarized to allow easier propagation.[32] Because they encompass both the technology and organization of work, these methods allow a sociotechnical approach[33] while providing attainable steps that make redesign a practical option. Other methods based on different concepts await further development.

5. REDIRECTING SPECIALIST STAFFS

In-house professional staff can help support local projects to design organizations and systems together, especially if they are helped to work cross-functionally. Management can impress specialists in industrial engineering, systems analysis, and human resources that it is important to work jointly in service of organizational renewal. The chosen method of organization design can make this an attainable objective by furnishing a practical agenda to guide cross-functional collaboration, perhaps between staff professionals in information systems and human resources. Eventually, managers can encourage the development of new staff positions that better combine multidisciplinary topics with advanced information technology (e.g., computing, communications, business strategy, government regulation, human resources). This development of new staff roles will require the investment of resources in new patterns of education, training, and promotion.

6. ENGAGING A VARIETY OF STAKEHOLDERS

The pervasive effects of advanced information systems will touch a variety of interest groups intersected by an enterprise. Conventionally, these stakeholders are viewed strictly as adversaries. There is a tendency to defer explicit relations with any stakeholder until polarization has already become excessive. Interest groups and managers of an enterprise may therefore find themselves irreconcilably at odds even if they can agree on some shared concerns.

But often these groups convey useful information, particularly about uncharted territory where there is no previous experience (like the adoption of a "smart" toolstock). Managers can be receptive to these stakeholders without capitulating and acknowledge their concerns before a crisis erupts. Many channels exist for listening: informal discussions, news reports, conferences, and family events. Keeping in mind the life cycle of external interests may help guide such effort by suggesting how different phases create different opportunities for stakeholder initiatives by management.[34]

These steps suggest a thoughtful, involved, and active management role with new information technology while avoiding empty slogans or predefined solutions. The problem is that managers often neglect this aspect of their jobs. In the past, other claims have seemed more urgent, and minimal management involvement has proven adequate with earlier generations of equipment. But the ground is shifting as information technology advances, and a reactive role becomes insufficient. Unfreezing structural and cultural factors will demand greater involvement and initiative on behalf of managers in every enterprise. The following case shows one manager's initiative.

HRM REFORMATION: A CASE EXAMPLE

As profitability declined, the distribution firm described at the beginning of this chapter moved to arrange a better match between their organization and a new information system. Drawing on a design method with the help of an outside consultant, a team of salespeople analyzed their organization and technology.

Their analysis indicated that to capitalize on the new computer system, salespeople needed to work more, not less, but that a different kind of effort was required. No longer was the salesperson an order-taker. That had become the computer's job. The nature of the salesperson's contribution would shift to involve two new tasks: (1) technical support for new product introduction, and (2) collecting strategic customer information. This work required a more consultative and less administrative effort.

To support this new kind of work, the design team proposed a thorough renovation in the structure and administration of the sales organization. This involved a new pattern of organization with different job content, supervision methods, reward systems, career paths, recruitment plans, and assessment procedures. Efforts were made to inform and involve people before the final design was proposed. Senior management approved the plan with a few modifications. As it was implemented, the growth of new products increased above plan, the customer base was expanded, salesforce turnover declined, and old product volumes rose unexpectedly.

Unfortunately, the computer system could have been designed initially to support this enhanced organization, but retrospective change after its installation was prohibitively expensive. Developed without regard for organizational factors, this computer system impaired the modified salesforce's ultimate effectiveness.

CONCLUSION: CHALLENGE AS AN OPPORTUNITY

In an era when microelectronics brings information-processing capabilities everywhere, the configuration of human resources around a system becomes vital as never before. The functionality and interconnectedness of equipment jumps abruptly, presenting a new technological infrastructure that makes novel patterns of organization viable and perhaps mandatory. A unique and fleeting window of opportunity is thus opened. Contrary to the public's fantasy, and despite the wrath of investment analysts, general managers lack omnipotence to renew an enterprise. Normally a web of issues restricts the range of feasible changes within the reach of an executive.[35]

Over the next twenty years, however, a contrary situation is likely to prevail. Once rare opportunities for renewal will become temporarily abundant because of the rapid and pervasive dissemination of advanced information technology. During this time, renovation of an enterprise—by design or default—will be inevitable as new toolstock quickly unfreezes numerous constraints on the management of human resources. Managers can seize this opportunity by working with various stakeholders to initiate renewal by forging a bridge between human resource management and the installation of advanced information technology. Enterprises that redesign strategic capabilities in this manner will prosper at the expense of those who do not.

5
Technologies That Informate: Implications for Human Resource Management in the Computerized Industrial Workplace

Shoshana Zuboff

In the 1980s the rapid development and diffusion of advanced information technology has focused attention upon industrial production and its automation. The label *information technology* reflects the convergence of several streams of technical developments, including microelectronics, computer science, telecommunications, software engineering, and systems analysis. This technology has dramatically increased the ability to record, store, analyze, and transmit information in ways that permit flexibility, timeliness, geographic independence, volume, and complexity; it is capable of fundamentally restructuring operations that depend upon information for the purposes of transaction, record keeping, analysis, or control.

The manufacturing sector offers wide opportunity for the application of advanced information technology. Besant and Dickson have enumerated some of the most typical manufacturing tasks that lend themselves to such applications:[1]

1. Controlled movement of materials, components, products;
2. Control of process variables;
3. Shaping, cutting, mixing, molding of materials;
4. Assembly of components into subassemblies and finished products;

103

5. Control of quality at all stages of manufacture by inspection, testing, or analysis;

6. Organization of the manufacturing process, including design, stock keeping, dispatch, machine maintenance, invoicing, and the allocation of tasks.

To this list I would add:

7. Process optimization;

8. Integration of internal and external business data with operational data to create real-time databases suitable for a wide range of analysis and decision support.

Efforts to optimize the production process tend to concentrate on three strategic objectives: increased continuity, controllability, and comprehensibility. Applications of advanced information technology are seen as uniquely suited to achieving these objectives.[2] For example, microprocessor-based devices, such as programmable logic controllers or sensors, can be integrated into production equipment and linked to a hierarchy of computer systems, increasing the continuity and controllability of operations. Comprehensibility is both a condition and a consequence of such applications. In order to be so automated, that portion of the production process must be made explicit and translated into the computer's binary logic.[3] However, the intelligence of the very devices that increase control means that new streams of data are generated, and these data become the occasion for developing an even more thoroughgoing understanding of the entire operation:

> Since the essence of control is processing information, it follows that any technology which offers improvements in the capability should find wide acceptance. Microelectronics is *essentially* an information-processing technology.[4]

It is in relation to this third dimension, comprehensibility, that information technology reveals the characteristics that most distinguish it from other automating technologies. As information technology is applied in the service of continuity and control, it can generate new streams of data, thus rendering transparent activities that had been either partially or completely opaque.

By its very nature, then, the application of information technology is characterized by a fundamental duality that has not yet been clearly recognized. The technology can be applied in order to *automate* operations. For example, a numerically controlled machine tool will operate by computerized instructions without the physical intervention of an operator, or a robot will operate according to its computer program to spray paint on the side of an automobile or weld pieces of metal without the addition of human effort.

In its second function, the technology creates information. Even when a given application is designed to increase automaticity, it simultaneously has what I shall call a capacity to *informate* the production process. That is, the intelligence of the microprocessor that resides at the base of virtually every application not only applies instructions to equipment but can convert the current state of product or process into information. In this sense, the concrete three-dimensional production process is, with the help of advanced sensing devices, programmable logic controllers, and hierarchies of computer systems, translated into digitized data that are then made available in a two-dimensional space, typically on the screen of a video display terminal or on a computer printout, in the form of electronic symbols, numbers, letters, and graphs. Consider the following examples of informatization, drawn from technical descriptions of microprocessor-based automation in industry:

> Programmable controllers (PCs) are being used extensively in both continuous-process and discrete manufacturing industries. PCs are small, dedicated computers which are used to control a variety of production processes. . . . Modern PCs, for example, are often used not only to control production processes but also to collect information about the process. PCs and numerical control devices for machine tools are very similar in concept. . . . CNC and DNC machines, through their computer screens, may also offer the operator more complete information about the status of the machine process.[5]

> The major catalyst to the robotics industry is their flexibility and their capability for increasing quality and doing it consistently. . . . The final justification . . . is the make up of robots themselves. Since they are computer-based products—and are becoming more so every day—they both draw from and depend

upon a database. Thus they are capable of generating management information, diagnostics, and tying into other forms of computerized automation.[6]

In its capacity as an *automating technology*, information has a vast potential to displace human effort and to substitute for much that has been familiar as human skill, but as an *informating technology*, its implications are not yet well understood.[7] As new forms of advanced information technology are applied to a variety of industrial processes, the extent to which either of its dual capacities is emphasized will determine many of the organizational consequences of technological change and thus its implications for human resource management. The choice of emphasis is above all a question of technology strategy. This choice derives from management's evaluation of the role that new information technology can and should play in the production process, its relationship to the work force, its compatibility with current organizational functions and structures, and the organization's ability to change in ways that best exploit the unique characteristics of new information technology.

This process of technology conversion, and the relative emphasis given to automating and informating capacities, becomes the occasion for revisiting many of the classic themes of the industrial workplace. What implications will advanced information and control technology have for the role of the worker in the labor process? What new skill demands will be generated? How effective is the Tayloristic approach to work organization as the context of production is altered by advanced information and control technologies? And finally, What implications will this new era of technological change have for the degree of antagonism or mutuality that characterizes the emerging industrial workplace?

FIELD INVESTIGATION: THREE PLANTS

In this chapter I rely upon field data collected in three plants during several visits over a three-year period. These plants represent three slightly different versions of the continuous-process form of production in the pulp and paper industries. Each was in a different stage of utilizing new microprocessor-based instrumentation that allowed operators to interact remotely with the production process. With digital control, data could be lifted directly from sensing devices in the manufacturing process and displayed on terminal screens in centralized control rooms. This distributed real-time control system created what I shall call an "information interface" through which operators could access, monitor, and analyze process information. Through this interface they were able to act upon the process remotely, using input commands to alter process parameters, control flows, and so on. The new systems also made it possible to maintain a vast record of hundreds of process variables as well as of manual inputs, thus providing managers with a complete history of plant functioning and operator activity within any time frame from several seconds to several months.

One plant, the Piney Wood Mill, was constructed with technology that was state-of-the-art in 1940. Its pneumatic control systems were, in 1981, being converted to microprocessor-based instrumentation. Approximately half of its operations had been converted at the time of my field visits. The unionized work force at Piney Wood had considerable experience, with an average tenure of fifteen years and many operators who had more than twenty-five years of operating experience. They were strongly identified with their craft-based functions, and a seniority system determined eligibility for promotion among those who qualified for higher-paying jobs.

Piney Wood was organized by an international union in the early 1970s, and since that time there had been a relatively high level of adversarial feeling between managers and the hourly work force. Piney Wood's top managers emphasized the value of the new technology not only as a means to improve process control but also as a way to increase the centralized coordination of plant functions. Technology conversion occurred without consideration of its potential for generating new skill demands, as there had been little investment in training or anticipation of potential organizational implications. Piney Wood's managers consistently emphasized the automating aspects of the new technology: its ability to increase the speed of operations, the product consistency, and the volume of "tons out the door."

The Cedar Bluff Mill was the smallest of the three plants. As a new start-up, it was built to be the most technologically advanced operation of its kind, and it began production in the early 1980s with highly sophisticated real-time information systems and microprocessor-based process control. In addition to the information interface through which the process was operated, an information system, known as the Overview System and accessed through terminals in control rooms and other plant locations, provided a complete real-time overview of 2,500 key pieces of operating equipment. This system's capabilities included a variety of analytic models that operators could use to discover ways to optimize process variables under distinct conditions.

Cedar Bluff was a nonunion plant with an innovative work organization characterized by a contribution-based system for compensation and promotion, a team structure for hourly workers, and a relatively flat management organization.[8] Like their counterparts in Piney Wood, Cedar Bluff's top managers saw new information and control technology as a way to significantly improve process control, but they also believed that an operator's ability to deal effectively with the vast quantities of information generated by their systems would be a decisive factor in the quantity and quality of production. Thus, there was a greater tendency in this organization to stress the informating aspects of the technology.

Tiger Creek, the largest of the three plants, was also constructed in the 1940s and combined pulping with papermaking and other finishing operations. During the past several years various plant modules had been converted to microprocessor-based instrumentation. Most recently, the pulping unit had been gutted and rebuilt, and a manually controlled operation had been replaced with a computer-based information and control system. In addition to process control applications, Tiger Creek had developed a unique passive information system to enhance operator decision making. Such systems differ from closed-loop process control applications in that they are not designed to enhance machine operation nor can they execute decisions without human involvement. Instead, passive systems are built to provide human beings with data for more informed decisions; they are passive with respect to the machine system but require the active engagement of the human mind. In this case, paper-machine operators received real-time cost data relevant to the more than 100 variables under their control (e.g., steam pressure, fiber utilization, moisture content). The computer was programmed to acquire and organize data, translate these data into actual costs, and display them on a terminal screen in the control room. The goal of this system, known as the Expense Tracking System, was to allow workers to manage that portion of operating costs over which they had direct influence. Operators could see the impact of their decisions and work to reduce expenses while maintaining quality.

Tiger Creek's work force had been unionized since the plant was purchased by the parent corporation in the late 1950s. Though there had been a tradition of adversarial relations, recent years had brought some success in labor-management cooperation and had resulted in several innovative approaches to work organization scattered throughout the plant. Moreover, there was a feeling shared by managers and the hourly work force that the plant would not remain competitive if it failed to develop a more collaborative and flexible work system.

In each plant, then, operators were required to work through the medium of an information interface. In both Cedar Bluff and Tiger Creek additional information systems were provided to enhance operator decision making. In Piney Wood and Tiger Creek the new technology presented a significant break with the past. In these plants people who had worked in a close relationship with operating equipment were now required to monitor the process from control rooms using the data interface generated by the new digital instrumentation and additional information systems. The inexperienced work force at Cedar Bluff was learning the pulping process for the first time in the context of the new technology.

The pulp and paper industry represents an interesting case in the spectrum of continuous-process operations. Unlike the processes of oil refinement and chemical production, these industries have been unable to create a complete scientific explication of their procedures, a situation that is further complicated by the constant variation in raw materials. As a result, the tradition of craftsmanship in these industries has persisted through the implementation of pneumatic controls and analogic measurement devices. Pulping has, for example, required a high level of manual involvement with the product at each stage of the process (cooking, bleaching, and so on). Thus, while these industries represent an excellent opportunity for the implementation of advanced technology, they have not shared in the traditions of innovation and automation characteristic of some other continuous-process operations.

Comparing and contrasting data from the three plants provides a special opportunity to assess the impact of the new technology from the vantage point of a more conventional kind of work involvement (Piney Wood and Tiger Creek) as well as to inquire into the new experience of work shaped by information technology (Cedar Bluff). It is likely that what can be learned from these sites about the experience of the worker at the information interface will have relevance for a variety of manufacturing operations as they confront the duality of new information technology and consider the organizational implications of their technology strategies.

THE BODY'S VIRTUOSITY AT WORK

The pulp and paper plants provide an occasion to observe the nature of those skills that derive from the worker's bodily involvement with the production process; sensual contact and the knowledge that it yields have traditionally formed the basis of the worker's competence. Instrumentation has been in close proximity to operating equipment, allowing the operator to combine data from an instrument reading with data from his or her senses. Workers have known what was going on at any particular moment because of what they saw and felt and their ability to relate these perceptions to a set of likely consequences. Under such conditions, the worker knows what to do and demonstrates that knowledge in physical actions—a valve must be opened, more chemical is required, the temperature must be raised, or a bearing must be adjusted. The required sequences and routines necessary to control certain parts of the process and proper adjustments for achieving best results are forms of knowledge that the worker displays in action as a continual reflection of this sensual involvement. Acquired experience makes it possible to relate current conditions to past events, and an operator's competence increases as the passing of time makes it possible to experience the action possibilities of a wide variety of operating conditions.

In both Piney Wood and Tiger Creek, where an older, highly experienced work force was making the transition to a new technology, operators had many ways of using their bodies to achieve precise knowledge. One man judged the condition of paper coming off a dry roller by the sensitivity of his hair to electricity in the atmosphere around the machine. Another operator could judge the moisture content of a roll of pulp by a quick slap of the hand. Immediacy was the mode in which things were known, and it provided a feeling of certainty, of knowing "what's going on." One worker in Piney Wood described how it felt to be removed from the physical presence of the process equipment and asked to perform tasks from a computerized control room:

> It is very different now. . . . It is hard to get used to not being out there with the process. I miss it a lot. I miss being able to see it. You can see when the pulp runs over a vat. You know what's happening.

The worker's capacity to know has been lodged in sentience and displayed in action. The physical presence of the process equipment has been the setting that corresponded to this knowledge, which could, in turn, only be displayed in that context. As long as the action context remained intact, it was possible for knowledge to remain implicit. Thus, the worker knew a great deal, but typically very little of that knowledge was ever articulated, written down, or made explicit in any fashion. Instead, operators went about their business, doing what they knew and rarely attempting to translate that knowledge into publicly accessible terms. When managers speak of "the art" involved in operating these plants, this is what they mean. As one manager at Piney Wood described it:

> There are a lot of operators working here who cannot verbally give a description of some piece of the process. I can ask them what is going on at the far end of the plant and they can't tell

me but they can draw it for me. By taking away this physical contact that he understands, it's like we have taken away his blueprint. He can't verbalize his way around the process.

When a process engineer attempts to construct a set of algorithms for automating some portion of the production process, a typical first step involves seeking information from those individuals who currently perform the tasks that will be automated. Only by learning the detail of their activity is it possible to translate action into a logical model. In the course of such detail gathering, an engineer is likely to run up against the limits of implicit knowledge. A worker may perform competently yet be unable to communicate the structure of her or his actions. As one engineer discovered:

> There are operators who can run the paper machine with tremendous efficiency, but they cannot describe to you how they do it. They cannot describe to you how to run a paper machine. They have built-in actions and senses that they are not aware of. One operation required pulling two levers simultaneously, and they were not conscious of the fact that they were pulling two levers. They said they were pulling one. The operators run the mill, but they don't understand how. There are operators who know exactly what to do, but they cannot tell you how they do it.

These aspects of the worker's know-how I shall refer to as *embodied skill*. The above comments reveal four components of embodied skill:

1. *Sentience.* Embodied skill reflects sentient information.
2. *Action Dependence.* Embodied skill is developed in physical performance. It remains implicit in action rather than becoming explicit in language.
3. *Contextuality.* Embodied skill only has meaning within the context in which the physical activities can occur.
4. *Wholism.* The action situation is grasped comprehensively. The actor is unconscious of detail while involved in the sweep or flow of the action process.

These four dimensions of traditional operator knowledge necessitate a fifth—individualism. It is the individual body that takes in the situation, and it is an individual's actions that display the required competence. Though every operator with similar responsibilities will perform the same functions, each will perform them in a unique way, fashioned according to a personal interpretation of what works best. A process engineer contrasted the personal rendering of skill with the impersonal but consistently optimal performance of the computer:

> There is no question that the computer takes the human factor out of running the machine. Each new person who come on shift will make their own distinct changes, according to their sense of what is the best setting. In contrast, the computer runs exactly the same way all the time. Each operator thinks he does a better job, each one thinks he has a better intimate understanding of the equipment than another operator. But none of them can compete with the computer.

The quality of knowledge at the core of embodied skill was described by the scientist Michael Polanyi as "tacit knowledge." He began with the need to explain why human beings know more than they can say:

> I shall reconsider human knowledge by starting from the fact that we can know more than we can tell. This fact seems obvious enough; but it is not easy to say exactly what it means. . . . We know a person's face, and can recognize it among a thousand, indeed among a million. Yet we usually cannot tell how we recognize a face we know. So most of this knowledge cannot be put into words.[9]

Polanyi contrasted this implicit way of knowing the world with the more explicit forms of knowledge characteristic of science. He argued that certain kinds of meanings are comprehensible only as a whole (the act of pulling versus how many levers) and can be destroyed when it is broken into its composite parts:

> We can see how an unbridled lucidity can destroy our understanding of complex matters. Scrutinize closely the particulars of a comprehensive entity and their meaning is effaced, our conception of the entity is destroyed. . . . By concentrating attention on his fingers, a pianist can temporarily paralyze his movement. We can make ourselves lose sight of a pattern or physiognomy by examining its several parts under sufficient magnification.[10]

Just as the aim of science is to establish objective and explicit knowledge, so computerization requires transforming the kind of tacit knowledge in which operator skills are embedded into explicit knowledge that is logical and programmable. The worker's tacit knowledge must be painstakingly brought to the surface and decomposed in order to be reconstructed in the form of the algorithms that constitute the heart of a computer system. As one Piney Wood manager put it:

> The whole point of developing technology in this business is to be able to duplicate what's in an operator's head and then have the outputs come faster and more consistently.

In plants like Piney Wood and Tiger Creek, where operators have relied upon embodied skill, management must convince them to leave behind a world in which things were immediately known, comprehensively sensed, and able to be acted upon directly in order that they might embrace a world that is dominated by objective data, removed from the action context, and requiring a qualitatively different kind of response. In this new world personal interpretations of how to make things happen count for little. The worker who has his "pet knobs" or knows just where to kick the machine to make it purr finds himself without these familiar landmarks.

In this transition the worker must trade immediate knowledge for a more explicit understanding of the science that undergirds the operation. One Piney Wood manager described it this way:

> The workers have an intuitive feel of what the process needs to be. Someone in the process will listen to things and that is their information. All of their senses are supplying data. But once they are in the control room, all they have to do is look at the screen. Things are concentrated right in front of you. You don't have sensory feedback. You have to draw inferences by watching the data, so you must understand the theory behind it. In the long run you would like people who can take data and draw broad conclusions from it. They must be more scientific.

Many managers are not sanguine about the ability of experienced workers to trade tacit knowledge for scientific inference:

The operators today know that if I do *x* then *y* will happen. But they don't understand the real logic of the system. Their cause and effect reasoning comes from their experience. Once we put things under automatic control and ask them to relate to the process using the computer, their personal judgments about how to relate to equipment go by the wayside. We are saying your intuition is no longer valuable. Now you must understand the whole process and the theory behind it.

As workers are removed from the physical context of the plant and are asked to monitor and control the operation through the medium of an information interface, what kind of skills and mental capacities do they experience as being necessary? As the value of traditional operator knowledge becomes obsolete, what replaces it?

A NEW HEGEMONY OF MIND

In contrast to embodied skills, the demands generated by new information technology require what I shall call *intellective skills*. The fundamental quality of these emerging skill demands, as it is experienced by workers and observed by their managers, is a reorientation in the means by which one can have a palpable effect upon the world. Immediate physical responses must be replaced by abstract thought processes, in which options are considered, choices made, and these choices are translated into the terms of the computer system. For many, physical action is restricted to the play of fingers on the terminal keyboard or screen; the real activity is now in the mind. As one operator put it, "Your past physical mobility must be translated into a mental thought process." A Cedar Bluff manager with many years experience in pulping contemplates the distinct capacities that have become necessary in a highly computerized environment:

In 1953 we put operation and control as close together as possible. We did a lot of localizing so that when you made a change you could watch the change, actually see the motor start up. With the evolution of computer technology, you centralize controls and move away from the actual physical process. If you don't have an understanding of what is happening and how all the pieces interact, it is more difficult. You need a new learning capability, because when you operate with the computer you can't see what is happening. There is a difference in the mental and conceptual capabilities you need—you have to do things in your mind.

"You have to do things in your mind." If you do nothing in your mind, nothing will happen. If you do the incorrect thing in your mind, the effects will not be what was intended. The scene of activity has shifted from the surface of the body and its ability to extend itself into the environment to the interior realm of mind. When operators in Piney Wood and Tiger Creek discuss their traditional skills, they speak of knowing things by habit and association. They talk about "cause-and-effect" knowledge and being able to see the things to which they must respond. They refer to "folk medicine" and knowledge that you don't even know you have until it is suddenly displayed in the ability to take a decisive action and make something work. Though embodied skills require the intelligent participation of the human brain, it is an intelligence that is seamlessly blended with the body's responsiveness and capacity to act. Thinking rarely has to stand alone, explicit and abstracted from this flow of action. The cognitive process of interference and interpretation can remain implicit throughout.

"We are in uncharted waters now," they say. "We have to control our operations blind." The metaphor reiterated countless times is one of being robbed of one's senses and plunged into darkness. Now the learning must begin all over again. It is slow and scary, and many workers are timid for not wanting to appear stupid and incompetent. Hammers and wrenches have been replaced by numbers and buttons. An operator with thirty years of service in the Piney Wood Mill (he was described by one manager as knowing so much about the process that his mind was "like a computer") described his experience at the new information interface:

> Anytime you mash a button you should have in mind exactly what is going to happen. You need to have in your mind where it is at, what it is doing, and why it is doing it. Out there in the plant you can know things just by habit. You can know them without knowing that you know them. In here you have to watch the numbers, whereas out there you have to watch the actual process.

"You need to have things in mind"—it is a simple phrase, but deceptive. For what it takes to have things in mind is far different from the tacit knowledge of former skills. Access to the process now depends upon explicit understanding. It is more complex, the ability to respond is slower, and there is greater opportunity for error. To accomplish one operation might require sixteen control actions spread across four groups of variables. Having decided what to do and executed that command, the worker must scan new data and check for results.

A line manager in Piney Wood, who had been actively involved with the design and implementation of the information and control system and had worked closely with his operators as they struggled for mastery in the new environment, attempted to enumerate some of the mental demands it exerted. He spoke of the importance of conceptualizing the process and understanding the interdependencies among variables; of the need to memorize many data points and their causal linkages; of the demand for written comprehension skills and the ability to anticipate instead of react to developments in the process. All these requirements fold back upon an interior act—the act of thinking. An operator summed it up this way:

> Before computers, we didn't have to think as much, just react. You just knew what to do because it was physically there. Now, the most important thing to learn is to think before you do something, to think about what you are planning to do. You have to know which variables are the most critical and therefore what to be most cautious about, what to spend time thinking about before you take action.

"We never got paid to have ideas," said one Tiger Creek worker. "We got paid to work." Work is, after all, the exertion that is known by its material results. The fact that a material world must be created necessitates exertion; without exertion such a world cannot be made. These workers believed that there are some in society who get paid to think but that they were not among them. They saw themselves as giving their bodies in effort and skill and through their bodies making things. Information technology has inserted itself among the assumptions of these men, accustomed to gauging their integrity in measures of strain and sweat, and thrown them into turmoil.

There is a gradual awareness that the rules of the game have changed. For some, this creates panic; they do not believe in their ability to "think" and are afraid of being revealed as incompetent.

Such feelings are no mere accident of personality, but the sedimentation of long years of conditioned learning about who does the "thinking"—a boundary that was not meant to be crossed. A Tiger Creek manager says:

> Currently managers make all the decisions. . . . Operators don't want to hear about alternatives. They have been trained to *do* not to *think*. There is a fear of being punished if you think. This translates into a fear of the new technology.

In each control room a tale is told about one or two old-timers who, though they knew more than anyone about the process, just "up and quit" when they heard the new technology was coming. From one plant to another, the reporting of these cases is remarkably similar:

> He felt that because he had never graduated high school, he would never be able to keep up with this new stuff. We tried to tell him different, but he just wouldn't listen.

But those who leave are not the majority. Most men and women need their jobs and will do whatever it takes to keep them. And beyond this, there are many who are intrigued with the opportunity. They seem to get pulled in gradually, observing their own experiences and savoring with secret surprise each new bit of evidence of their unexpected abilities. They discuss the newness and strangeness of having to act upon the world by exerting a more strictly intellective effort. Under the gentle stimulus of a researcher's questions, they think about thinking. What does it feel like? Here is an operator who had spent twenty years in one of the most manually intensive parts of the Tiger Creek Mill that had recently been computerized:

> If something is happening, if something is going wrong, you don't go down and fix it. Instead you stay up here and think about the sequence and you think about how you want to affect the sequence. You get it done through your thinking. But dealing with information instead of things is very . . . well, very intriguing. I am very aware of the need for my mental involvement

now. I am always wondering where I am at. What is happening? It all occurs in your mind now.

Another operator discussed the same experience but added an additional dimension. After describing the demand for mental involvement, he observed:

> Things occur to me now that never would have occurred to me before. With all of this information in front of me, I begin to think about how to do the job better. And being freed from all that manual activity, you really have time to look at things, to think about them, and to anticipate.

As information technology restructures the work situation, it turns action into thought and replaces physical involvement with mental engagement. Absorption, immediacy, and organic responsiveness are superseded by distance, coolness, and remoteness; such distance brings an opportunity for reflection. There is little doubt in these workers' minds that the logic of their jobs has been fundamentally altered. As another worker from Tiger Creek summed it up, "Sitting in this room and just thinking has become part of my job. It's the technology that lets me do these things."

Beyond this essential shift from a know-how lodged in sentience to a know-what that resides in thinking, what are other components of the intellective skills that the operator must now bring to the data interface? The first and most immediate fact that forces itself upon the operator is the presence of a vast quantity of explicit data:

> The amount of information available now makes the background detail of the process much more visible and it's harder to discern which outcomes to gauge your work by. . . . Some of this information was theoretically available before, but we never paid any attention to it because it just wasn't easy to get.

In each plant the microprocessor-based control system registers hundreds of data points updated at five-second intervals to provide a complete picture of real-time functioning. One salient demand upon the operator involves the capacity to approach the data analytically. He or she must be able to grasp how the various data points are related to one another: What will a change in one variable mean for the web of variables to which it is linked? Managers stress the fact that a systematic and logical thought process is a necessity. Operators must be able to approach the data as problem solvers and use it to build and refine their deductions.

Because Cedar Bluff was conceived and constructed around these advanced information and control capabilities, it is an advantageous setting in which to develop an understanding of intellective skill demands. Operators in Cedar Bluff were new to the industry and marveled that it was ever possible to run a pulp mill without such advanced systems. The Cedar Bluff start-up represented one of the most advanced automation experiments in the mill's parent company and as such was its first opportunity to learn what might be involved in training an entire work force to become competent in a highly informated environment.

Cedar Bluff's managers were trying to understand what operators "do" at the information interface. One systems engineer worked closely with operators during the early years of the plant's operation. His comments illustrate the new demands on the analytic capabilities of the worker:

> When you want to know what is going on in a part of the plant you roll through several screens of data. You must keep important data in your mind as you continue to scan. People learn how to organize data in their minds. They build models in their minds about what is really happening and they build on the model with the data until they have a complete picture.

Workers themselves had come to believe that analytical thinking and data-based reasoning were essential elements of competence. As one younger operator put it:

> Management wants to know how you are going to handle problems. They want to see your logical thinking, your deductive reasoning. We need to be systematic; we need to analyze problems. The reasoning is all in your head.

The plant manager goes one step further. He views the technology itself as a learning tool, the means by which the work force will actually be educated in abstract thinking and data analysis:

> We are depending on the technology to educate our people in abstract thinking. . . . You can no longer make a decision just based on local data. There is so much going on in the plant . . . you have to derive your decision from the interrelationships among the variables.

For workers and managers in Piney Wood and Tiger Creek, controlling the process through the information system represents a shift in orientation, and sometimes it is perplexing. The physical process is now represented by an interlocking set of variables. In order to "do" something, operators must know how to make their way through these variables, as well as the logical sequence that reflect cause and effect. Even relatively routine control actions require monitoring data instead of actual equipment. A Piney Wood operator describes his experience:

> Monitoring the screen takes a different kind of thinking. . . . You can do more, but you have to know more to do more. There is more to manage and more to think about. For example, if you want to get one washer ready before filling it with pulp, you have got to go through three or four programs and they must be in sequence. Then you got to jump down the line of flow and start bringing up steam and chemicals gradually. You go back and forth continuously monitoring the flow, the chemicals, and the steam until it is all leveled out. In the manual environment you could just see everything.

The capacity to understand data, to approach data logically, and to use data-based reasoning ultimately depends upon having an overarching theoretical conception of the processes to which the data refer. It is only such a theoretical grasp that can guide operators through the data, provide the basis for generating hypotheses, and inform operators' judgments as to how to search the database for evidence of the consequences of their actions and how to design future actions. An operator's understanding of the production process was previously implicit and displayed in action. Now understanding must become explicit—a consciously articulated theory that guides data analysis.

A theoretical understanding of the process had become one of the principal criteria by which Cedar Bluff management discriminated among its operators. Those with a theoretical grasp of the process were most likely to be promoted to the higher pay curves. Top managers stressed the value of such theoretical knowledge among the operating work force and believed that without such knowledge it would be impossible for operators to develop the quality of insight that would allow them to improve plant performance:

> The hope in Cedar Bluff is that people will discover ways to improve the process because they understand the basic theory.

Such emphasis was borne out among the operators who perceived theoretical knowledge as a salient factor in the development of their own competence.

> The more I learn theoretically, the more I can see in the information. Raw data turns into information with my knowledge. I find that you have to be able to know more in order to do more. It is your understanding of the process that guides you.

In the traditional operating environment such theoretical knowledge had been the exclusive domain of managers and engineers. Operators knew how to do things but had little understanding of what they were doing and why. In the transition to data-based reasoning, they must learn to embrace theory as well. As a Piney Wood manager explained:

> We've never expected them to understand how the plant works, just to operate it. But now if they don't know the theory behind how the plant works, how can we expect them to understand all of the variables in the new computer system, and how these variables interact?

Piney Wood's operators felt this new pressure to approach their work in a more explicit, systematic, and conceptual mode than they had ever before considered:

> To do the job well now you need to understand this part of the mill and how it relates to the rest of the plant. You need a concept of what you are doing. Now you can't just look around you and know what is happening, you can't just see it, you have to check through the data on the computer to see your effects. And if you don't know what to look for in the data, you won't know what's happening.

These components of the new intellective skill base—abstract thinking, data-based reasoning, and theoretical apprehension—require a fourth skill dimension that I shall call *attentional commitment*. In the conventional plant environment workers were engaged with the production process through the natural involvement of their bodies in physical activity. The senses at the surface of their bodies were available to be put on alert in response to noises, sights, and smells. This represented a kind of polymorphous attentional involvement in which each sense organ attended in its own way to relevant stimuli in the immediate environment.

Now, surrounded by electronic data, a different kind of attention is required. It is a cerebral attention and is experienced by the operators as demanding a new kind of conscious cognitive commitment to their work. Industrial administration has long accepted that technological change calls for a reevaluation of the effort bargain between management and the worker. A new technical means for accomplishing a task requires each side to reassess the acceptable level of effort that the worker must give and the appropriate means through which managers can control the stability and intensity of that effort.[11] In each of the plants informatization had done more than simply reduce or increase the worker's effort. Effort itself had undergone a redefinition; the terrain of effort had shifted, not simply from muscles to brain but from the complete sensual involvement of the worker to an involvement that depends on quality of mind. Attentional commitment is the sign of this new modality of effort.

For those of us who have never worked with our bodies, such a change would seem an obvious invitation to a better world. But for the worker whose skill has been inextricably bound up with physical activity, cognitive effort does not necessarily seem better or easier:

> Sometimes hard work is the easier kind of work to do. I find that now I have to pay more attention. I have to watch things closer. . . .
> There is less manual work and a lot more mental strain. You can't break your concentration from what you are doing in the

middle of a sequence. You have to concentrate; you have to pay attention.

Frequently, when operators begin to discuss the attentional demands of their new roles, they will act out their appraisal by gripping their foreheads and feigning sudden pain:

> At least in the manual operation there are no headaches. It is hard to pay attention for such a long time.

Maintaining an attentional commitment to the data interface can be difficult, and operators repeatedly describe the ease with which their attention lapses:

> It's a problem keeping up your attention, particularly when things are running smoothly. You have a tendency to be looking at something and at some point you realize that you are staring and you don't know what you are seeing . . . you are staring at something when you thought you were looking at something.

This worker has identified the interior structure of attentional commitment. It is not sufficient to look; one must see. Attention implies intention, without which it is merely a superficial activity, the appearance of engagement without active deliberation.

Managers in each plant found themselves having to invent ploys to engage the operators' attention. When they supervised a worker's physical activity, fostering attentional commitment was never perceived as a problem. The physical engagement necessitated by the work activity assured an organic involvement in the work at hand. But as effort comes to be situated in the domain of the mind, how does a manager keep others mentally engaged?

The problem was most pronounced in Cedar Bluff, where information systems dominated the environment and operators had no history of manual involvement with the pulping process. Some Cedar Bluff managers insisted that operators keep written logs of their activities. Though there was little information an operator could record that was not already available through an information system, these managers saw the physical requirement of recording information as one way to ensure that attention was being paid. One manager explained:

> With our information systems we don't need the operators to keep logs but we have them do it anyway, because we think the

activity of logging in will force them to pay attention to certain parameters. The underlying issue is how to get them involved with the process. Physically writing down certain numbers is thought to maintain some kind of involvement. . . . As a manager, I have to think of ways to keep people consciously involved, rather than just staring at the screen.

The technology itself was designed to take into account the difficulty of ongoing attentional involvement. The control interface was equipped with alarm capabilities that could be programmed to sound when a given variable strayed out of its optimum parameters. The alarm system substituted for a certain amount of supervisory attention. It cajoled operators into paying attention, even as its very presence recognized and legitimated lapses of attention. No manager or operator felt it was possible to survive in a computerized environment without such alarms to help maintain attentional commitment. As another Cedar Bluff manager put it:

We need alarms because we find that operators stop paying attention. The computer lulls us into not having to pay attention, not having to be involved. So we need alarms.

INFORMATIZATION AND THE LIMITS OF TAYLORISM

As the new systems make a wide variety of information immediately available in a centralized location, plant functions are integrated in a single database. In the previous technological context each plant module would have some objective mill-wide data, but more typically individual workers would handle specific pieces of equipment or aspects of the production process with little information about their activities or other relevant operations ever made explicit. Information about the production process remained more private than public. Process information was recorded in logs, but such data were cumbersome and used only by managers or engineers in time-consuming analyses.

Residing at the interface of such a powerful information system changes a worker's relationship to the production process. No longer does he or she concentrate on one boiler, digester, evaporator, or chlorine tank. Instead, data that reflect the functioning of a wide range of process variables and are constantly within view. The assumption here, only occasionally made explicit, is that such newly visible information becomes the responsibility of those who see it. It is further assumed that the individuals who behold the data actually see the data and that they will respond to what they see.

A Piney Wood manager who had worked closely with his operators in the conversion to the microprocessor-based control system explained:

> In computerizing the controls we exposed people to information that had nothing to do with their jobs, but they couldn't ignore the information once they identified it. So they are taking the responsibility without being formally assigned the responsibility. Before they did not cross the borders between jobs.

Operators agreed with his assessment:

> The computer brings all your information to you. You can watch the whole plant operating from your screen. It's different from a conventional plant, where you would be spending most of your time with each piece of equipment. Everything now is brought right in front of you.

The very structure of the situation implies that those before whose eyes the information passes will see it, comprehend it, and respond to it.

In each plant the accessibility of such data did offer operators an extraordinary opportunity, when they had the skills to adequately understand, analyze, and explore what they saw. Experienced operators found they had a broader range and greater depth of information than ever before. In many cases, the data to which they were now routinely exposed were only a short time ago considered to be for management eyes only. With sufficient intellective skill development, many operators were able to develop a better grasp of the production process. They discovered that the contributions they were able to make could go beyond simply controlling to actually developing new insights into the process and how it might be improved. Such activity, known as optimization, is the result of thoughtful analysis and data-based insight. It is the kind of contribution that an organization typically depends upon its managers and engineers to make. A Tiger Creek operator commented:

> Having access to so much information makes you think ahead.
> Many problems can be avoided if you are just monitoring the
> information, concentrating on it, thinking about it, understanding what it means, seeing the patterns in it, and being alert to
> the things it is showing you. Once you gain confidence with the
> new technology you have time to think about how to do the job
> better. That is the real potential of this equipment. That would
> never have occurred if we had just stayed with the old technology.

Thinking about how things might be done differently has never been the worker's domain, at least not since the advances of scientific management gave rise to the management superstructures of the modern organization. The worker has not had access to the kind of information that would make such insight possible. In many industries management itself has had to apply enormous diligence in order to be able to compile the data that could be subjected to systematic analysis as a basis for process or product improvements. One older worker in Piney Wood mused:

> They hired us from the neck down. In all the years that I have
> been working here, they were only interested in me from the
> neck down. Now with computers, they seem to only care about
> us from the neck up.

The significance of the new opportunity that faces operators can only be appraised in light of the legacy of Taylorism that so dramatically limited the legitimate contribution of the worker to the production process. The logic of scientific management rested on three key elements: (1) the worker's implicit know-how was analyzed in order to generate data that could serve as the basis for (2) the development of a series of management functions that enabled (3) management to take more responsibility for coordination and control of the production process.

The process of automation in these plants follows a similar course. Process engineers must interview workers in order to learn what they actually do. Only with such information can they program automatic control or set appropriate process parameters. A Tiger Creek engineer describes debriefing one of the oldest hands in the digesting area of the pulp mill undergoing a complete conversion to microprocessor-based instrumentation and computer control:

> We thought there were six important steps in the process. But when we debriefed George we found that there were more like forty steps, each one requiring various decisions and judgment calls. Those guys were acting like computers on that process.

If the work of the engineers only gives weight to the automating capacity of advanced information technology, thus reducing both the effort and the skill requirements of the operator, the structure of Taylorism is replicated along with its inherent antagonisms. In one area of Piney Wood, where an emphasis had been placed upon automatic control and staffing reductions, many operators agreed:

> They need the operators to help them figure out what the computer should do. But why should you tell a man all your knowledge about how this place runs so he can put it into a machine and then it's going to take your job away?

When the application of computer-based technology emphasizes the informating capacity of the technology, the results can be markedly different. As intelligent technology turns the production process into information, and when that information is made accessible to operators, the essential logic of Taylorism is shattered. For the first time, technology returns to workers what it once took away, but with a crucial difference. The worker's knowledge had been embodied, implicit in action. Informatization makes that knowledge explicit; it holds up a mirror to the worker, reflecting what was known, but now in a form that is precise and detailed. In order to reappropriate his or her reflection, the worker must be able to grapple with a kind of knowledge that now stands outside the self, externalized and public. Intellective skill becomes the means to interact competently with this now objectified information, to reappropriate it as one's own, and to engage in an ongoing learning process that can transform information into insight. A Piney Wood operator reflected:

> Before we did not have any way to know what we were learning or to understand the effects of our actions. Now we have so much

information and feedback—not to be able to conceptualize it is the real crime.

The Expense Tracking System at Tiger Creek provides an example of the impact that such reappropriated knowledge can have. The system informed the operations of two paper machines and computed the associated costs in real time. Operators were encouraged to use the system to improve their understanding of the process and to seek ways to minimize costs while maintaining quality and preserving the integrity of the equipment. Within the first year of operating with the new system, the operators had suggested changes that generated several hundred thousand dollars in savings, an amount approximately one-third greater than had been predicted in the original justification. The operators maintained they had known all along how to make such improvements, but their point of view was only acknowledged when they were able to transform their sense of what was right into the objective terms that their managers found legitimate:

> The Expense Tracking System is a vehicle for us to talk to our managers. Managers only believe quantitative data. If our managers read the printout and it says that snow is black, they will believe it. All along we have known the best way to run this process, but we couldn't prove it to them. Now we have a common ground for talking to them.

LIFE AT THE INFORMATION INTERFACE

In each of the plants the operator's world came to be dominated more by data than by equipment, required effort that was more cognitive than physical, and engendered skills that were more intellective than embodied. In a world such as this, what are the sources of meaning and motivation that men and women find in their work? What will ensure that when an operator is face-to-face with a broad array of relevant operating information, he or she will actually be responsive to it and make the intellective effort that is necessary to go beyond the surface of the data and learn from it?

The intricacies of life at the information interface are not yet well appreciated. There is a tendency among managers to assume that human beings will respond to data displays like obedient servomechanisms, immediately recognizing the significance of the data and responding appropriately. The image of the human subject as another factor in a feedback loop does not take into account some distinctly human realities. The meaning with which humans invest their work, their levels of motivation and commitment, and the quality of their skills will each mediate the relationship between information and the human observer.

Indeed, as the work people do and the effort they must make become more abstract, the need for positive motivation becomes more pressing. It is relatively easy for a manager to determine that a worker has not properly repaired a boiler (it continues to malfunction) or has failed to adequately monitor the levels of a surge chest (it overflows). But how does a manager determine that a worker has failed to respond to something in the data? How does a manager evaluate the possibility of missed opportunities to learn more about the production process and improve operations? In the final analysis, it is only operator skill and commitment that can ensure that intellective effort will be exerted and that the opportunities made available by an informating technology will be exploited.

In many cases it seems that operators are more aware of the importance of managing their psychological relationship to the information interface than are their managers. As one Piney Wood operator remarked:

> You have to know what information to pull out and how to get it. But it's your attitude that plays a big part in whether or not you are willing to learn.

The new control interface meant that Piney Wood operators were being exposed to an array of data that tended to dissolve many of the boundaries traditionally defining job responsibilities. The expectation that operators approach the data as an integrated whole with an eye toward monitoring the interdependencies of the production process also provided them with a new way to express resistance. Some Piney Wood managers had begun to notice that in those areas of the plant where there were pay disputes or hostile relationships between managers and workers, operators had discovered the power of selective inattention:

> We are exposing them to all this information now, which means more responsibility because you can't ignore it. But in one module the operators are digging their heels in. They want more pay and they are mad. So they are ignoring the data they see.

A growing number of managers in each mill were becoming aware that the new relationship between workers and their work was subtly problematic. A Tiger Creek manager summed up the concern:

> The $64,000 question for us today is how to get the operator to own the data, how to get him or her to feel personally accountable for what the system displays.

The problems of managing motivation are shaped in part by the history and culture of each plant, but the options that managers take for eliciting work motivation will finally depend on how the duality of information technology is perceived and exploited. To the extent that these new systems are narrowly perceived for their automating potential, managers will want to maximize the self-correcting capacity of computer systems and minimize the need for human intervention, contribution, and understanding. There are powerful forces driving managers in this direction. Justifications for investment in new technology tend to rely on conventional accounting formulas, in which computer power is treated as a direct substitute for human labor. Managers are rewarded on the basis of their ability to get more done, more efficiently, with fewer people. Such structural pressures reinforce an underlying but potent managerial fantasy of achieving perfect control through total automation and thus avoiding the messiness and potential conflict of human interaction. One operator in Piney Wood told the following story:

> One of the higher ups brought some customers in here for a tour. He showed them one of the new computers we have controlling the process. The man came in here and stood in front of the machine. He rubbed it back and forth. It was like he was

lusting after it. He just kept stroking it and we were all in here and he said to these customers, "This is a marvelous machine. It is a wonderful piece of equipment. It doesn't take coffee breaks or come in with a hangover. And it does a better job than a man can do." He said all this to them just like we were not there, like we were not human or something.

I wanted to tell him off right then, but I waited until we were out of the plant. I saw him on the street in town on Saturday and I called him a motherfucker. I told him that the computer may not take coffee breaks but it cannot do anything unless it got information from people who do take coffee breaks. We are the ones who feed it information and have to tell it what to do.

This adoration of the computer in its transcendence of human needs is not unusual. Managers frequently comment on the pleasure they take in robots that do not require coffee breaks or automatic systems that perform continually without demands for overtime pay. This allure is understandable as long as managers perceive the technology as a straightforward substitute for human labor.[12]

The alternative is to emphasize the informating power of the technology. This does not mean ignoring opportunities to automate. It does mean recognizing the distinctive contribution that human beings can make through their ability to recognize unprogrammed events and discern patterns. The computer as automation is subsumed in the computer as information, supporting an individual's potential to think inventively and critically. Informatization does not only imply human monitoring of a data flow. It is a recognition that human beings cannot reasonably monitor without having responsibility for what they see. Such responsibility depends upon being able to exert influence, and there can be no influence without the intellective skills that define competence at the information interface.[13]

PROSPECTS FOR SOCIAL INTEGRATION IN THE COMPUTERIZED INDUSTRIAL WORKPLACE

The likelihood of a socially integrated workplace in this new era of information technology will depend upon the design and application strategies that managers adopt. A strategy that gives priority to the automating capacity of the technology is likely to diminish social integration. It will create a definitive and probably irreversible gulf between managers, whose understanding empowers them to influence the operation, and workers, who function as adjuncts to the system with minimal critical understanding. In this scenario the organization becomes more sharply hierarchical. Though there would be a reduced number of jobs at the lower levels of the organization, opportunities for advancement would be slight, since the activities of those at lower levels would have little relevance for the kinds of knowledge required in higher status functions.

In contrast, a strategy that recognizes the informating capacity of the technology and emphasizes the opportunities associated with informatization by providing broad access to the information interface and investing in the development of intellective skills is likely to be better positioned to exploit the unique potential of intelligent technology and dramatically increase social integration. Three dominant features of the informatization scenario contribute to this.

The first concerns the social character of life at the interface. Though managers often envision the ultimate centralized control room staffed by one highly trained individual, the realities of problem solving and sense making at the interface are very different. The proper interpretation of information as it appears on a video screen is rarely self-evident. Whenever the viewer perceives something unusual or potentially problematic, there are soon four or five people crowded around the screen, each offering hypotheses and suggesting methods for testing them. In addition, it frequently requires individuals from several disciplines—systems engineers, process operators, instrumentation specialists—to generate the best solutions. An operator explains:

> The new technology really brings people together. You need people who can understand electronics, programming, and the complexity of the information it presents requires teamwork because you need to have different specialties and understandings to work together. You need to talk about what you know. This type of computer system will always bring people together be-

cause you have to discuss what you see, what you understand, what you know, and what should be done.

A second integrating feature involves the organizational visibility that is created by the continual presence of real-time data. For example, in Cedar Bluff the Overview System automatically generated a database that reflected plant functioning as well as operator performance. When access to such a database is primarily top-down, hierarchical control is strengthened and the potential for conflict is increased. When the data are widely accessible, as they were at Cedar Bluff, a different scenario unfolds. Organization members can monitor their own performance as well as that of their peers. While an exploration of all the psychological dynamics associated with such a phenomenon is beyond the scope of this discussion, it does appear true that such transparency is a powerful force for social integration. Managers and operators report less conflict, because the volume of objective data stands as a dispassionate arbiter of truth. People can spend less time arguing the facts and more time identifying and implementing solutions. Individuals may be "observed" remotely, but their own access to the data decreases the tendency to feel that they are victims of oppressive surveillance. Instead, organization members become brethren in the data, and the world that is created comes closer to Frederick Taylor's dream of mutuality born of a perfect science than anything the time-study experts ever conceived. Managers need no longer closely observe subordinates in order to have detailed knowledge of their conduct. In each of the plants the memory associated with the control interface made it possible for managers to track results and to deduce many of the important elements of operator behavior. This dynamic is described from an operator's point of view at Tiger Creek:

> Managers don't have to be standing guard over you to find out what is happening. They can come back in ten days and from the computer they can see everything that happened. This eliminates the middle man. It is like going right to the farm to buy your eggs. The exactness of the information means that managers can trust folks on the floor because they can see everything that is happening. And it is easier for operators to run the business because they have all the data too.

This final comment foreshadows the third and most dramatic integrating feature in the new technological context. As the salient demands at the point of production shift from embodied to intellective skills, the fundamental distinction between worker and manager breaks down. The physical exertion and bodily involvement that has been the experiential basis for defining the worker role have, for the most part, vanished. The intellective skills that are required by those at the interface do not differ in kind from the skills required by those at higher organizational levels. The differences between organizational levels are now defined more by the comprehensiveness and range of responsibilities than by differences in everyday work experience. For the first time, the manufacturing organization faces the possibility of creating a homogeneous skill base, where the skills at the point of production ground the skills needed for other organizational functions.

The most direct implication of this change is that there is no longer a stark functional difference between workers and managers. The shift to intellective skills means that those at the point of production can take on many of the tasks and responsibilities that have been associated with the lower levels of management. Comments from managers in each of the three plants show that this realization was beginning to emerge, but with varying degrees of acceptance:

> There is a subtle power shift as the technology takes the decision making out of manager's hands and gives it to operators. . . .
>
> The technology can finally get the information to the workers that allows them to manage the process. Everyone will be operating with the same kind of technology and will feel confident no matter who is running it. . . .
>
> Now people have to be involved and on top of their own data. We don't need people in the mode of telling others what to do. The data is there and people should be able to deal with it. . . .

For operators, the psychological impact of this realization can be extraordinary. Most operators believe, along with so many other blue-collar workers, that there are people in the world who call the shots, make decisions, and are in the know, but they do not believe themselves to be among that group. Operators see themselves as the people who are told what to do and who do what they are told. Informatization can provoke an abrupt change. The well-defined boundaries of identity begin to melt. In the process, there is learning about the self and learning about the other:

> I learned that I could do these things. It helps you understand yourself. It helps you understand other people. It gives you an opportunity to understand managers better, the pressure they are under. . . .
> So much of the adversarialism, so much of the anger that we feel against one another is really a kind of sore-headism. We are angry that we don't get to call the shots, that we don't get the same respect that they get, that they don't respect us, that they have opportunities and privileges that we don't have. But with all the new changes, the more chance operators have to do things that are managerial, the more those barriers will be broken down. It isn't one group against another; it shouldn't be.

But hierarchies do not simply wither, and the advantages of power and privilege are painful to relinquish. Managers can feel deeply threatened by such change and prefer to ignore this emerging sense of new potential or, more forthrightly, utilize the new technology in ways that continue to assure their own dominance. The most significant barrier to fulfilling the organizational implications of an informatization strategy may be the ambiguity it creates for the manager's role. A Tiger Creek operator describes how perceived managerial resistance interfered with the operators' ability to fully utilize the Expense Tracking System:

> The managers discouraged us from exploring more aspects of the data and trying new things. They started taking it over themselves. They wanted the glory from the system. They want to make the innovative discoveries and present it as their thing.

Another operator expresses his perception of the worker's ability to move into a new role:

> In terms of our ability to really use this information, we are like a reed in a wind storm. The winds are managers and the extent to which we can do anything is determined by the pressures they exert and how much room they give us.

Until the function of the manager in this new context is better understood, it will be difficult for managers to enthusiastically embrace change. They too must be able to sustain their feelings of competence and control.

SOME IMPLICATIONS FOR HUMAN RESOURCE MANAGEMENT: A SUMMARY

An emphasis upon the automating or the informating aspects of advanced information technology will have determinative consequences for human resource management. To summarize those implications that have been identified in this discussion:

1. Information technology has a special relationship to human effort. As an automating technology it can replace physical labor. As an informating technology it creates new demands for intellective skills. Managers have tended to underestimate the importance of these skills and have typically neglected to identify appropriate forms of training or to commit sufficient resources to this educational process. However, the informating aspects of new technology cannot be adequately exploited without a sound intellective skill base. These skills become *the* crucial organizational resource in its efforts to deploy new information technology for comparative advantage.
2. Managers will have to pay special attention to the differences between the problems of workers in transition, who have mastered embodied skills, and those of workers who learn their tasks in the context of new information technology. The data suggest it is not necessary to "write off" older workers. Their experience can provide a valuable framework for the new analytic skills. For the new worker, a depth of intellective skill will be crucial if he or she is to make a valuable contribution to the business.
3. Activities related to selection, development, promotion, and recruitment will need to be aligned with these changing skill demands. For example, in many plant organizations, entry-level jobs are the simplest and most repetitive. It makes little sense to select tomorrow's intellective work force on the basis of their ability to perform such routine tasks.

4. Excellence in intellective work depends upon individual motivation and commitment. Traditional methods of supervisory control will not elicit high standards of intellective effort. A technology strategy that stresses informatization will require a human resource management philosophy that emphasizes commitment and mutuality as well as work systems that support such values at each organizational level.

5. A strategy that emphasizes automation will have to address issues related to employment security for workers and managers alike, as the logic of labor substitution affects all organizational strata. A strategy that stresses informatization will also have to consider employment impacts. However, in this approach human contributions are considered essential to a full exploitation of the technology. As workers can take on more "managerial" responsibility in the informated environment, it will be necessary to rethink the total configuration of organizational roles, functions, and structures. What new managerial activities will add value to the organization, and what structural changes (as they affect rewards, communication, authority, power, and so on) will be required to support such activities?

6. Informatization, with its implications for new skills, roles, and structures and its demand for motivation and commitment at the information interface, renders inadequate the Tayloristic approach to work organization. New forms of work organization will have to consider the sociality of problem solving, the depth of intellective skills, the mutuality of supervision, the degree of technical integration (e.g., as reflected in data displays that express organization-wide functioning), and the presence of a vast quantity of real-time data. Creativity, and collaboration, and innovation replace control as guiding managerial objectives.

Advanced information technology releases a potent set of possibilities for business improvement, with implications for the psychological experience of work, the nature of skills, roles and organization structures, quality of social integration, and the strategic framework for human resource management policies.

The pattern according to which these possibilities are selected and exploited will depend upon how managers resolve many of the issues raised in this chapter. The stakes are high, both for the robustness of our industrial organizations and for the values they foster. One worker from Tiger Creek offered this thought:

> If you don't let people grow and develop and make more decisions, it's a waste of human life—a waste of human potential. If you don't use your knowledge and skill it's a waste of life. Using the technology to its full potential means using the man to his full potential.

6

Threatened Industries: Can Collective Bargaining Adapt?

Janice McCormick

Many traditional industries that have long sustained American prosperity now face competitive challenges of a previously unknown magnitude. Whether from abroad or domestically, from new products or cheaper ones, the new competitive environment has threatened the survival of many U.S. companies. To help regain their advantageous position many unionized firms are attempting to cut costs by negotiating more favorable collective-bargaining agreements with their unions. The results have been mixed.

Among the highest in the world, American unionized labor costs may not have caused the loss of market leadership, but they have certainly exacerbated it. Examples of managerial attempts to seek concessions appear daily in the press. According to one survey, in 1982 one-third of all managers of unionized firms said they had sought concessions from their unions.[1] In many cases, management has been disappointed by the slowness and complexity of the process and by the moderate savings. Further, the permanence of the concessions is doubtful; unions that had granted concessions during one bargaining round are demanding a restoration of wages, work rules, and benefits three years later during the next round.

Cooperation between labor and management seems most elusive where it is needed the most—in older, major industries. Through a historical analysis of collective bargaining in four industries—coal, steel, automobiles, and trucking—this chapter examines why this is the case.

141

It is the argument of this chapter that the pattern of labor-management relations as it evolved over the last fifty years, was to the mutual satisfaction of both sides—perhaps an early version of mutuality. Management found a compromise that could satisfy its major stakeholders. Sheltered from foreign and major domestic competition, managers gave in to labor's wage demands and paid dividends to their shareholders; however, they failed to innovate and invest sufficiently in their companies, preferring to pass the cost of their policies on to their consumers. When the economic circumstances changed, this practice was no longer feasible. Expectations and established patterns of relations are difficult to change even when the need for change is urgent. These patterns have outlived their usefulness and may have accelerated the decline of these industries by impeding their adaptation to a new competitive environment.

This chapter begins by examining the origins and content of the historical pattern in these four industries. It then analyzes the economic challenges faced by the four industries and their attempts to use collective bargaining to reduce costs; in all four cases, there were similar difficulties. Since wage costs are only one cause of the industries' competitive problems, reducing costs may not be sufficient to turn the industries around. However, wage and work-rule concessions are a necessary first step. In order to facilitate these, certain issues must be addressed if labor and management are to work together more effectively to meet the competitive challenge, achieve better results, and ultimately improve the health of their industries. Their survival is at stake.

THE TRADITIONAL PATTERN

THE FORMATIVE PERIOD

Historically in the industrial world the employment relationship has been characterized by the managerial few commanding the managed many. But as society and technology have evolved, the ideology and content of that relationship have undergone a series of profound transformations. After decades of a relationship where the scope of legitimate managerial rights appeared virtually limitless and the managed merely had negative rights of opposition, demands were heard for a new balance of rights and responsibilities in the workplace. The terms of the old employment relationship were losing their legitimacy. The state responded to citizens' demands to limit the perceived excess or capricious powers of management by legislating new terms of the mutual rights and obligations of the managers and the managed. Employees were granted defensive rights of unionization, the right to strike, and collective bargaining. Managerial rights and control in the workplace were thereby given legal limits.

Since the labor legislation of the 1930s a new pattern of rights and responsibilities in the employment relationship evolved, which both parties found mutually beneficial. Management attempted to preserve as much as possible its traditional authority over business decisions and the organization of work, and in exchange union members made significant gains in wages and benefits.

The degree to which management was able to preserve unlimited direction in the workplace varied among companies and industries. In some instances, management preferred to grant its union a considerable degree of rule-making authority. But even in these cases—like the railroad and the construction workers—the terms of the quid pro quo were still high wages for preserved managerial authority.

With today's hindsight, a different compromise between labor and management would have been a more mutually satisfactory long-term solution. Cost control, efficiency, quality, and job satisfaction would have been possible had management shared control and labor shared responsibility for the firm's competitiveness.

Relations between labor and management followed a similar evolution in the coal, automobile, steel, and trucking industries. The early years shaped and set the tone for subsequent labor-management relations. The pattern was as follows: Labor organizations emerged as a challenge to managerial discretionary authority; management fought their efforts to represent employees, and often violence ensued. The sit-down strikes at Ford, the violence in the smaller so-called "Little Steel" firms, the hunger marches and gun battles over coal mine lockouts, and the Teamsters union seeking the help of organized crime to unionize trucking employees were part of the labor history of these early years. Demanding recognition, unions attempted to use their labor-market power to achieve their aims. Management in each case sought to protect itself from any encroachments on its authority by these intermediaries for their employees.

In a few cases, the early union organizing efforts were successful. John L. Lewis, president of the United Mine Workers of America, understood the labor-market power of his industrial union organizing efforts; begrudgingly and not without violence, the largest mines recognized the union in World War I, even before the passage of national legislation guaranteeing unions the right to organize. Management began negotiating immediately with UMWA.

But for most manufacturing companies, the government had a key role in establishing collective bargaining as a practice in labor-management relations. As a political response to the violence of those early years, the government passed the National Labor Relations Act, or Wagner Act, in 1935. The purpose of the Act was to help balance the power of labor when facing management. According to Section 1 of the Act, "the inequality of the balance of power between employees and employers . . . substantially burdens and affects the flow of commerce." The law embodied the conviction that free negotiations between labor and management only result from a roughly equal balance of power at the outset. Although the legislation was not specifically prolabor, it restricted managerial prerogatives in human resources. Under government pressure for stable wartime production, companies that had remained hostile to the unions' efforts gave in and complied with the new laws. The traditional pattern of labor-management relations was developed in response to political pressure on the government to limit the power of management and mediate the conflicts over rights in the workplace. Management's role was reactive to environmental forces.

This early pattern indelibly marked subsequent relations in the four industries. Battling for recognition, labor challenged management's rights and authority to make workplace decisions. In this setting, labor's gain was management's loss. Unable or unwilling to meet its employees' challenge, management awaited the government's decision as arbiter of the rules of the game. Labor-management relations and collective bargaining in these industries became like trench warfare, with a series of advances and retreats mediated by legal rules.

ADAPTATION AND INSTITUTIONALIZATION: SETTING THE QUID PRO QUO

This win-lose power play between labor and management became institutionalized in public policy. The procedures for organizing, for union recognition, and for contract negotiation and administration became highly bureaucratized. The legal framework for collective bargaining provided an orderly resolution to labor and management's "distributive" battles.[2] Strikes would occur only at predictable intervals, enabling management to better plan production; employees would be guaranteed stable compensation for the duration of the agreement. For both sides, this was an improvement.

Although strikes were now predictable, taking place at contract expiration, some of these were damaging to the industries. In the late 1940s there were protracted strikes in all four industries. The General Motors strike of 1947, the U.S. Steel strike of 1948, and the national coal strike of 1952 were watersheds for establishing a new phase in labor-management relations. The strikes were long and costly: The steel strike was held responsible for the earliest penetration of foreign steel on the American market; in the 1947 strike GM lost market share and vowed to avoid such long shutdowns in the future. In coal and trucking, management recognized the need for greater industry preparation for collective bargaining when confronting strongly centralized unions. In all four industries management recognized that unions were here to stay and that further efforts would be needed to avoid costly strikes.

There were two changes made to overcome these problems: first, union members would be guaranteed greater wage gains; and second, employers in the industry would more closely coordinate their efforts for collective bargaining.

General Motors was first to initiate bargaining practices that would later prevail in American contracts. After the strike of 1947 General Motors chief Charles Wilson and the president of the United Automobile Workers, Walter Reuther, negotiated a groundbreaking contract. Under the label progress sharing, the agreement granted a cost-of-living adjustment to insulate wages from inflation in addition to an annual improvement factor pegged to productivity gains in the entire American economy. In exchange, the union agreed to a three-year, strike-free contract. The principle of inflation-resistant wages plus annual increases over a three-year term became the new labor-management quid pro quo.

The second element of the new pattern—greater employer coordination and, later, national bargaining—also was seen as an improvement over the earlier chaos. In these four industries the earliest settlements were negotiated by individual companies with their unions and became the key to these companies' competitive position within the industry.

In steel and automobiles the task of employer unity was facilitated by the oligopolistic industry structure. In coal and trucking, with hundreds of companies, the task of unifying employers for negotiation was much more difficult. In the last two industries the unions were the key to the unification of employers.

John L. Lewis of the United Mine Workers believed that a national agreement would be mutually beneficial for labor and management. He believed it would give labor increased bargaining power. Management would not be able to shift production to nonstriking facilities to force the union to strike. A national bargaining unit meant that the union could shut down all facilities in the industry, thus forcing the hand of management. Lewis helped create BCOA (Bituminous Coal Operators Association) to sit opposite him at the bargaining table. In return, he agreed in principle to facilitate the mechanization of mines and the shutdown of smaller inefficient ones, even if it meant the loss of union jobs. The first national agreement was signed in 1951, guaranteeing that all coal operators would pay the same wages and have the same benefit plans.

In steel and trucking strong union leadership was also responsible for the creation of a national bargaining unit. Philip Murray of the Steelworkers and Jimmy Hoffa of the Teamsters convinced management in their industries of the benefits of a national agreement. In return, under their tightly centralized leadership, these union leaders guaranteed their members' compliance.

In steel the United States Steel Corporation had always taken the lead. In 1937 it had been the first to sign a companywide agreement with the union. For twenty years the leaderships of the two organizations worked closely to coordinate their efforts for their mutual good. In the late 1950s conditions changed; a recession hit the nation, and the demand for steel declined. To meet the new threat, the steel companies decided to pool their efforts for negotiation. But the first national negotiation of a three-year contract in steel had an unfortunate outcome. U.S. Steel's attitude to the union had hardened, and as leader of the industry group it demanded a series of concessions on work-rule control of the shop floor. Its language was aggressive despite the opposition of other members of the industry bargaining group; a costly 116-day strike followed. But management swore never again to risk this type of disruptive strike. After 1959 the basic steel agreement was coordinated by the companies and carefully planned with the USWA. Joint committees were set up to study mutual problems, and difficult issues were sent to arbitration. For another twenty years there would be union-management cooperative relations at the top and coordination within the industry group around a national contract.

In trucking, where operating margins were slim and competition was cut-throat, the companies were eager to coordinate their efforts. Jimmy Hoffa's efforts were successful, and the first National Master Freight Agreement was signed in 1964. The National Master Freight Agreement between the International Brotherhood of Teamsters and the trucking industry determined a target national increase in the package of wages and benefits and set a standard for hard noneconomic provisions. Because local conditions were so diverse, regional supplements gave local labor and management the flexibility to adapt the national settlement to local conditions.

There were several advantages for the companies in following these nationwide patterns. First, these industries faced strongly centralized unions capable of shutting down the companies; a national coordination or organization of employers increased management's bargaining power vis-à-vis the unions. Second, closer coordination of wages reduced the differentials between companies; there was a tacit agreement that the wage costs would not give one company a competitive advantage over the others. Finally, no one company alone would determine the terms of union employment for the whole industry. The companies would cooperatively coordinate their efforts to their mutual advantage. In coal, trucking, and steel this pattern was considered superior to individual bargaining; rubber, copper, and aluminum also followed this pattern of a national three-year contract.

The automobile industry, on the other hand, has never had a national collective-bargaining agreement. In a variation of national bargaining, one company sets the pattern for the other companies to follow. Competitive characteristics of the industry were responsible for this variation. Since no one company dominated the industry throughout the postwar period, the competitors were wary of sharing cost information with one another. The automobile companies preferred the pattern bargaining to a national agreement. The union targets one company for negotiating the pattern-setting agreement. Generally it did not target General Motors. The two times GM had been selected to set the pattern, 1949 and 1970, lengthy strikes had ensued. Ford was the innovative pattern setter in six of the ten negotiation rounds from 1955 to 1982. Ford developed a reputation as a more favorable negotiator with the union. General Motors was considered a hard bargainer, though often more willing to grant money than power sharing or innovative work practices. With tight competition between the Big Three producers, the incentives for the smaller companies—Ford and Chrysler—to settle were greater.

The pattern of relations that evolved in all four industries preserved much of management's control over the workplace in exchange for relatively high blue-collar wages. Both management's and labor's organizational goals—self-preservation—

were satisfactorily met through an adversarial collective-bar-gaining compromise. Under intense economic pressure from the domestic and international competitive environments, this pattern began to break down. It no longer seemed to satisfy both labor's and management's organization goals.

THE CHALLENGE TO THE PATTERN

This quid pro quo of collective bargaining had served these industries well in times of prosperity. The challenges to it did not come from either management or the unions; neither expressed dissatisfaction with their relations. The initial challenges came from the outside—from the changing economic and political environment.

In steel and autos, where foreign competition was a serious threat, the pattern of high wage settlements had exacerbated the problems of the industries' maintaining an advantageous market position. *Table 6-1* compares the increases in compensation costs (wages and benefits) from 1975 to 1982 in the automobile and steel industries. In the steel industry the big cost advantage to Europe and Japan grew larger, despite slower American increases. The data for automobiles, comparing U.S. compensation costs with those of Japan and two Third World nations, explain both the $1,500 landed cost advantage per Japanese car and the desire of American carmakers to outsource the manufacture of parts to other nations. In the early 1980s the problems of the two industries were dramatic. With sales down, huge losses, plant closings, and layoffs, management and labor entered their negotiations under changed conditions.

The first of the four industries to feel the crisis was steel. Labor relations and poor investment decisions were two causes for the import crisis. Every three years, at the contract expiration, long strikes ensued. During these strikes steel companies' customers purchased foreign steel, resulting in a loss of sales for the American companies and a loss of jobs for American workers. This practice opened the door for foreign steel. Although only 5 percent of steel sold in the United States in 1960 was foreign, by 1970 this figure had risen to above 15

Table 6-1

Hourly Compensation Costs (Wages and Benefits) for Production
Workers (in U.S. Dollars)

	Iron and Steel Manufacturing			
	1982	*Percent of U.S.*	*1975*	*Percent of U.S.*
United States	22.20	100	10.24	100
Germany	11.68	53	7.12	70
France	9.52	43	5.86	57
Japan	10.15	46	5.26	51
Mexico	3.28	15	2.27	22
	Motor Vehicle and Equipment Manufacturing			
	1982	*Percent of U.S.*	*1975*	*Percent of U.S.*
United States	19.37	100	9.44	100
Japan	7.24	37	3.56	38
Mexico	3.53	18	2.90	31
Korea	1.95	10	0.50	5

Source: Office of Productivity and Technology, Bureau of Labor Statistics, U.S. Department of
Labor (December 1982), unpublished data.
Note: Changes in the dollar value of compensation abroad are due to changes in amounts of
compensation *and* to changes in the value of the dollar.

percent. Although both labor and management recognized the
problem as early as 1959, when they created a joint committee
to study the strike-imports link, the first joint solution was agreed
to in 1974. An example of short-sightedness, the Experimental
Negotiating Agreement (ENA), designed to limit imports, in
fact increased the steel wage bill. In exchange for an annual 3
percent wage increase above the cost-of-living allowance, the
Steelworkers agreed not to strike. There were no convincing
indications that ENA had halted the surge of imported steel on
the American market. Costing less because of lower labor costs
and heavy government subsidies, foreign steel was also often
high quality, with a better product mix to meet the needs of
American manufacturing.

Wage gains had been high in the U.S. steel industry because
of several factors: union bargaining power, the high value added

in steel processing, the quality of steel labor as measured by training and skill, high capital investments per worker, and strong industry concentration, allowing the companies to pass any increases on to the consumer through higher prices for certain safe market segments.[3] Although real wages increased an average of 2 percent per year, productivity declined. Restrictive work rules, old technologies, and an eroding work ethic were blamed for this decline. Until 1982 concessions on wages, benefits, and work rules were not seriously sought. The 1980 steel negotiations took place in an environment in which both labor and management were deluding themselves about the crisis in the industry. Imports were blamed, and the crisis was seen as cyclical.

The crisis in the American automobile industry was more sudden and unexpected but also precipitated by international events that shook its competitive position. The 1973 oil crisis surprised world markets and reshaped international politics. Auto sales plummeted. When sales picked up, consumer preferences had changed; Americans no longer wanted large, uneconomical vehicles. Instead they wanted smaller, more efficient engines. However, because the American producers had not kept abreast of the technological advances in small, energy-efficient autos, foreign automakers took advantage of the new American demand. As in steel, scrutiny of labor costs came later. The American automakers reacted defensively, clamoring for protection. Not until the 1979 Chrysler crisis and the 1982 auto negotiations was the traditional labor-management quid pro quo challenged.

In coal and trucking, the precipitants of the crisis were organizational and political and then, as a result, economic. Labor negotiations in trucking have an impact that far exceeds the several hundred thousand truckers covered by the agreement. Most of the nation's raw materials, food, and finished products are carried by truck. A work stoppage in trucking could cripple the nation's economy. This enormous market power gave the organizationally strong Teamsters even greater bargaining power. For these reasons, public policymakers carefully monitor the negotiations and intervene directly and indirectly to shape their outcome.

In recent years the National Master Freight Agreement has also been watched by other industries. Many believe it to be the pattern setter for other industries. Since 1967 it has led the national three-year cycle known as a bargaining round. In both 1976 and 1979 trucking negotiations immediately preceded those in rubber, autos, steel, and coal, originally setting the tone if not the content of these subsequent agreements.

For years the Teamsters had the upper hand with experience and bargaining power. A strong union with a very loyal membership and a violent history, the Teamsters dominated the industry. Though influenced by charismatic leadership at the top, the regional units kept tight reins over their local unions. Union bargaining power also derived from a virtual monopoly over important carriers in the business. When the industry prospered, the companies were willing to grant large wage increases in exchange for cooperation. From 1950 to 1973 Teamsters' wages increased about 300 percent compared with 200–250 percent in all other American unionized industries.

The union's bargaining power was also enhanced by management's organizational weakness, reflected symptomatically in the series of name changes of the employers' negotiating arm—first called TEI, Trucking Employers, Inc., then CMI, Carrier Management, Inc., then TMI, Trucking Management, Inc. Management had difficulty keeping the organization together. Many small firms would give in to the union and settle on their own; lacking the financial resources to resist a strike of more than a few days, they would undermine the leadership of the employers' organization.

The high settlements in the industry were also due to government intervention. Management gave in to union demands for high increases, knowing that the regulatory agency, the ICC (Interstate Commerce Commission), would allow them to pass the increases on to their customers in higher hauling rates.

In 1976 and 1979 the union was master in the trucking industry talks; the International Brotherhood of Teamsters flexed its muscles to extract generous agreements from management. In 1976 the union exercised its bargaining power against a very weak employers' association; playing on that weakness the union divided the ranks of management and conquered. In 1979 the union's power was exercised against the Carter administration. At the first negotiations under the Carter inflation-fighting program, the administration wanted a settlement within its wage guidelines. When the Teamsters refused, demanding a package that exceeded the guidelines and threatening a nationwide strike, the government conceded and engaged in what was called "guideline math." After some clever accounting the government agreed that the union's demands fell within the guidelines, virtually undercutting the power of management to negotiate a less costly agreement. In both bargaining rounds management's bargaining position was very weak.

A force outside the bargaining relationship drastically altered conditions in the industry, forcing labor and management to reconsider the pattern of bargaining that had evolved over the years. In 1982 the National Motor Carrier Act was passed, deregulating the industry and removing the protective shelter from which most of the big unionized carriers had benefited. Financial barriers to entry into the business were lowered, and interstate commerce rates were freed, introducing new competition into the industry.

Both the Teamsters and the trucking owners' association had actively opposed deregulation. Both felt that it threatened their organizations. Negotiation of a concessionary labor agreement in 1982 resulted from an attempt to respond to this external threat.

New and existing owner-operated firms were generally nonunion and thus not subject to the high labor costs of the unionized firms. In the past these firms had found it difficult to meet regulatory standards and to compete with the larger, unionized firms on the more lucrative interstate routes. With deregulation, their lower costs gave them a competitive edge. Their numbers grew, and the ranks of the trucking owners' association dwindled. Almost 65 percent of the unionized firms' expenses went to labor costs; with deregulation they could no longer pass these on to their customers through higher rates. Some unionized firms went bankrupt; some withdrew from the national agreement; and still others went "double-breasted"—setting up nonunion subsidiaries with lower-cost labor. The unionized trucking owners actively opposed these developments, which they saw as "excessive rate cutting and chaos in the industry." Side by side with the Teamsters they lobbied Congress for a return to regulation; each side hoped to cut the losses of its weakened organization.

The Teamsters opposed deregulation, recognizing that their union had no foothold with the smaller carriers who were most likely to benefit from it. They also feared a loss of membership, since their share of the industry was declining. These losses weakened their bargaining power and threatened their survival in the industry.

Labor and management in the unionized trucking firms agreed to cooperate for concessions in the 1982 National Master Freight Agreement. Their mutual interest lay in a more flexible, less costly agreement. The Teamsters were willing to make concessions in order to preserve the unionized trucking firms' share of the market, thus preventing a further decline in membership. The unionized firms also sought concessions through collective bargaining to help prevent further losses of market share to owner-operated, nonunionized firms. The stage was set for negotiation.

In coal the traditional quid pro quo came under challenge from forces internal and external to the industry. The economic and market changes were complicated by internal union problems. As in trucking, the unionized portion of the industry was rapidly losing its share of production to the nonunion. Previously mining over 70 percent of American coal, unionized mines saw their share decline to around 40 percent by the end of the 1970s.

There were market and organizational explanations. First, the strip mines of the western United States were more mechanized and productive. Second, the Mine Workers had had little success organizing these mines. Many of the smaller unionized mines could not compete with the western mines' higher productivity and lower nonunion wages and benefits. Third, the instability in the industry resulting from the massive shifts in demand had also benefited the western mines. Prior to the oil crisis the demand for coal had declined with the decline of the steel industry and with cheaper alternative fuels; when coal demand picked up again, the western coal was more readily usable as an energy source.

The organizational explanations for the decline of unionized coal are an indictment of labor-management patterns as they evolved in the industry. First, total output per mine in the unionized pit mines had declined because of the accumulation of restrictive work rules and regulations and poor miner morale. Second, there were many strikes in the unionized mines at contract expiration and during the contract. This led many customers to seek foreign or nonunion coal sources. Some coal operators closed their union operations, while others actively campaigned to keep the union—and its bad work relations—out of their operations. Unionized coal mines had the reputation for being unruly, unproductive, and unprofitable. Third, the United Mine Workers had seemed unwilling or unable to control their own rank and file. They had difficulty gaining contract ratification and getting their members to obey the contract language once ratified. The coal operators' association, the negotiating arm for the unionized coal industry, sought greater control of strikes and work-rule concessions to prevent a further erosion of market share. With over 25,000 unionized miners out of work, UMWA also had an interest in keeping the unionized mines profitable. But as the stage was set for the 1981 negotiations, the prospects for a strike-free concessionary agreement did not look bright.

In all four industries the quid pro quo of traditional labor-management relations was called into question. The compromise that was thought to have served these industries so well for almost thirty years was now held responsible for their decline. In steel and automobiles it seemed that the survival of the industries was at stake. In trucking and coal, the survival of the unions and the unionized companies was uncertain.

In the immediate postwar years management and labor had worked out a system that they perceived to be of mutual benefit—high wages in exchange for labor peace and preserved managerial decision making in their plants. While these industries were sheltered from competition, this relationship thrived to their mutual benefit. With competition from abroad, as in the cases of steel and autos—or from other products, as in steel and coal—or from nonunion producers, as in trucking and coal, the quid pro quo was no longer feasible. In this changed economic situation management groped for solutions.

CHANGING THE TRADITIONAL PATTERN

Once management recognized the need to cut labor costs, the next step was to decide what types of cuts to seek and how to get them. In autos, steel, and trucking, management had concluded that it could no longer afford the old pattern of annual increases. The well-established and mutually beneficial pattern had inflated labor costs and had become a barrier to the competitiveness of American steel, autos, and unionized trucking carriers operating in a deregulated environment. Management knew it needed cost relief, but in all four cases union consent and cooperation were needed.

In autos, trucking, and steel, management sought to reopen the previously negotiated collective-bargaining agreement. For the companies, this would mean postponing, delaying, or renegotiating downward the wages and benefits that had been fixed for the three-year period. In nationwide company bargaining the Chrysler Corporation set the precedent. The UAW had agreed to reopen Chrysler's three-year contract and to decrease wages by almost two dollars per hour as a condition for government financing of the bailout.

At General Motors and Ford and in the trucking industry the unions agreed to "begin contract talks early" instead of reopening the agreement as management had requested. The difference was semantic; for organizational reasons, the union leadership could not violate the sacred union tradition of "winning" a three-year contract and yet keep the support of its own rank and file. Since ratification of any renegotiated contract was necessary, the leadership felt that this formulation would be easier to sell. Beginning talks early also decreased the likelihood of a strike at contract expiration, which both sides knew the companies could ill afford and the unions could not win.

TRUCKING INDUSTRY

Management had first requested a reopening of the contract two months after the Motor Carrier Act was signed into law. Although the Teamsters union refused, it did allow its local unions to agree to certain work-rule changes that would improve the companies' labor productivity. Both sides knew this would not suffice; by 1982 one-half of the unionized firms had filed for bankruptcy and over 20 percent of the unionized truckers were on layoff. In this morose atmosphere the Teamsters accepted an "early opening" of talks in which a contract covering the next three-and-a-half years would be negotiated.

The ensuing negotiations occurred quickly and were carefully managed by both sides. The two parties officially used the months of October and November to seek contract suggestions from members and to develop bargaining proposals. An initial session between the union and the carriers gave the go-ahead for thirty-one local negotiating committees to begin. The parties exchanged bargaining proposals at the opening of formal talks and expressed the hope of reaching a new pact in three weeks.

The entire negotiation as well as the preparation for negotiation operated under a news blackout. Both sides did not want news of interim bargaining proposals leaking to the rank and file or to individual carriers. Agreement was reached within several weeks.

The speed of the agreement on concessions can be attributed to the careful management of the respective organizations and to the common goal of the two sides—to keep the unionized carriers competitive.

The company negotiator thought that negotiations were made more fruitful because of the solid, nonadversarial relationship that existed between himself and the Teamsters president. Since they had a common background and a common goal, they respected each other and seemed to understand the difficulties of the other's position. Each hoped that this understanding would allow a new, mutually beneficial "realism" to pervade their talks. Because of the speed with which the contract had been settled, some industry experts believed that the actual negotiations had occurred in earlier private meetings between the two men. Some held the view that the actual talks were only a formality and the real contract had been settled before employers had officially requested to open the talks early. They were purported to have discussed what their various memberships would accept and then to have agreed to support one another.

Finally, neither side blamed the other for the decline of the industry. Although both sides recognized that the 1979 agreement had been too costly, the government deregulators were the "common enemy" who had precipitated the crisis. For both sides, the concessions were to be temporary remedies until the legislation could be reversed and health restored to the industry; both sides believed they could return to the traditional pattern.

The proposed new contract froze basic wage levels for two years and modified the cost-of-living adjustment (COLA) to be paid annually instead of semiannually. This change alone would save employers $100 million per year.

The two most radical provisions under the new national agreement consisted of diverting COLA payments and work-rule changes. Through the diversion of COLA payments, employees actually paid for increased health and pension benefits by "giving up" COLA payments.

Work-rule changes consisted of such provisions as flexible work, that is, work time arranged according to available work as opposed to an arbitrary schedule; over-the-road haulers allowed to make one pickup and delivery within the former jurisdiction of city drivers; and elimination of pay incongruities like two days' pay given to drivers completing two short runs in the same day. The contract also provided for lower starting pay for new employees and prorated benefits for part-time workers.

In exchange for "give backs" the union received job security guarantees, including preferential hiring of laid-off union members, prohibiting carriers from setting up nonunion subsidiaries, and extending by three years the seniority of laid-off workers. The union hoped that this would halt the loss of union membership resulting from double-breasted carriers.

The union ratified the contract by almost 2 to 1. Unionized employers had more difficulty selling the contract to their members. Many companies who were not members but who had traditionally used the national pattern for their own bargaining held out in an attempt to get better terms from their local unions. In some cases, the union acquiesced, allowing the locals to determine the conditions with their companies. But worried about the breakdown of the agreement, the union warned the locals that companies who receive additional concessions often go out of business anyway.

The double-breasted operations allowed their management to bypass the National Master Freight Agreement conditions and to seek a new, cheaper work force. With lower wages and employees who had never known the union's restrictive practices, these companies hoped to take advantage of the new economic environment. Both sides were concerned about the implications for their organizations.

THE AUTO INDUSTRY

Prospects for a successful settlement had looked bright at the outset of the negotiations. The union councils had heralded the talks as coming at "a time for a fundamental reassessment of the collective bargaining relationship in the U.S. auto industry." Both the union and management stood ready to work toward a mutual resolution of the problems of the failing auto industry, which had experienced a thirty-four-month recession, its most severe downturn since the Great Depression.

Although the contract was not due to expire until September 1982, the union had agreed to reopen it in January after nine months of company pressure for modifications. This was only the second time a contract had been reopened in the history of the UAW and the first time it had been reopened at the company's request.

Although the UAW leadership was uncertain which company—General Motors or Ford—would set the 1982 pattern, General Motors made the first move. Early in the talks, it had shocked the business community by agreeing to a union proposal to pass all wage concessions on to the consumer through lowered car prices. The UAW had been trying to gain a say in car prices for years. With this GM concession, a contract agreement seemed imminent.

Despite these favorable beginnings, within three weeks the union had broken off talks with both companies, reopened negotiations with GM, and dissolved talks with the largest automaker a second time. A disappointed Douglas Fraser, president of the UAW, stated firmly that talks with GM would not begin again until July.

Each side publicly blamed the other for the breakdown. On both sides the problems were organizational. Both GM and the UAW spoke with many voices, making coordination difficult.

At General Motors the strategy was unclear and the union felt that the tactics were duplicitous. The company sent mixed signals to the UAW, vacillating between cooperation and hostility, and sent shock waves through the business community, which was suspicious that the groundbreaking offer to the UAW had a hidden agenda to gain competitive advantage.

The UAW was also in flux. Its GM and Ford department heads were competing to succeed Doug Fraser for the UAW presidency. Whoever "won" a better agreement first might receive an added advantage in the eyes of the rank and file. The personal rivalry between the two union men was intense.

Another factor was that the workers viewed each company differently. The rank and file perceived Chrysler and Ford as financially weak and were more likely to feel that these companies needed wage concessions from the union. The Chrysler bail-out of 1979 set a precedent for concessionary bargaining in the rest of the industry. GM was still making a profit. As Doug Fraser explained, "There is no doubt about the attitude of our workers to GM. They view them as rich even when they aren't rich and arrogant."

GM's quality-of-work-life programs, which encouraged employee involvement, had been fairly successful in many plants. At the top, however, the company seemed to have grown ambivalent to QWL and at times had made statements that seemed overtly hostile to the union. While the president and the vice president of industrial relations at GM advocated QWL and called UAW president Douglas Fraser their best friend, the chief executive officer seemed more ambivalent. An old-style GM manager, he wanted more control of the 1982 negotiations. Under his direction, GM's initial proposal to the union took an extremely hard line. The company requested wage concessions of five dollars per hour, which would have represented a 25 percent cut in pay. In exchange, GM offered the union some protection from outsourcing and an equality-of-sacrifice clause for white-collar workers but nothing in the way of job-security guarantees for workers. Talks at GM broke down amidst mutual acrimony, since the union did not feel it could sell these cuts to its members.

At the urging of the Ford department of UAW, talks re-opened at Ford with both sides feeling hopeful. UAW leader Don Ephlin and Pete Pestillo, vice president of labor relations for Ford, took a realistic attitude toward the negotiations, each taking into consideration the needs and constraints of the other. A union negotiator summed up the attitude by saying, "Ford wants economic relief, but we [UAW] have to decide what we can sell. We have to have enough to offset it." The negotiators first decided how much relief the company needed. The union insisted that it would decide how to take the cuts. After two weeks of intense joint problem solving, the union negotiating committee unanimously endorsed the Ford agreement. Four days later, 132 out of 144 attending Ford UAW council members voted to approve the contract.

What had been impossible at GM seemed easy at Ford. The organizational and strategic barriers facing GM and the UAW were absent at Ford.

First, Ford's organization for negotiations was unambiguous and unified. Ford president Donald Peterson publicly and privately endorsed the strategies of his hand-picked vice president of labor relations, Pete Pestillo. Hired from outside the company specifically to change the direction of Ford's labor relations department, Pestillo quickly gained the confidence of top management, which helped him gain the support of his staff. As a sign of his power at Ford, Pestillo approved all public statements made by top management at Ford on labor relations or the upcoming negotiations, placing him squarely in charge of the talks.

Second, Pestillo and UAW vice president for Ford, Don Ephlin, were committed to a mutually beneficial solution. After a joint trip to Japan they fashioned a strong employee-involvement (EI) program and together visited all Ford plants to sell it to their organizations. Ford's employee-involvement program went further than GM's QWL and soon became a prominent example of a new union-management relationship in Ford plants. This greater trust between labor and management engendered by the program facilitated ratification of the agreement.

Finally, a resolution may have been facilitated at Ford by the severity of the problems it faced. Financially, Ford could not risk a strike; it set in place a different style of labor relations. Having lost over $1 billion in 1981, Ford publicized its problems: it thus had little difficulty convincing employees of the severity of the crisis. The UAW ratified the contract by a 3 to 1 margin. Having more options, GM chose the old style, since its competitive position was not as dangerous. It could afford hard bargaining. But with pattern bargaining it would be tied to Ford's pattern.

After the Ford settlement, it was once again General Motors' turn. According to the union, management continued to play hard ball. Since it was now the high-cost producer, GM continued to pressure the UAW to reopen talks. The giant automaker had closed ten plants and laid off an additional 10,000 workers since the breakdown of negotiations in January. GM management began talks with a Japanese carmaker for a subcompact in the United States. The union feared that with Japanese parts outsourced for these jointly produced cars, more American autoworker jobs would be lost. GM stated firmly that it would not resurrect the wage-price linkage and would pattern its first proposal after the Ford contract; GM would begin over again. Relations between the two sides were frosty.

Despite the pattern set at Ford, talks did not go smoothly. Though the negotiating teams bargained, they could not agree on the dollar amounts for the contract. But, after thirty-seven hours of nonstop bargaining, the exhausted negotiators announced that they had reached an agreement.

The GM council of UAW approved the contract by a vote of 229 to 25. But the rank and file ratified the agreement by only the narrowest of margins. Observers wondered if the close vote would spell labor trouble for GM. As one local union official explained, "You start out with almost half your work force mad at you." The good feeling between labor and management at Ford was absent at GM.

The content of the new Ford agreement, which had been signed without a strike, broke new ground in collective bargaining. Instead of passing the savings on to the consumer, the newly ratified agreement helped ease the company's cash-flow problems. The union agreed (1) to give up nine paid personal holidays and Sunday bonus pay; (2) to allow the company to hire new workers at 85 percent of the hourly base pay; (3) to defer the next three cost-of-living adjustments; and (4) to relinquish the traditional 3 percent annual pay increase that all contracts since 1948 had provided. In exchange, management agreed (1) to a twenty-four-month moratorium on plant closings due to outsourcing; (2) to give the union sixty days' notice prior to making an outsourcing decision; (3) to attempt to maintain the number of currently existing jobs; (4) to provide a "guaranteed income stream" of 50 percent of the hourly rate until the age of 62 for employees with at least 15 years of seniority; (5) to establish profit sharing; (6) and to set up "mutual growth forums" to promote sound union-management relations and employee development and training programs for employees displaced by changes in the industry.

GM was rumored to be unhappy with all Ford had "given up." But following the Ford pattern, GM made minimal alterations of the contract. GM added both a new health advisory board and a more generous profit-sharing plan. As one GM manager noted, "Ford was desperate and gave away the company." The four plants, whose closing GM had threatened during negotiations, remained open.

Ford had sought to alter the style of labor-management relations from the traditional conflictful one to a more cooperative one. The company needed the union to help cut labor costs and to improve productivity and quality; without labor's cooperation, management could not achieve its organizational goal of protecting the firm. Similarly, without management cooperation, the union's goal of protecting its members' jobs was endangered. Both sides chose a cooperative style to achieve their congruent goals. The groundwork for this greater co-operation at Ford had been laid by employee-involvement programs that had fostered greater trust between the two sides. Agreement and ratification were made easier.

STEEL INDUSTRY

The attempts to shape a new labor-management equilibrium were difficult in coal and steel. In both cases, attempted remedies were late in coming, as conditions continued to deteriorate. Organizational problems plagued the attempts to hold the bargaining units together. In steel the companies were divided over the means to achieve their organizational objectives. Many member companies left the basic steel organization over differences with U.S. Steel, to negotiate alone with the Steelworkers union. In coal internal battles made it impossible for the leadership to convince the rank and file of their congruence of interest with management. As a result, negotiating labor cost or work-rule relief was difficult in steel and impossible in coal. Individual companies sought to go it alone. Newer nonunion companies emerged. Union jobs in these industries declined. The old adversarial style of labor-management relations was too difficult to change.

The 1980 steel contract had been expensive and ignored many of industry's most serious problems. For their duration the two previous agreements had increased labor costs by 41 percent and 29 percent in the years when steel was facing its greatest competitive challenge.

Both sides soon realized the problems with the agreement. The contract was reopened after one year. The companies still had to decide whether to renew the Experimental Negotiating Agreement (ENA), which had expired in August 1980. Both sides had discussed it intermittently since 1981, but so far they had not made progress on an agreement. The Steelworkers desperately wanted to renew ENA, which provided workers with a guaranteed 3 percent wage increase and a yearly bonus. Steel producers, led by David Roderick of U.S. Steel, believed that ENA was too expensive and proposed to link its renewal with an elimination of the cost-of-living adjustment (COLA), which had represented 65 percent of the growth in labor costs over the past ten years.

The union finally acknowledged the severity of the industry crisis; the president of the Steelworkers, Lloyd McBride, noted that "our successes have caused some problems." To stop the losses of union jobs, the Steelworkers were willing to make some cost concessions. But in an example of poor timing, U.S. Steel announced the $6.3 billion purchase of the Marathon Oil Company just as McBride was trying to convince his rank and file that concessions were needed because the steel companies were in financial crisis.

U.S. Steel did not anticipate the strongly negative response from Congress, the public, and the workers. Congressional leaders criticized U.S. Steel for not investing in steel.

The USW responded with disbelief and anger to the news of the takeover. The takeover exacerbated the union's historical suspicion of management and decreased the likelihood that a cooperative concessionary bargaining round would occur.

Some industry analysts believed that companies were not only getting out of the steel business through diversification but also allowing steel plants to "die a slow death" through lack of investment in plant and equipment.

The early talks did not go well. The industry proposed a package of "adjustments" that would last until 1986 and save the steel producers $6 billion over three years. The package, amounting to a net decrease of fifty cents per hour excluding the cost of maintaining current health benefits, consisted of elimination of four COLAs and the imposition of a fifty-cent limit on COLA raises in the next two years. The companies hoped eventually to phase out COLA payments. In return, the companies would increase their contribution to the Supplemental Unemployment Benefit (SUB) funds by fifty cents per hour to assist laid-off steelworkers.

The USW returned with a counterproposal of a three-year freeze on general wage increases, elimination of one COLA payment of twenty-five cents per hour, and the deferral of three

COLAs for eighteen months, resulting in an increase of three dollars per hour in labor costs over three years, assuming inflation of 8 percent.

The talks broke down as the union rejected the final industry proposal; COLA was the major stumbling block. The union refused to give up the COLA principle, which the companies wanted to eliminate.

Both sides criticized each other viciously after the breakdown of talks. U.S. Steel publicly rebuked the union for rejecting the industry proposal. The producers and the union attacked one another in separate letters to steel employees. In August 1982 the management of the major steel producers refused to renew the ENA, leading the way for the first national steel strike since 1959.

Profitability of the steel industry continued to erode. Producers incurred losses of more than $2 billion in the first three quarters of 1982, and steel production dropped steadily. The industry's giant was operating at a record low of 38 percent capacity. U.S. Steel reported a loss of $290 million in the third quarter of 1982 alone, and it sold $750 million of assets, including the company headquarters building in Pittsburgh, Pennsylvania. It was predicted that at least three of the Big Eight firms would file for bankruptcy by August 1, 1983, if expenses were not reduced. There were 140,000 steelworkers on layoff or on a short work week.

On September 21, 1982, the union met to review the desperate situation. The locals' presidents decided that McBride should explore the possibility of further negotiations and perhaps compromise by linking COLA to company performance, something they had previously refused.

In October 1982 talks resumed. As the first step, the union and the industry agreed to put a COLA due on November 1, 1982, into escrow to give them more time to renegotiate.

A new agreement sent to the union council for approval was immediately rejected. With an August strike deadline that could be suicidal for both sides, they agreed to resume efforts to reach an agreement early in 1983. The mood was grim. The previous failures and propaganda wars had stirred up both sides; man-

agement sent employees letters accusing the union of irrespon-
sibility, and the union accused management of "union busting."

In March 1983, however, an agreement was reached. Both
sides felt pressure to settle. The companies could not afford to
lose sales in a strike; GM and other steel customers had made
provisions for buying foreign steel in case of a strike. The union
could not afford a strike and could not win it. Both sides wanted
to use the concessionary pact to help win congressional approval
for limiting steel imports.

The agreement was expected to save the companies $2 billion.
Pay was temporarily cut 9 percent; benefits were reduced; the
first-year COLA was eliminated; one week of vacation for the
first year and one holiday were conceded; and Sunday work
would be paid at 1¼ wage instead of 1½. It was called the least
expensive concessionary agreement in any major industry.
However, most of these concessions were for the first of three
years only. They would be fully restored by the contract expiration in 1986.

In exchange, the companies agreed to invest their labor savings in steel facilities and to strengthen the supplementary unemployment benefits. But relations between both sides remained
hostile, and neither seemed pleased with the settlement.

The process in steel had been complicated by the magnitude
of the crisis in the industry; by U.S. Steel's tight control of
negotiations and its miscalculation of the impact of the Mara-
thon Oil purchase; by the heterogeneity of the companies in
the industry and their different financial positions; and by lack
of imagination in the companies and the union. The steel negotiating group and the union continued to distrust one another
and to proceed by the rules of the old quid pro quo. Each side
behaved as if it could still "win." Neither completely recognized
its dependence on the other to further its own organizational
goals.

COAL INDUSTRY

Labor and management leaders in the coal industry acknowledged their common goal: to avoid another lengthy strike at

all costs in order to protect the union mines and union jobs. Acceptance by rank and file of a proposed contract would be necessary; and the diverse company interests within the Bituminous Coal Operators Association (BCOA) would have to be satisfied. Both sides agreed to concentrate on building support within their respective organizations and to help the other side gain its membership's support. The negotiations were thus off to a positive start.

The two chief negotiators coordinated their efforts, and four days before the expiration of the 1977 contract they reached an agreement. Approval by the UMWA bargaining council seemed likely, but both the UMWA leadership and BCOA were only guardedly optimistic about whether the new agreement would be ratified by the union's militant rank and file. If ratified, this contract would have been the first since 1964 to be concluded without a protracted strike.

Both sides felt they were better organized for the successful conclusion of the agreement. BCOA restructured its organization and consolidated its leadership. The UMWA had also elected a new president, Sam Church, who vowed to win a good settlement and avoid another long strike. The two negotiators were rumored to have met secretly before the opening of official negotiations to set the parameters of an agreement; their efforts seemed to have paid off.

The proposed contract did not restrain wages or limit the COLA. But management was more concerned with avoiding a strike and limiting wildcat strikes. Wages and benefits would be increased 35 percent over three years, but there would be no change for the cost of living. No work-rule changes or Sunday work were included in the contract, although work would be allowed on holidays. Pensions for the 44,000 miners' widows were to be raised to $100 a month. In return, the UMWA gave up a thirty-five-year-old provision requiring unionized coal companies to pay the UMWA pension fund royalties for non-union coal that they buy for resale; this provision in 1981 alone had cost the union mines almost $1 million per month.

The UMWA bargaining council ratified the contract by 21 to 14. However, on a tour to promote the settlement, UMWA president Sam Church lost his hopes for its ratification. Booed at rallies and snubbed by local unions, he was accused of having sold out.

Church still argued that when the votes were counted, the "silent majority" of the membership would be with him and not with the local dissidents. Instead, the agreement was defeated nationally by over 2 to 1. A seventy-two-day strike ensued.

Labor-management relations turned sour as the talks resumed, but a second agreement was reached. The new contract, however, was generous. It reinstated the $1.90 per ton royalty fee that the coal operators paid to the union's health and pension fund for processing coal from nonunion mines. This was what seemed to have defeated the first contract.

The pact also provided a $150 back-to-work bonus and wage increases of $3.60 per hour over forty months—thirty cents more than under the first proposed contract; and the forty-five-day probationary period for new employees that had been added under the first tentative agreement was dropped. The union also retained the monthly pension for the miners' widows, a new benefit that was included in the rejected contract, but the benefit amount was cut to $95 per month. Operators retained the right to subcontract labor to nonunion contractors but only if this would not deprive UMWA members of work that was normally theirs.

Both sides felt that the failure to ratify the first agreement had resulted from internal union politics. Local union leaders had used the ratification campaign for their own union election campaigns. Traditionally suspicious of outsiders, many Appalachian miners distrusted their own national union leaders. Church and BCOA had not carefully planned how to sell the agreement, although it is possible that no one could have succeeded at this impossible task except John L. Lewis himself. Church lacked Lewis's charisma and leadership; later that year Church was defeated in his bid for the UMWA presidency by a local union dissident leader.

In 1981 the market for coal improved dramatically. Production in union and nonunion mines increased, and many laid-off UMWA miners were called back to work. But the more modern and productive nonunion mines, with better labor-management relations, were in a better position to take advantage of the upsurge; their market share increased.

THE FUTURE

The difficulty and modest outcome of attempts to alter the wage quid pro quo of collective bargaining have disappointed management. Unless two issues are addressed, no further progress can be made toward mutuality: (1) The future conditions of national bargaining must be decided; and (2) the mutual expectations for local or national negotiations must be clarified.

THE CONDITIONS OF NATIONAL BARGAINING

First, industrywide agreements are increasingly an obstacle to the competitiveness of U.S. firms. National contracts evolved in response to dissatisfaction with separate company agreements; both labor and management preferred the stability of one major agreement. Companies with diverse characteristics negotiated as one unit to counter union whipsawing; in times of growth, this uniformity benefited both weaker and stronger firms. Labor's legitimacy as a national political actor was also enhanced. However, because of a changed labor market, management is no longer a victim of whipsawing and now tolerates diversity. In a new competitive environment, uniformity becomes a constraint on many firms, limiting their ability to respond. And circumstances require the unions to be more flexible.

National bargaining complicates the process of reaching more concessionary agreements. Achieving employer cohesion and managing internal union dynamics across different companies are difficult and make efforts toward satisfactory compromises slow and ineffective. National bargaining has also overloaded the content of bargaining. During the years of postwar growth, a national or pattern agreement preceded and took priority over plant-level contracts. Many plant-level conditions became issues on the national bargaining table. Now there is a gradual recognition that the terms of an agreement must be closer to local production, product, and market conditions. National agreements are often insensitive to local conditions and actors and remote from the plant or company level, where there is greatest awareness of potential areas for flexibility in wage costs and work rules. Needing cost relief, member firms have their hands tied by national agreements; some go bankrupt, others suffer losses or set up nonunion facilities.

There are three possible scenarios for the future of national bargaining. We can continue as is; work to eliminate national bargaining and return to local agreements; or build greater flexibility for local responses into the agreements. Each scenario would have different costs and benefits.

National bargaining can be eliminated at the companies' initiative if they disband their associations and negotiate separately. Although there are no legal constraints, this would be difficult. In trucking and coal the industry associations jointly manage pension funds with the union; it would be difficult to disengage from them. More important, in all four industries the unions would oppose the unilateral elimination of a national agreement or a national pattern. The unions' cooperation could help return union firms to an advantageous market position; therefore, union hostility, strikes, or political actions could work *against* the long-run health of business. This strategy would involve a test of management's bargaining power. In the present economic situation many companies are choosing to "go it alone," confident of winning the test.

Maintenance of the status quo in national bargaining would be the easiest option for both sides. But it, too, has many costs. Parallel union and nonunion firms would continue to grow, and unionized firms would continue to lose their positions, as collective bargaining would be slow to adapt. Neither labor nor management in unionized firms would have control over the direction of the changes that threaten the elimination of their organizations; the market would determine their fate. This could be a missed opportunity to structure a new, more productive, and mutually satisfying relationship.

In either of these scenarios—directly abandoning the national agreement or allowing it to die a slow death—the industries will never be the same. By outsourcing in autos, going double-breasted in trucking, diversifying out of basic steel, or opening nonunion mines, management can decrease its labor costs in the short run and better compete with foreign autos and steel and with nonunion coal mines and truckers in the long run. Either choice will diminish the impact of the national agreement and weaken the trade unions.

The third scenario involves a compromise between labor and management. It is easier to implement than the first, and it has greater potential for positive outcomes for both labor and management than the second option. This choice would acknowledge the positive roles unions play in the workplace when providing a check on local management and guaranteeing respect of workers' rights. Under this compromise both sides would try to make agreements more relevant to local conditions and to seek more input from local managers and labor leaders. A national agreement would set the major terms and conditions, while union and management at the company or local level could negotiate the specific policies and practices relevant to their firms. Joint local problem solving would be encouraged by the agreement.

While national unions have opposed the breakdown of the national pattern, this added flexibility could save jobs and perhaps improve working conditions. There has been evidence of some movement in this direction. To meet the external competitive threat, the auto and steel negotiations began local contract talks well before the initial national talks. Since 1978 the local agreements have been settled first in order to regain greater responsiveness to local conditions. However, for specific companies, this compromise is not sufficient to generate rapid or extensive wage savings. According to some managers, the possibility remains that the industries may not survive the competitive challenge while waiting to work out a compromise. For them, these changes could be too little, too late.

EXPECTATIONS FROM NEGOTIATIONS

The second issue to address is that of management's and labor's expectations from concessionary agreements. In most cases, management has the choice of changing policies or changing the quid pro quo. Changing specific policies or conditions of a labor agreement is a temporary solution. It implies that the crisis is cyclical and that piecemeal adjustments in labor costs are sufficient to remain competitive. By this model, no major changes in attitude and behavior of either side are sought; labor has temporarily lost and management has gained bargaining power. When the companies return to profitability, the same labor expectations are expected to reemerge. Yet we have seen that a return to postwar growth rates in the older unionized firms is unlikely. Further, the cycle of expectations created by the old quid pro quo has been in part responsible for their decline in competitiveness. The entire system must be altered.

Instead of a mere change of policies, a more positive and audacious objective should be sought. The culture of labor-management relations should be challenged to build a new mutually beneficial quid pro quo. To change the culture, care must be paid to building trust with the union and with employees outside the collective-bargaining relationship. To change attitudes, expectations, and behavior to be more mutually beneficial, information and power must be shared. Management must offer employees something in return besides wages; traditional managerial prerogatives in the plant could be shared. The old quid pro quo must be abandoned by both sides and a new one developed. However, there are many obstacles to be overcome, and even the most optimistic analyses provide little hope for these changes.

At GM and Ford, management and the UAW worked to establish a new understanding of their mutual rights and responsibilities in the workplace. Quality-of-work-life and employee-involvement programs set a new tone of trust and understanding; trust is slow to build and easy to destroy. Many observers blame a threatened 1984 auto strike on the bad feelings that resulted from the spring 1984 announcements of the auto executives' compensation. While asking the UAW for further wage concessions, top management was awarded million-dollar bonus packages. This insensitive, poorly timed announcement resulted in considerable worker cynicism. The longer-term impact on the labor-management relationship on the shop floor is yet to be determined.

In unionized coal a changed culture appears most remote,

because a 200-year tradition of hostility in the mining communities is so difficult to reverse. In 1984 there were some signs of a change. A change in union leadership and statutes solidified the hold of the UMWA over its contentious rank and file. In 1982 Richard Trumka, a dissident candidate, defeated Sam Church for the presidency of the union. Although elected on a platform of greater rank-and-file control, his first act was to request a reform of the collective bargaining ratification process that would decrease the role of local officials. Trumka asked the union convention to eliminate the bargaining council—the forum where local district leaders had rejected so many settlements in previous negotiations before they were even put to a rank-and-file vote. In 1984 Trumka proved to be a skillful negotiator, an effective salesman of his agreement, and for the first time in twenty years, the coal contract was negotiated and signed without a strike.

A cohesive union under a strong leader may halt the disintegration of national bargaining in coal. Trumka has been successful in bringing some stray companies back into the agreement. He has also stated that his goal is to unionize the new pit and strip mines. While the coal market is expanding, the unionized Appalachian mines will continue to operate, but the more cost-effective nonunion mines will increase their share of production. Although the 1984 contract held the line on costs, restricted wildcat strikes, and granted other cost savings to management in exchange for some job security, the long-run prospects for union coal are bleak.

The choice in all four industries is between piecemeal policy changes that will only be temporary palliatives and a changed culture in which management and labor would work together to shape the future. The early phases of a change are very slow and fragile and often depend on the personalities of the individuals involved. The upcoming automobile negotiations will be affected by the change in principal union actors, who are less committed to a new relationship with management. The rank and file is also clamoring for a restoration of their wage increases now that the companies are not losing money. In order to avoid reversing the progress toward more cooperation, managers must understand internal union dynamics and manage the consequences; their task will not be easy.

In steel we may be witnessing a breakup of the national agreement in order to allow for more local or companywide flexibility. Bethlehem Steel, Armco, and others have begun to seek a new relationship with their employees, while others have returned to hard bargaining with their union.

The trucking industry has long had an adversarial relationship with its union. The industry is being forced to question the expectation of a return to growth and restoration of wage losses. Many local unions are willing to seek a new relationship, and in some cases the international union has gone along. The choice for the managers in the unionized companies is either to seek these changes or to go double-breasted to avoid the union.

For most of the twentieth century these industries have helped make the United States a major economic power. Labor's role in the industries' development and growth has been crucial. Now changes are necessary in traditional labor-management relations. Under the first two scenarios management is not assured of a competitive victory, but labor is the biggest loser as the base of its organizational strength erodes. It may be too late for the third scenario of flexible bargaining and a changed culture to solve the problems of our older unionized industries. Either way, management will decide the fate of national bargaining, of unionized firms in their industries, and ultimately of their trade unions.

7

From Protest to Partnership: The Dilemmas of Managing Change in the Democratic Union Organization

Bert Spector

Both the popular press and management journals have, over the last several years, been heralding the emergence of a new era of industrial relations. Concession bargaining, especially when coupled with joint union-management efforts to enhance the quality of working life, and attempts to increase employee participation in management as well as work performance are taken as signs that unions, management, and employees are responding mutually to new competitive realities. They have begun edging away from the adversarialism that has traditionally characterized labor relations. However, contrary trends are also acknowledged: decertification campaigns, concessions not tied to a redefinition of the legitimate role of unions in corporate governance, the movement of plants and the assignment of work out of the country, fast growth in traditionally nonunion industries like high technology, the use of work innovations in greenfield sites to help maintain a "union-free" environment, and the inevitability of continued tough adversarial bargaining over issues such as wages. But the fact that two of the nation's most powerful unions, the United Steelworkers of America and the United Auto Workers, have committed themselves to some degree of cooperation has helped emphasize mutuality of interests rather than adversarialism.

To the extent that unions are seeking to change their traditional concentration on narrowly defined bread-and-butter issues to the more intangible goals of improving quality of work life, union leaders must foster changes in their unions. This chapter looks at two of the nation's largest unions, the United Steelworkers of America and the United Auto Workers, where an attempt to redefine direction and goals seems to be taking place. Rather than evaluating the broad assertions made elsewhere that American industrial relations is undergoing a major transformation,[1] I will use the example of these two unions to suggest the particular challenges and opportunities now facing union leaders and some implications of these for managers who have decided that labor-management collaboration can improve organizational effectiveness.

BACKGROUND: MOVES TOWARD UNION-MANAGEMENT COLLABORATION

The opening salvo in the move toward greater union-management cooperation in the auto industry came in 1973, when the United Auto Workers added a Letter of Agreement to their contract with the Big Three automakers calling for the establishment of joint national committees to improve the quality of work life. Increasing foreign competition; shifting work-force demographics and societal values; innovative personnel practices initiated by nonunion companies, which appeared to be giving these companies a competitive edge in labor costs and quality; and a national recession—all combined during the 1970s to increase the interest of management in exploring new avenues of working with union leaders to strengthen the competitive position of the companies and the unions. Interest seemed particularly strong at General Motors, and in 1979 executive vice president James McDonald made mandatory at plants throughout the company a commitment to improving the quality of work life for their employees. That same year, Ford demonstrated its first real interest in a joint union-management effort to increase employee involvement. Responding to many of the same pressures, the Basic Steel Conference and the United Steelworkers created a joint problem-solving committee during their 1980 talks as an addition to the usual myriad of contract committees. Out of that effort came Appendix 15, which committed the union and the industry to a national joint committee whose structure would be echoed in each participating company from companywide to plant levels.

Each of these committee structures are aiming in some way to improve the quality of work life, competitiveness, and, implicitly at least, productivity. The joint structure of these committees is meant to signal a commitment by both parties to the idea that they share mutual interests. The emphasis on business as well as on human goals was explicitly recognized in the 1973 Letter of Agreement between the UAW and the auto companies:

> These and other projects and experiments which may be undertaken in the future are designed to improve the quality of work life, thereby advantaging the worker by making work a more satisfying experience [and] advantaging the corporation by leading to a reduction in employee absenteeism and turnover.

Even stronger language can be found in Appendix 15 of the Basic Steel Agreement, which set dual goals for joint union-management committees: "To improve the effectiveness of the company's performance, and to provide employees with a measure of involvement adding dignity and worth to their work life." The view that worker and employer interests are inherently and exclusively conflictful is superseded in these cases by the idea that while there are *some* inherently distributive and conflictual issues, which require traditional collective bargaining, there are other issues for which the collaborative approach is appropriate.

Whether such programs are called labor-management participation teams, quality-of-work-life committees, or employee-involvement groups, there is a great deal of similarity in their functioning.[2] Union and management plant leaders form oversight committees, while shop-floor work teams attend to both specific job-related problems, like reducing scrap or improving equipment maintenance, and to more general concerns, like communication, coordination, and relationships throughout the plant. Scientifically collected and systematically analyzed data on the impact of these efforts are just beginning to emerge.[3] But anecdotal evidence and statistics derived from related measures of scrap reduction, productivity, machine utilization, absenteeism, even the number of filed grievances—all point in the same direction: Such teams have a positive impact on organizational effectiveness. Further evidence from attitude surveys indicates a strong positive employee response to such teams.

CHANGE IN A DEMOCRATIC ORGANIZATION

Unions are formally democratic organizations;[4] that is, they have some mechanisms, usually including a written constitution, that ensure opportunity for members to hold office and influence decision making. While the mechanisms that ensure democracy in trade unions are undoubtedly imperfect, most available measures—participation in union meetings and elections, turnover of office holders, expressions of satisfaction by members concerning the internal operations of unions—consistently reflect the fact that such formal democracy is translated to a significant extent into democratic behavior, especially at local levels.[5]

The evolution of a collaborative relationship between unions and management requires that both sides change the manner in which they conduct business with the other. Change within the union occurs in a fundamentally different context than in a company, however. Corporations are hierarchical organizations, in which power, authority, and legitimacy flow downward from the top.[6] Unions, on the other hand, are formally democratic organizations, in which power, authority, and legitimacy ultimately flow upward from the consent of the governed. As a consequence, the ability of union leaders to articulate new goals and to establish new mechanisms for achieving those goals, without abandoning their use of collective bargaining for mediating some conflicts, ultimately depends on the approval of members. Elected leaders inevitably weigh new initiatives against political realities. Any alteration in the mission and direction of the union will, in the end, be tested by union members themselves through their election or rejection of union leaders.

If leaders in democratic organizations tend, in fact, to be followers of what they perceive to be the popular consensus, then from where will the thrust toward change come? In the case of trade unions, there are three likely, highly interrelated sources of change: a shifting environment, a newly emerging consensus on the part of members, and the appearance of influential leaders who are willing to articulate a bold new future for their organizations.[7]

The environmental changes that have led union leaders to realize the need for a new labor relationship are the same ones that have encouraged management to explore new avenues of collaboration. While it would be difficult to provide longitudinal evidence of a shifting consensus within the work force on such matters as employee participation, labor-management collaboration, and quality of work life, there is evidence both from research findings and from private attitude surveys that a large majority of workers favor such initiatives.[8] This seems especially so under two sets of circumstances: first, if they have experienced such involvement either directly or indirectly (through observing trial projects and experiments within their work setting); and second, if workers are convinced that the union is able to protect them from possible abuses by management. The insistence by the United Auto Workers and the United Steelworkers that the union remain an equal, joint, and voluntary partner in such efforts is correctly seen as a mandatory step toward overcoming a distrust of management, especially corporate management, that lingers among many workers.

The potential exists, it would seem, for a powerful internal consensus for a more collaborative relationship if the benefits of that new relationship include enhanced participation and involvement. As with any new consensus in a democratic society, it becomes necessary for forward-looking leaders to help articulate that consensus, mold it into a more specific vision, and translate it into a political agenda for that society. In the case of unions, particularly the two unions under consideration here, there are influential leaders who look into the not-so-distant future and see employee participation and union-management collaboration as the centerpiece of the trade union's mission within American society. Sam Camens, assistant to the president of the Steelworkers, for instance, suggests that joint committees will operate at a corporate level to advise on strategic decisions as a logical and hoped-for extension of labor-management cooperation on the shop floor. UAW vice president Don Ephlin points to his union's recent "blueprint" for national industrial policy, with its call for joint union-management strategic efforts on both the industry and national level. Many of these same leaders insist further that such a thrust represents not a discontinuity with the past mission of trade unions but rather a natural extension of their historical efforts to promote democracy in the workplace—first, by winning for workers certain material security; and second, by enlarging the workers' right to "participate in making decisions that affect their lives before such decisions are made."

But among other leaders of these two unions there is, at best, an uneasiness over this vision of the future. The highly centralized structure of the Steelworkers, together with the industrywide nature of its bargaining, has led to a somewhat unified policy direction for that union. But the decentralized United Auto Workers has found itself without the strong support of its presidents or the endorsement of its executive committee for the idea that quality of work life or employee involvement should be core goals of the union. At their 1980 convention the UAW did generally endorse the notion of enhanced employee influence. Certain language was dropped from the union constitution—"The worker does not seek to usurp management's functions"—and new provisions were added advocating workers' having "a voice in their own destiny" and participating "in making decisions that affect their lives before such decisions are made." But without the official backing of the union's executive committee, the Auto Workers have not made these a central union goal for the future nor developed specific mechanisms for grooming new leaders who would turn such visions into practical realities. As a result, companies and union leaders in the auto industry have found the process of changing the nature and direction of their relationship somewhat difficult. Assignments to head various Auto Workers departments, for instance, are made with little regard for the impact on such initiatives.⁹ Changes at the plant level have been blocked by appointed international service representatives who seem willing to tolerate joint union-management efforts only insofar as the higher-ups within their departments forcefully promote such an idea.

Perhaps as damaging to the momentum of change can be the creation of mechanisms for cooperation under one regime that are deemed to be inappropriate, even detrimental, by new leadership. The 1982 contract between General Motors and the United Auto Workers illustrates the problem. That contract contained a so-called Competitive Edge Agreement, which encouraged joint activities at the local level to build plant competitiveness not only in the international marketplace but also "among ourselves." From the 1930s through the 1970s periods of low demand or high competitiveness have regularly been accompanied by increased management attention to local work rules. But this new effort represented more than just cyclical response to certain environmental conditions. The intent of the Competitive Edge committee structure was to enlarge the scope of quality-of-work-life deliberations by encouraging local unions and plant managers to discuss contractual matters such as work rules, production standards, and seniority, all of which are formally off-limits to QWL activities.

While QWL supporters discouraged explicit talk about business goals like productivity or quality, Competitive Edge articulated its goals in precisely those terms. Its emphasis on interplant competition, with the inevitable consequence of competition between UAW locals, raised the ire of union leaders. "They're trying to have it both ways," complained one regional director. "It makes it really hard to try to work together with the companies when they do this." When Don Ephlin arrived at General Motors, he became convinced that the manner in which the Competitive Edge idea was being translated into specific plant-level actions was seriously eroding rank-and-file support for QWL:

> Under Competitive Edge, the locals are being told to change the local contract in order to become more competitive with one another. They are threatened by local management, who says

that either they give up benefits that the union has already won for them or they risk losing work to other plants that have made such concessions. This undermines the faith of local leaders and members in their management, and if they think management is bad, they'll think we shouldn't be working with them on QWL.

The important point to make concerning the controversy over Competitive Edge is not so much the merit of this particular effort as the inevitable confusion and deleterious impact that the lack of clear goals (and strategies to achieve those goals) has had on the change process in the UAW.

Even among those union leaders in the UAW and the Steelworkers who are fully committed to this change, it is assumed that increased influence and participation by workers on the plant floor, or even in the management of their companies, cannot replace traditional calls for improved wages and enhanced job security as a union rallying cry for the future. Most believe that the issue of participation is too complex to be supported a priori by workers; or that it does not quite carry the emotional impact of calling for higher wages; or that, especially among nonunion workers, the battle is still to be waged over the "first step" of industrial democracy: the traditional concerns of collective bargaining.

Underlying this analysis of quality of work life by union leaders is another widely held viewpoint: Trade unions are, by nature, reactive rather than proactive organizations. They depend largely on the initiatives of management rather than on the wishes of their members or their leaders to set the agenda. "The leadership of the union reflects the leadership of management," said one vice president. "If management sincerely changes, the leadership of the union will change."

THE CONSTRAINTS OF HISTORY

Such a conception of union organizations is deeply rooted in the history of American unions. Trade unions are essentially protest organizations fighting perceived abuses of workers in the work setting and, occasionally, in the larger society, as seen in the support by a number of labor leaders for the civil rights movement of the 1960s. In moving beyond protest, American unions have strayed little further than narrowly defined bread-and-butter remedies for such abuses: the eight-hour work day, minimum wage, health and safety laws, improved wages, and job security for members.

The historical context of the development of trade unionism in this country can help explain the conservative manner in which those unions have moved beyond protest. In the late nineteenth century, at the very time that the American Federation of Labor was formed and began to flourish, economic growth placed skilled labor in a strong bargaining position over wages. (Because of immigration and internal migration, unskilled labor was in overabundant supply; the American Federation of Labor aimed mainly at organizing skilled workers.) As craft unions successfully used that bargaining position to gain higher wages for their members, the concentration on higher wages came to be accepted by members. Union leaders, furthermore, saw the emphasis on higher wages as being positively correlated with institutional growth. In addition, the political environment in the United States strongly discouraged attempts by the Populist Party (in the late nineteenth century), the Socialist Party and the Industrial Workers of the World (in the early twentieth century), and the American Communist Party (in mid century) to widen American trade unions into a reformist/revolutionary movement with broadly defined social, political, and economic goals.

Labor law further reinforced this view of unions as institutional representatives of employees with the main goal of reacting to specific grievances and needs in the workplace not being met by management while seeking to enlarge the slice of the economic pie being allocated to members. By specifying wages and working conditions as the proper scope of collective bargaining, the National Labor Relations Act (1935) made it easier for union leaders to negotiate over bread-and-butter issues and to respond to specific grievances against management than to suggest bold new directions. When the Taft-Hartley Law (1947) outlawed strikes in pursuance of nonmandatory collective-bargaining issues, the narrow focus and reactive nature of trade unions was further reinforced.

THE CONSTRAINTS OF DEMOCRACY

But the widely shared opinion that the agenda of unions will largely be set by management is also a pragmatic response to assumptions concerning change in democratic organizations. Nearly all the leaders with whom I spoke agreed that because of the democratic nature of their unions, shifts in policy can occur only slowly and gradually. The various change levers available to top corporate executives—selection and placement of key personnel, succession planning, performance appraisals, pay systems, even top-down mandated change—are either missing entirely or are weak tools in the arsenal of any organization where most key positions are filled by election and any significant change in policy must be ratified by management. Even if the executive committee of the United Auto Workers were fully behind the QWL/EI process, it is difficult to conceive of a union mandate parallel to General Motors' 1979 declaration that all plants must initiate some kind of QWL process. The more democratic the organization, in fact, the weaker are the top-down levers.

This is not to say that unions are entirely without change levers. Some are being employed currently within these two organizations. Under Lloyd McBride's tenure as president of the United Steelworkers, for instance, frequent executive committee meetings were held for national and district officers and staff to help build a consensus among them around joint cooperation. Within his own staff organization at both Ford and General Motors, Don Ephlin held long sessions in which the pros and cons of participation were discussed and individual feelings and misgivings aired freely. Because of their positions as staff who reported directly to him, however, Ephlin was able to insist that publicly these people would all "sing from the same hymn book."

But neither Ephlin nor top leadership within the Steelworkers has the luxury of being able to issue such marching orders to elected officials. While national leaders might have clear preferences for local, and, in the case of the Steelworkers, regional candidates for election who are compatible in both values and skills with the direction in which they are seeking to move their union, officers in union headquarters are reticent to become involved in local elections. Based on past history, they fear that such involvement may be viewed as high-handed by local membership, resulting perhaps in a popular backlash against the very candidates they are supporting.

Such centralized control, in addition to being difficult to administer, implies some significant long-term risks for unions. Centralized control could jeopardize internal union democracy by pulling the union leadership further away from members, thus increasing dissatisfaction and alienation between leaders and the rank and file. The use of top-down change levers in a centralized, formal manner might increase the efficiency of the change process, but it could threaten the democratic foundations on which unions are built. In some ways, this dilemma may be viewed as the flip side of a dilemma faced by managers attempting to make their organizations more democratic. While managers must ask how efficient democracy can be, union leaders must ask how democratic efficiency can be.

The democratic nature of unions, then, makes succession planning such as corporate management can engage in difficult if not counterproductive. The Steelworkers have attempted to mold both the vision and skills of local and regional leaders following (rather than preceding) their election through regular meetings of the executive board and through a mandatory training program that is just beginning to emphasize behavioral and interpersonal issues. At a recent six-week staff education program held at the union's Linden Hall training facility, three of the fifteen seminars dealt specifically with skills or content areas designed to address new needs arising from the union's involvement in participative efforts: labor-management participation teams, worker participation concepts, and group dynamics. There is also some indication that staff positions, both at the regional and national levels, are increasingly being filled by better-educated members and even occasionally by outsiders. This is a change strategy with, at best, long-range payoffs that is further limited by the lingering emphasis in union educational programs on more technical issues (collective bargaining, arbitration, pensions, standards and incentives) and by severely limited training resources.

To convert resisters, the Auto Workers have relied heavily on word-of-mouth, coupled with orchestrated visits to innovating work sites and assurances that no local official has ever lost a reelection campaign based on support for quality of work life or employee involvement.[10] The Auto Workers and the Steelworkers have come to rely on outside consultants for helping to plan change strategies and for training. These consultants are hired by management, however (with the unions possessing veto power over the selection of particular consultants) and thus serve unions and management jointly rather than concentrating on the internal change process of the unions. Further, both unions have, with the cooperation of their counterparts in management, carefully avoided imposing collaborative efforts where local resistance remains strong. The hope of such a strategy, yet to be proved in practice, is that eventually local resisters will either be swept up by the ever-widening tide of change or will be swept out of office by restless local members anxious for the kind of workplace reform they see occurring elsewhere.

BOTTOM-UP SUPPORT: LESSONS OF THE PAST

The support or opposition of local leaders is, of course, critical to the success of the process of collaboration. Training and consensus building are helpful in the process, but there are also political and institutional considerations that must be met. Local leaders, for instance, wonder whether their early support for collaboration will be viewed by members as "getting into bed" with management.[11] They also worry about the impact that the direct involvement of employees in problem-solving groups and joint committees will have on their local union structure. If collaboration involves only union leaders talking with plant management, there is little likelihood of substantive improvement on the shop floor and high likelihood that the effort will eventually collapse. The history of past collaborative efforts clearly points in this direction.

In the 1920s industries such as textiles, garments, and railroads saw a number of joint efforts. Occasionally, as in the Naumkeag cotton mills of Salem, Massachusetts, the company agreed to work with the local union to cut down operating expenses as an alternative to laying off workers. The local union committee made cost-saving suggestions, which were then evaluated for the company by an outside industrial engineering consultant.[12] Labor-management cooperation at railroad companies assumed a somewhat broader agenda: defining jobs, training and recruiting workers, improving the quality of the product, and measuring output.

By the middle of the following decade, however, most such initiatives had disappeared.[13] The failure of these joint efforts can be laid, in part, to the economic devastation brought about by the Great Depression of the 1930s. But even without the Depression, the joint efforts of the 1920s would likely have disappeared without making a lasting impact on the nature of labor relations within their industries. The mechanisms created to facilitate cooperation were fatally flawed, particularly given the democratic nature of one of the two participating parties. Look, for instance, at the mechanisms for cooperation within the railroad industry:[14]

1. Union committeemen met biweekly with representatives of plant management in management's offices.
2. Additionally, top union officials met once a month with the heads of their company's maintenance and equipment departments.
3. The content of such meetings included discussions of "the quality of services, elimination of waste, increased production, and stabilization of employment" and specifically excluded any discussion of grievances.
4. All suggestions generated in such meetings were considered by management in consultation with outside industrial engineers, often from the (Frederick) Taylor Society.
5. Minutes of all meetings were made available to the local shop management and union leaders.

While the *content* of this collaboration may seem similar to more recent forays into labor-management cooperation, the *process* of collaboration is fundamentally different. Virtually no attention was paid to changing the nature of the relationship between unions and management. Factors that are today recognized as roadblocks to the development of a trusting, problem-solving relationship—power inequities, poor interpersonal skills, for example—were not addressed. Cooperative mechanisms in the railroad industry, for instance, offered no real power sharing with local union leadership, since all decisions were made unilaterally by management. As a result of not paying attention to the need to offer situational power parity as a way of building an enduring, trusting relationship, none of the mechanisms common to virtually all of today's collaborative efforts (the use of third-party process facilitators, extensive behavioral training, off-site meetings) were in evidence.

But perhaps most crippling to the long-term viability of such initiatives was the total lack of direct involvement by rank and file in the collaborative process. The early structures of cooperation failed even on a most basic level: to provide for widespread dissemination of information to the rank and file concerning what decisions were being made and how they were arrived at. Thus, both management and local union officials ignored one of the basic constraints on democratic organizations: the need for leaders to build and maintain support among their critical constituencies. Labor-management cooperation became, on the union side at least, a program without a constituency. Traditional rank and file suspicions of the motives of management could easily develop into deeper distrust concerning what was taking place behind the closed doors marked "labor-management cooperation." That distrust made a favorable consensus impossible to develop and eventually helped destroy these efforts.

THE DIFFICULT BALANCING ACT

The lesson of the early efforts seems clear: The democratic nature of unions dictates that the lack of direct member involvement will prove fatal. But it seems equally clear that the local union leadership must also play a critical role. Efforts that involve members directly but contain little or no formal role for the local union bring into question the institutional survival of that local and are thus bound to generate suspicion and opposition from the leadership. Much of the union opposition to recent quality-circle efforts derives from just that fact: union leaders as representatives of their institution feel shut out of the participative process. If managers downplay or even ignore this concern for institutional survival, then they become vulnerable to charges that they are using such direct participation to weaken or even destroy the local union. In such a circumstance, management may find itself not only bucking the local union but also building animosity and distrust within the work force itself.

Thus, local union leaders find it necessary to balance carefully two separate but critical imperatives: the need to get the rank and file directly involved in the process, and the need to carve out a meaningful, ongoing role for the local union. Unions and management in the two industries under consideration here have attempted to strike a workable balance. While members get involved in shop-floor discussions, joint committees of local plant management and union leadership oversee these efforts. But the balance is an extremely delicate one, requiring constant attention by union leaders at all levels of the organization and a good deal of sensitivity on the part of local and corporate management as well.

Consider a recent incident in which involving workers directly in a participatory process threatened to bypass the role of the local union. A worker team in an auto plant asked their union representative to speak to the plant management about placing a fan in their work site. When the union declined to pursue the matter with management, the team approached plant management directly. Instead of realizing the inherent threat to the institutional integrity of the local union, the plant manager agreed to the request. In bypassing the local union in favor of the team, local management emphasized the latent fear held by a number of local leaders that "too much" or "the wrong kind" of direct involvement by members will shift the loyalties of workers away from the local and toward participation committees and, ultimately, management. In this case, the local union committee appealed to corporate staff, who explained the realities of local union life to the plant manager. This incident is admittedly limited in scope. However, if repeated often and widely, similar occurrences could severely undermine the necessary commitment of local union leaders to the collaborative process.

A comparison of the collaborative structures being utilized by the Auto Workers and the Steelworkers indicates that the union's own role in the change effort may also be posing a threat to the delicate balance that needs to be struck at a local level between institutional and direct involvement. Unlike the early efforts in the railroad industry, both the auto and steel industries provide ample opportunity for rank-and-file members to participate directly in the process of collaboration through shop-floor teams. But while the auto industry and the United Auto Workers are turning entire shops or departments into work teams, the practice within at least one major steel company is to compose work teams only of elected representatives of that shop or department. By allowing for the creation of separate elected bodies of workers with ever-increasing responsibilities and powers but with no direct organizational links to the local union (the local unions in these cases play only an oversight function), the Steelworkers may themselves be perilously tipping the balance of collaboration away from their own local structure. It would not be surprising if local leaders eventually see such a structure as a threat to their own long-term survival.

THE SHIFTING ROLE OF THE LOCAL LEADER

What is becoming increasingly apparent is that the local union leader has a critical role to play in the process of changing union-management relations, and that the role differs significantly from what it has been in the past. The previous role of local leader was that of a protester and an adversary to local management, standing up for the rights of members against the abuses of management, and negotiating with plant management over local issues like work rules. Members expected local leaders, as adversaries of management, to "beat" management, and elected leaders based their success on ability to "win" in that relationship.

While this role will not be replaced entirely, it must be supplemented if the collaborative process is to succeed. Local union leaders will be dealing less and less with the content of union-management relations. Increasingly, discussions of work rules and assignments, supervisory attitudes, even (at least informally) grievances against management will be held by members themselves within their work teams.[15] The primary role of local leaders will then be to oversee and facilitate the problem-solving process while removing themselves from the content issues involved in the process. But local leaders will need to do more than play a consulting role, and herein lie new avenues to increasing influence and power. As shop and department teams flourish, local union leaders will increasingly be called upon to play a coordinating/integrating role, keeping track of all the various efforts, pulling them together when cross-boundary problems arise, helping to ensure that they are all moving in a common direction. As the oversight process builds a stronger relationship between union leaders and plant management, those leaders become the voice of workers as a stakeholder group to plant management and the voice of plant managers as a stakeholder group to workers. Finally, local leaders will become strategists, working with local plant management—as they are already doing to some plants—to help develop business plans for their plant in conjunction with the strategic plans for the company. At the same time they will work with both local members and national leaders to plan for the future course of the union.

The United Auto Workers and the United Steelworkers have both recognized that such a future role will require a new set of talents and skills on the part of local union leaders. Shifts in the content of the Steelworkers' training programs for new leaders toward behavior-oriented skills represents a small but important sign of such awareness. The process that will most likely have a more far-reaching impact on the type of leader that emerges from the union ranks, however, is the appointment of local coordinators or facilitators from within the union ranks.

Local union coordinators are explicitly not meant to become leaders of the local union in any formal or institutional sense. Both the Auto Workers and Steelworkers, in fact, insist that such coordinators be appointed rather than elected to ensure that they are not seen as alternative union leaders to the local presidents, committeemen, and so on. But there is a more subtle process taking place, beyond sensitivity to local concerns. The electoral process cannot be counted on to serve up the "right" kind of leader for the collaborative process. Particularly at an early stage of the change process, as the rank and file still harbors strong suspicions of management motives and the collaborative process itself, elected leaders may well be oriented more toward the protest or adversarial functions of the union. Union officials who support the change realize that a collaborative relationship requires union representatives who "think neutral," that is, who are able to go beyond purely parochial points of view by seeing the future of the union as ultimately tied in with the future of the company. As long as such "unbiased" representatives, along with management's appointed facilitators, work within the guidelines established by the joint plant oversight committee, the union will not be placed at a disadvantage by the collaborative process.

IMPLICATIONS FOR MANAGEMENT

An important caveat to this notion of a "new" union leader is that there must be a new kind of leadership from management as well if the collaborative process is to succeed. Managers who engage in this process must, like their union counterparts, be "unbiased." Their own strong company orientation must be tempered by a recognition of the legitimacy of workers and their unions as powerful stakeholders. This is especially true in industries like the ones considered here, where the unions, while significantly weakened in recent years, will certainly continue to be a powerful force among employees. Further, if the change process in democratic organizations is necessarily slow, then a change in the industrial relationship becomes all the more dependent on management. Only long-term commitment sustained by sincere beliefs will allow the change process to edge forward. Missteps by management at any point in the inevitably long process can severely undermine that process, undercutting the direction being offered by top union leaders by reinforcing suspicions and distrust of management motives that exist within the rank and file.

Managers would also do well to be sensitive to the political realities of local union politics. Clearly, management at both the local and corporate level is anxious to do what it can to promote the kind of labor relations it believes will be beneficial to the company. But such eagerness must be tempered by a keen awareness that unions are political organizations, democratic in nature, and as legitimately concerned with their own institutional survival as the companies are with theirs. Otherwise, the long-term effects of insensitivity on the part of management may move labor relations in precisely the opposite direction from the one desired. The controversy within the UAW over the GM Competitive Edge program indicates a lingering distrust at both the local and national levels of the union of an explicit emphasis on the business outcomes of participation programs. The 1984 GM-UAW contract finally sought to allay such suspicions with a written guarantee that no job losses would result from jointly negotiated productivity improvements at the plant level. Failure to take such sensitivities into account risks future union support, which management depends upon to make collaborative efforts possible.

Finally, a reading of the assumptions of top union leaders concerning the reactive nature of their organizations would suggest that bold initiatives from management might be accepted, even welcomed, by those leaders as an additional tool for changing their organizations. But such boldness must be restrained by a recognition that if a change process is slow within large corporations, it is even slower within unions. If the democratic nature of the organization largely negates the use of top-down change levers and requires instead the emergence of a consensus among rank-and-file members and local leaders, then management must resist the urge to expect too much too fast. "Management tends to be impatient," cautioned one union vice president. "They'll say, 'I've been treating those bastards nice for a whole week now! Why won't they change?' But the process takes time." By understanding the nature of change within unions, management can both develop patience for the pace of change and learn something about how and where to push and how and where to refrain.

IMPLICATIONS FOR UNIONS:
A REVITALIZED FUTURE

An organization that conceives of itself primarily as a protester may well find the role of partner to be an uncomfortable one. The new presidents of both the unions considered here insist that they can continue to play each of these two roles simultaneously and well. The United Auto Workers President Owen Bieber now sits on the board of directors of the Chrysler Corporation (as did his predecessor, Douglas Fraser), and the Steelworkers' Lynn Williams assures the steel industry that as long as a company is willing to recognize fully the legitimacy of the union as a voice for the collective interests of workers, he is willing to work as a partner for that company. But there remain important factions within each of these unions that openly challenge such a view, wondering whether the union abdicates its protest role by becoming a partner. The democratic nature of unions will act, both sides hope, as a corrective force: If either the protest or partnership role becomes overplayed to the detriment of the union, members will send a strong signal to their leaders through the ballot box.

Once a union decides to try to change its relationship with management, certain important benefits can accrue to the union from the process. Denials by many current union leaders to the contrary, it offers unions another rallying cry in their attempt to attract new members. The rising educational and expectation levels of the work force may well make calls for increased meaningful involvement in work an important addition to the union's more traditional emphasis on unity, shorter work days, and improved wages. This may be especially true among white-collar workers, who have in the past found little appeal in the promises of working-class solidarity. Around these issues, unions have the opportunity to shed their reactive assumptions and move into the forefront of demands for participation, involvement, and empowerment, insisting now that management follow their lead.

The change effort can also work to the long-term benefit of unions by providing them with a new stream of leadership. A new generation of union activists will emerge from the process of participation and collaboration, who may well dominate leadership in upcoming decades. Further, these new leaders will bring with them a different perspective from that held by the previous generation of leaders. Their orientation will be more strongly toward the company than toward the union as a separate entity when compared to the orientation of their predecessors. But such a shift does not bespeak a weakened loyalty to the union. Far from it. The company orientation of these new leaders will involve, at its heart, a concept of "company" that clearly recognizes both workers and their union as powerful and legitimate stakeholders. Far from suggesting a stunted view of unions, these new leaders may well emerge from the process openly wondering where, or even if, the limits of such a legitimate role for employees and unions within their companies should be drawn. Those current leaders within the United Steelworkers and the United Auto Workers who are truly looking into the future and thinking about the new type of leadership that may result, welcome that change and hope that their unions will emerge from it revitalized.

8
Challenges in the Management of Technology and Labor Relations

Richard E. Walton

This chapter explores the possible future of two issues: First, what are the emerging human problems and opportunities associated with the management of the new computer-based work technology? Second, will a new pattern of union-management relations evolve, tailored to the changing philosophies of management (oriented to eliciting commitment) and adaptive to the new competitive realities in U.S. industry? My basic assumption is that we urgently need to develop new concepts and know-how in managing each of these issues, and my forecast is that we will. This chapter analyzes these needs as they merge in practice and proposes how they might be met.

The two challenges merge in practice when a unionized company has an extensive long-term program for introducing new work technology. This situation exists in many major industries—automobile, aerospace, steel, rubber, electrical equipment, and others. In many of these cases, information technology affects unionized professional and clerical workers as well as blue-collar workers. The situation also exists in the AT&T system; in some unionized white-collar service companies in insurance, retailing, and utilities; and in the Internal Revenue Service, the Social Security system, and the Post Office.

The first section of this chapter outlines the critical importance of work technology in shaping employee commitment. The next section analyzes how management and union officials in the unionized sectors typically deal with the work-force issues

199

associated with new technology. The third section explores an alternative strategy to set the stage for union-management discussions.

THE IMPLICATIONS OF WORK TECHNOLOGY FOR EMPLOYEE COMMITMENT

The new work technology referred to here includes robotics, numerical control machining, computer-aided design, computer-aided manufacture, manufacturing planning requirements, automated storage and retrieval, automated process controls, point-of-sale systems, word processing, and many applications of new information technology to the unique requirements of the telecommunications industry, such as automated test equipment and work-force scheduling.

An earlier Harvard research project investigated a number of office applications of advanced information technology and their human and organizational consequences for clerical, professional, and managerial personnel.[1] Most, but not all, of the research sites in this earlier project were nonunion. The applications of computer-based technology were found to have profound implications for the way work is organized and managed. This technology can either be designed and implemented in a way that reinforces the control model or shaped so as to facilitate movement toward the commitment model.[2] To date, the directional effects have been variable and mostly unplanned. The following illustrate the variability:

1. Applications of this technology sometimes narrow the scope of jobs and sometimes broaden them.
2. They may emphasize the individual nature of task performance or promote the interdependent nature of the work of groups of employees.
3. They may change the locus of decision making toward centralization or decentralization, with further implications for the steepness of the hierarchy.
4. They may create performance-measurement systems that emphasize either learning and self-control or surveillance and hierarchical control.

5. They may transfer certain work functions from the unionized work force to supervisory or professional groups, or they may provide developmental opportunities for the workers.

6. They can increase the flexibility of work schedules to accommodate human preferences, or they can decrease flexibility and introduce shift work.

7. They often contribute to social isolation, but sometimes they have the opposite effect.

When the new technology modified work so as to make it more routine and controlled, requiring less operator skill and knowledge, the employees tried to ameliorate the adverse effects or to retaliate. Whether worker reactions were spontaneous or deliberate, protective or aggressive, these reactions undermined the technical and economic performance of the new work technology.

On the other hand, when the new technology provided meaningful employee discretion, promoted decentralized decision making, emphasized learning, and clarified the individual employee's role in the larger work flow, it generated greater employee commitment, which led to improved utilization of the technical capability and economic performance of the technology.

Based on my personal values and encouraged by the research findings just cited, I offer the following definition of effectiveness in managing technology:

> By "effective utilization" I mean that the applications of the technology are designed and implemented so as to (1) yield the cost, quality, and service benefits for the enterprise that are potential in the technology; and (2) minimize adverse effects on the work force and promote positive organization effects.

Our research found that, with rare exceptions, managers had not been guided by such a concept of effectiveness as they developed and implemented the new work technology. When a technological application had effects that promoted commitment, these effects were as likely to be accidental and unanticipated as were effects that reinforced the control model. The directional effects often were not inherent in the technology;

that is, the control effects could have been minimized or reversed had they been attended to early in the design and implementation process.

Thus, on the basis of formal research and other observations
of nonunion settings, I conclude that the new work technology
is being developed according to economic and technical criteria
but not social or human organizational criteria, and the result
is less effective utilization of the technology. Two major reasons
for this are lack of awareness of the potential and absence of
methodological know-how to tap this potential.

As a rule, neither the professionals who develop the applications nor the managers who approve them recognize at present the extent to which new work technology can be better
managed in the way defined here. They share with many others
in contemporary society an assumption about "technological
determinism"—the idea that the side effects of technological
progress are given and that individuals, organizations, and society must learn how to cope with them. Even in organizations
otherwise pursuing the commitment strategy, there has been
relatively little appreciation of technology policy as a manageable element of a human resource strategy. In fact, it can be
argued that computer-based technology is the least deterministic, the most flexible technology to affect the workplace since
the beginning of the Industrial Revolution. Because this technology is less hardware-dependent and more software-inten-
sive, and because of the rapidly declining cost of computer
power, the basic technology offers an increased number of options, all economically acceptable. Thus, one can solve the business requirements with a greater variety of technical
configurations, *each with a different set of human implications.* Progress in making better use of new technology, and in using it to
promote the commitment model, requires a recognition of this
potential by professionals and managers. (Later we will extend
this point to labor leaders as well.)

Progress also depends on another type of knowledge—how
to influence the technology-development process at the design
and early implementation stages. Line managers who are at
least one step removed from the process are often awed by the
technology-development process and do not know how or when

they could intervene to ensure that social criteria as well as economic and technical criteria, are considered. Thus, a second need is to develop methods that influence but do not encumber the technology-development process. These methods will need to include involvement by workers who will operate the new work technology.

ADVERSARIAL LABOR RELATIONS AND THE MANAGEMENT OF TECHNOLOGY

In the previous section we argued that at present, in settings where the employees are not unionized, management does not plan for the human effects of new technology and therefore fails to utilize it effectively. That general picture also applies to unionized settings. But collective bargaining introduces some additional complexities with important implications for the utilization of new technology. On the one hand, the union prompts management to address some potential or actual work-force effects that they typically do not address in the absence of a union. This may have some positive effects, in human terms, on the utilization of technology. On the other hand, adversarial bargaining over technology issues and the solutions it produces often decreases the effectiveness of the technology in technical, economic, and human terms.

The introduction of new work technology has always been of interest to both management and unions. New work technology often plays a critical role in improving a company's competitiveness in terms of cost, quality, and service. In addition, it can have several kinds of adverse effects on the work force:

1. *Employment effects.* New technology usually reduces the total number of jobs available. It may result in the unemployment of current job occupants or simply in a reduction in the number of employees by attrition.
2. *Relocation effects.* New technology may require employees to make a physical move.
3. *Health and safety effects.* New technology may introduce new health and safety risks.
4. *Bargaining unit effects.* New technology may result in a basic

redesign of the work system, affecting tasks performed by employees both within and outside the bargaining unit, including supervisors. Often, judgments are made about which tasks in the revised work system will be performed by employees in the bargaining unit and which will be performed by other employees. Unions are concerned about the transfer of work out of the bargaining unit.

5. *Skill and income effects.* New technology may reduce skill requirements, resulting in new jobs that are lower-rated and lower-paying.

6. *Job qualification effects.* New technology typically requires different skills and knowledge, whether the new jobs are rated higher or lower. Some workers may have considerable difficulty performing the new job satisfactorily.

7. *Job advancement effects.* New technology may alter job families and job ladders, thereby decreasing an employee's or worker's current status.

8. *Job control and job pressure effects.* New technology may change work loads. It may also subject workers to greater external controls and more frequent and detailed monitoring of their performance and job-related behavior.

9. *Job satisfaction effects.* New technology may result in jobs that are more routinized and that involve less discretion, less physical freedom, less social contact, and less privacy. Simpler jobs that use fewer skills can result in lower individual self-esteem and other unhealthy symptoms.

How have unions responded to protect their members against the potential adverse effects of new work technology?

In 1960 Slichter, Healy, and Livernash distinguished a number of policies in relation to new technology ranging from opposition to encouragement.[3] The dominant approach was to accept the introduction of technology but to influence timing if possible and then to attempt to limit some of the work-force effects just listed. This pattern continues today.

This union approach is not surprising given the legal framework for collective bargaining in the United States. The National Labor Relations Act of 1935, amended in 1947, established that "wages, hours, and other terms and conditions of employment" constitute mandatory bargaining material.

> The National Labor Relations Board has interpreted this provision to mean that labor and management may negotiate over issues in two categories, one category of issues for which bargaining is mandatory, and one category for which bargaining is permissible but not mandatory. NLRB and court rulings on the adoption of (conventional) automation through the 1970s, generally imposed a requirement to bargain as to the effects of automation, but not on whether and when to introduce automation.[4]

Nor has management been required to bargain about the design or configuration of the technology. Thus, decisions about which technology will be introduced and when have been protected as "managerial rights" when management's unilateral decisions in that area have been challenged:

> . . . Arbitration rulings regarding the interpretation of existing contracts suggest that management is accorded broad discretions for implementing new technology, altering work rules, and reallocating work between employees in the bargaining unit and others as a result of technological change in the absence of specific contract language governing such changes.[5]

Unions have had some success in expanding the scope of labor contracts in the past two decades in relation to technological change and other job threats. To cite a few examples:

> Agreements limiting plant movement rose from 22 percent in the 1966–67 survey to 36 percent in the 1980–81 survey of some 1,600 contracts, while worker coverage rose from 38 to 49 percent. . . . Agreements dealing with relocation allowances increased from 34 to 41 percent, while worker coverage went up from 60 to 65 percent.[6]

The range of contract provisions negotiated by unions and the grievance activities and other influence attempts utilized by unions are shown in *Table 8-1*, along with the particular workforce effects they are intended to ameliorate. This list reflects considerable ingenuity as well as union perserverance. However, in general, these initiatives have been only moderately

Table 8-1: Union Approaches to Technology Effects

Type of Work Force Effects of New Technology	*Prevailing Union Responses to Potential Effects*
1. Employment effects	Slow down rate of introduction Influence proposed staffing plans for new technology Retraining for displaced employees to qualify for other jobs Expanded bidding rights Shorter work week Advance notice Attrition versus layoff
2. Relocation effects	Expanded job transfer rights at same location and retraining to qualify for other jobs
3. Health and safety effects	Request studies; access to studies Grieve conditions
4. Bargaining unit effects	Assurances precluding "transfer of work" Challenge management actions
5. Skill and income effects	Challenge appropriateness of lower ratings Assurances that revised jobs will pay as much as the jobs they replaced
6. Job qualification effects	Training for new job Longer period to demonstrate mastery Burden of proof for disqualifying
7. Job advancement effects	Training Bidding rights
8. Job control and job pressure effects	Assurances that new system will not be used to monitor individual performance Constraints on load and other job conditions Grieve conditions and direct action
9. Job satisfaction effects	(Only recently have employee-involvement and quality-of-work-life programs set the stage for addressing these effects directly)

effective in ameliorating the adverse work-force effects of new technology. Unions have had less leverage over the work-force effects in the bottom half of *Table 8-1* than over the first ones.

Thus, current practice involves managers who are preoccupied with technical and economic criteria in designing technology; and unions that attempt to impose conditions on implementation in order to limit the technology's adverse effects on the work force. To complete the picture of prevailing practice, we need to consider how management copes with the union's influence attempts and how it has acted in other ways that intensify the union's concerns. Within this adversarial context, management has shown three additional tendencies.

First, the most constructive management response to union challenges is to do more advance planning and, as a result, for instance, to rely on attrition rather than on abrupt work-force reductions.

Second, management also compromises on certain human resource policies. Two types of compromises accepted by management were reported by Slichter, Healy, and Livernash[7] and are common today:

1. Managers have tended to give to the holders of jobs on the new machines or new processes somewhat higher wages relative to other workers in the same plants—in other words, they have tended to introduce distortions in the wage structure of the plant.
2. Managers have tended to a slight extent to allow the new techniques to be operated with excessive crews and under make-work rules.

The third and the most self-defeating set of coping responses by management are (specifically) to add social control to the other criteria that shape the design of new technology and (generally) to intensify the adversarial battle to protect managerial prerogatives. These responses virtually ensure a pair of interrelated self-reinforcing cycles, which are depicted in *Figure 8-1*.

Management's pessimistic assumptions about workers lead to a work-technology strategy that involves deskilling and routinizing work, which in turn generates worker apathy or antago-

Figure 8-1
Some Self-reinforcing Dynamics

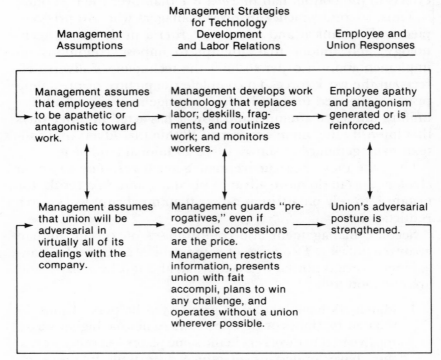

Management Assumptions	Management Strategies for Technology Development and Labor Relations	Employee and Union Responses
Management assumes that employees tend to be apathetic or antagonistic toward work.	Management develops work technology that replaces labor; deskills, fragments, and routinizes work; and monitors workers.	Employee apathy and antagonism generated or is reinforced.
Management assumes that union will be adversarial in virtually all of its dealings with the company.	Management guards "prerogatives," even if economic concessions are the price. Management restricts information, presents union with fait accompli, plans to win any challenge, and operates without a union wherever possible.	Union's adversarial posture is strengthened.

nism, thereby justifying both management's earlier assumption and the strategy. The development of intense adversarial labor relations in many unionized companies has reinforced the dynamics surrounding technology design. An assumption of adversarial relations by management leads it to pursue objectives and utilize tactics that increase the union's tendency to challenge, control, and constrain management actions.

These management assumptions are related to the inevitability/intractibility of apathetic labor and adversarial labor relations. Each of the two self-reinforcing loops depicted in *Figure 8-1* is strong by itself. In combination, they further reinforce each other. For example, preoccupied with its position in an adversarial relationship, management will be especially interested in work technology that deskills work, controls workers more closely, and permits the removal of tasks from members of the bargaining unit, because these effects will increase management's operational flexibility and minimize certain labor-relations "hassles."

As suggested throughout this book, some people are revising their assumptions about the inevitability of worker apathy and the intractibility of adversarial relations in favor of assuming a potential for commitment and mutuality. There is growing recognition that the assumptions about apathy and adversarial relations have led to suboptimal use of technology—from any point of view.

By way of summary, management assumptions that employees tend to be apathetic (have low commitment to work) and that unions tend to be adversarial (will pursue own self-interest at expense of company's) lead to the following patterns of work-technology development:

1. In the design of new work technology, jobs are deskilled, fragmented, and routinized. This increases management's control over the work force, but the new jobs also demoralize employees and limit the positive contribution they can make to service and cost effectiveness.
2. As new technology is designed and implemented, the full potential of retraining employees is seldom realized, even though such retraining could be advantageous to both the company and the employees. Management fears that contract provisions will force them to fill positions with unqualified persons.
3. In the design of new technology, tasks are sometimes moved up and out of bargaining units. This shift may give management certain tactical labor-relations advantages, but it assigns to professionals and supervisors work that neither uses nor develops their potential and takes away from workers in the bargaining unit some work that would have utilized and developed their potential.
4. In the design and implementation of new technology, monitoring capabilities are built into the work system that may ensure achievement of minimum performance but

that discourage workers from providing any more than the minimum. The result is to limit both employees' contributions and the satisfaction, pride, and self-esteem they may derive from work.

5. To ensure an orderly implementation of the new technology, management often agrees to compromises in the classification of jobs (rating them higher than otherwise warranted by the new work content itself). Such agreements are responsive to the equity concerns of the immediately affected group of employees, but they distort and decrease the integrity of structures and procedures intended to ensure reward equity among employee groups. They can also decrease the cost competitiveness of the company.

6. Similarly, management may agree to excessive manning levels as new technology is implemented. This may limit the immediate adverse employment effects on the affected group, but it leads to effort inequities and can detract from the competitiveness of the company.

Thus, the prevailing combination of unilateral and adversarial approaches to technology development falls short on two counts: It results in adverse work-force effects that could be avoided and in applications that do not make full use of the performance potential in the technology and in the work force.

MUTUALITY AND TECHNOLOGY

In the previous section we discussed how management and labor usually treat the work-force issues associated with new technology strictly within a familiar collective-bargaining format. The union attempts to negotiate guarantees and rights addressing as many of the work-force issues as possible. Management resists most of these provisions and shares only that information about its technology that it is obligated to share. Once the new technology is implemented, the union utilizes the grievance process and other forms of influence to minimize any adverse work-force effects. Management in turn utilizes tactics at its disposal that minimize the union's influence. The process is basically reactive: The union is reacting to management's implementation, and management is reacting to the union's influence attempts. The decision process is primarily bargaining.

In this section we explore an alternative union-management strategy. Some unions and employers are trying to develop a different approach to technology issues, not as a complete substitute for the one just described, but as a major additional approach. An element of such an approach is the creation of joint committees that address the work-technology issues in a planning and problem-solving mode. Examples are Ford-UAW (United Auto Workers) mutual growth forums and AT&T-CWA (Communications Workers of America) technology change committees. These newly created forums have not yet developed a track record, but we can consider their potential.[8]

Whereas the strict bargaining approach is *reactive and after the fact* (technology design has long been determined and an implementation plan is in place), the joint committee/forum offers the potential for employee representatives to influence technology plans and the design features of proposed work technology *before the fact*.

Whereas the bargaining context often produces decisions that involve trade-offs between company and employee interests, the problem-solving forums offer greater possibilities for finding solutions that integrate the needs of these two stakeholders. This is one source of potential joint gain.

Although the traditional bargaining approach may be relatively well designed to address some work-force issues listed in *Table 8-1* (such as income effect, health and safety effects, and some employment effects), it is not well designed to treat the issues of deskilling, job control/autonomy, job pressure, and job satisfaction. These often neglected issues offer the greatest potential for solutions that integrate human needs and business requirements.

I am aware of certain pilot efforts in this collaborative mode. For example, Ford and the UAW have a pilot project in a crankshaft machining unit that involves joint planning by union and management for the introduction of a variety of automated processes. The project also provides for workers to participate directly in the project planning process. The planning apparently has addressed many work-force effects, including noneconomic ones, which have not been explicitly attended to previously by either party.

When I have discussed the potential benefits from cooperation regarding technology with top union leaders and business executives (sometimes in the same session), they have all pointed out that progress on this front depends upon the more general development of mutuality between the two groups. In response to their assertion of this precondition for the more effective utilization of technology—an assertion with which I agree—I have begun to study directly the development of greater mutuality in labor relations.

The concept of mutuality proposed here is more than an increase in mutual trust and respect; it is more than a recognition by the parties of their common fate; it is more than self-restraints and concessions by one party or the other, even unprecedented self-restraints and concessions; it is more than one party accommodating to the institutional realities of the other. My interviews with representatives of management and labor indicate that they both understood that the above factors are all elements of mutuality. But mutuality is more.

Mutuality involves *a change in the modal decision-making process*. There will be more reliance on joint planning and problem-solving processes and correspondingly less on power bargaining to determine policies and on the legalistic approach to resolve grievances arising in the implementation of policies. Mutuality also *expands the substantive agenda* discussed by the parties, as new items are brought in. The full implications of these last two aspects of mutuality often were *not* recognized by the labor leaders and managers with whom I have discussed this issue.

Figure 8-2 should clarify the general conception of mutuality proposed here, as well as its application to technology. Technology policies and practices may be determined in at least four ways. First, government regulations determine or constrain related practices in some areas, such as health and safety, shift work, and the privacy of personal data. Second, some technology issues are decided unilaterally by management, such as size of investment, the functions automated, the design of jobs which operate the new technology. Third, in the unionized sector other issues will be resolved by adversarial processes between union and management, such as the pay associated with revised jobs and the rights of employees to bid into new jobs. Adversarial procedures have gradually come to be used in more and more areas originally left to unilateral decisions by management: for instance, in negotiating advance notice of technological change that affects the work force and in receiving assurances that attrition will be used to achieve reductions in work-force levels made possible by new technology. Fourth, in a relationship based on mutuality (*Figure 8-2(b)*) many of these issues become subject to mutual planning and problem solving, including participative processes that directly involve employees.

As *Figure 8-2* shows schematically, the area of practices determined by mutual and participative processes is created at the expense of *both* the adversarial and the unilateral agenda items. This symmetry is not always recognized by those who consider a strategy of mutuality. Managers typically foresee that with greater mutuality unions will be willing to adopt a joint problem-solving process in some policy areas previously subject to adversarial bargaining—for example, policies governing wage classifications and seniority bumping rights. On the other hand, union officials expect that management will bring to the joint agenda matters it previously controlled unilaterally, such as technology plans, priorities, and timing.

Managers and unions both tend to overlook what their own side must bring to the joint problem-solving agenda. Yet, in my view, this symmetry specifies the basic quid pro quo that is required if the mutuality strategy is to be initially acceptable to both parties and a sustainable pattern of labor relations over the long term.

This way of looking at the problem suggests many tactical issues in the development of mutuality. What are the best technology-related issues to transfer from the adversarial bargaining agenda? From management's unilateral planning agenda? Do participative job design, retraining, and the skill profile of the work force constitute a promising cluster of technology questions in which management, union, and employees can all gain from joint problem solving?

Figure 8-2
Determination of Technology and Work-Force Practices

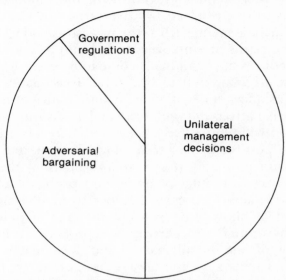

Government regulations

Unilateral management decisions

Adversarial bargaining

Under Adversarial Union-Management Relations

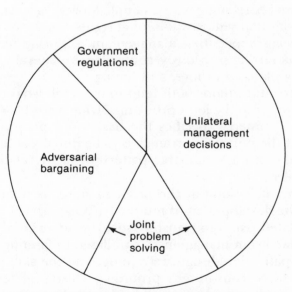

Government regulations

Unilateral management decisions

Adversarial bargaining

Joint problem solving

Under Mutual Union-Management Relations

Note: Proportions shown in these diagrams are illustrative only.

The mutual labor-relations agenda will include both items that were formerly handled by management unilaterally and items that were already on the joint agenda but were approached adversarially. In the case of technology, this means bringing technology planning to the agenda and using a problem-solving mode to address job design, job evaluation and other pay questions, jurisdictional questions, training, seniority rights, work-force adjustments, and work rules.

In a mutuality strategy, the parties jointly consider a balanced set of decision criteria. Specifically, they would strive to develop and use new technology in a way that satisfies three criteria. New technology must be (1) technically sound (reliable); (2) economically justified (return on investment); and (3) socially congruent (serving human needs and organizational health). There are abundant opportunities to increase both the social and the economic effectiveness of new information technology applications at the same time. Of course, design ingenuity has its limitations, and it is not always possible to avoid trade-offs. Although the parties strive for integrative solutions, compromises are sometimes necessary en route to consensus.

The potential benefits of labor-management planning and problem solving in relation to new work technology include better utilization of basic technology because of attention to economic and social effects; stronger labor and management institutions; and greater employee voice. In addition, the mutuality/participation system is expected to be *more inventive* in developing new solutions to both old and new problems; *more adaptive* to changing conditions; and more productive of *a higher level of commitment* to solutions on the part of employees, unions, and management.

A major risk for management is that the technology-development process will become too complicated and therefore less effective in certain respects even while it becomes more effective in others. A major risk for union officials is that while they gain influence they also gain responsibility, and they may prefer not to be so closely associated with certain decisions that some union members may later take exception to (even if the decisions were by far the best ones available for the work force).

SUMMARY AND CONCLUSIONS

New computer-based technology is employed to improve industry competitiveness in terms of cost, quality, and service. However, this technology often has adverse consequences for workers, ranging from job and income insecurity to job pressure and dissatisfaction.

Many of the adverse consequences for the work force are not inherent in the technology and can be minimized or reversed if attended to early in the design and implementation process.

It is in the self-interest of both union and management to give priority attention to these work-force effects. "Effective utilization of technology" means serving both human concerns and business requirements.

Generally, neither union officials nor managers recognize the extent to which new work technology can be better managed. They share a widely held assumption about technological determinism—the idea that the side effects of technological progress are inevitable and that individuals and institutions must learn to cope with them. Yet, computer-based technology may be the least deterministic, the most flexible technology to affect the workplace since the beginning of the Industrial Revolution.

Progress depends on knowledge about how to influence the technology design and implementation processes. Line managers and union officials do not know how or when they could intervene to ensure that social criteria are attended to along with economic and technical criteria. Thus, a second step is to develop methods to influence the technology-development process.

Progress also depends on changes in union-management relationships. If the relationships were based more on mutual trust, management's policies shaping the application of technology would probably change. Moreover, some issues, especially job skill and job satisfaction, are difficult to address in a bargaining mode; integrative solutions can only be invented in a joint planning and problem-solving process. Thus, a change toward mutuality involves an expansion of the problem-solving agenda at the expense of both the adversarial agenda and the agenda previously handled unilaterally by management.

Part Three:
Managing Change in Human Resource Practices

9
Corporatewide Transformations in Human Resource Management

Michael Beer
Bert Spector

Innovations in the management of human resources have been taking place in American industry over the past decade. Increasing foreign competition, an upgrading of the educational levels of employees, and shifting societal values toward such matters as traditional authority and compliance have combined to produce a growing sense of dissatisfaction with both the traditional practices and the underlying assumptions that guided the management of people in organizations. Important shifts, with particular emphasis on increasing the autonomy, responsibility, and influence of employees at all levels, are significantly altering the traditional relationship between organizations and their employees, amounting, we believe, to a new model of human resource management (HRM).

This chapter reports on a study we are conducting of HRM transformations in American companies. Specifically, we have targeted for in-depth field research six companies that are broadly redefining their HRM policies and practices. Our research is to be supplemented by visits and case writing in a number of other companies undergoing similar transformations. At this stage, we have conducted studies in three large companies (sales of $4 billion to $6 billion), two of which can be characterized as largely single-business, "smokestack" companies; firms operating in old industries that have been buffeted by severe crises in the past decade. Both these companies are unionized. One bargains at the industry level, and all its production employees are unionized. The other company bargains at the plant level, and not all its plants are unionized. The third company is a multibusiness firm operating in newer industries. With the exception of unionization at its headquarters location and a few other plants, it is mainly a nonunion company. While this third company has not undergone quite the same competitive pressures as the first two, it also faces challenges that require product innovation and cost reduction. Our final sample will include an equal number of smokestack companies and companies operating in newer industries.

Our field research has involved interviewing key players, observation, and analysis of available documents in each of our sample companies. In selecting key players we have been careful not to focus just on one constituent or stakeholder group. Thus, we are looking at the HRM changes that are taking place not just from the point of view of top management but also from the points of view of human resource specialists at both the corporate and field levels, line managers at all levels of the organization, blue- and white-collar workers, outside consultants assisting with the transformation, and where applicable, union representatives. We are seeking to understand what new HRM policies and practices are coming into effect, and how these changes influence the different stakeholder groups and the organization's culture at all levels. In other words, we are seeking to understand not only what HRM changes are taking place but also the underlying assumptions that provide the foundation, coherence, and form of this new HRM model. Finally, we are seeking to analyze *how* these HRM transformations are being implemented. We are interested in characterizing those aspects of the change process that seem to facilitate change and those that slow down change or cause difficulties.

CHANGES IN HRM POLICIES AND PRACTICES

An overview of the changes that are occurring in our sample companies leads us to two conclusions. First, the content of the HRM changes are far from being identical. The older smokestack industries, for example, tend to focus their initial attention on such matters as labor costs, productivity, and quality. The presence of powerful unions also draws attention to the impact of a long-standing adversarial relationship. While these are issues faced to some extent by companies in newer industries, there seems to be a greater emphasis in the latter, at least initially, on the need to attract, satisfy, and motivate highly skilled professional employees. Thus, while smokestack companies often start their transformation process by paying attention to labor relations and productivity at the plant level, companies in the newer industries often start by reexamining their policies in areas such as recruitment, promotion, career development, and pay.

Although we are aware of the existence of such differences, we would like to suggest a second conclusion—that there are underlying similarities, common themes, that run through the changes that are taking place. An examination of the content of those changes begins to clarify some of these themes. But it is the surfacing of the assumptions that underlie the content changes that most powerfully points to a single and appreciably different HRM model than the one that has guided American industry in its past management of human resources.

Before examining these assumptions, though, we would like to describe the content of the HRM changes within each of four HRM policy areas: employee influence, human resource flow, reward systems, and work systems. We believe these four policy areas define fairly simply the key tasks of human resource management and the strategic HRM issues that face general managers.

EMPLOYEE INFLUENCE

Employees may be given influence through direct involvement in decisions affecting their work and their departments. (We will review these changes when we discuss work systems.) Where unions exist, employees have a voice in their pay and working conditions through collective bargaining and a grievance system. In nonunionized settings employees may be given a voice to influence affairs of the company by management-created mechanisms such as open-door policies, a grievance system, representative committees, task forces on special issues, opinion surveys, and a network of ombudsmen and employee-relations representatives.

In unionized settings HRM changes typically start with increasing collaboration between union and management in the form of labor-management committees, sometimes around specific issues such as product quality, quality of work life, or a joint employee attitude survey. The nature of these agreements is that they recognize a certain mutuality of interests between the company and the union as the representative of employees. Both the auto and steel industries, for instance, have signed agreements with their unions for joint programs to promote increased employee participation, involvement, and improved quality of work life. And while none of the agreements openly acknowledge improved productivity as a specific goal of such collaboration, there is explicit recognition of a long-term coincidence of interests. A recognition that increasing employee influence over the accomplishment of the task, innovations in work practices, and improvements in quality of work life are in the interest of both the employees and the company is contained in a commitment by top management to the "democratization" of the work force of a largely nonunion company in our study. "At our company," noted the vice chairman, "we are currently trying to make democracy of the workplace a reality."

Collaboration is providing management, employees, and their union with greater influence over each other concerning both business and employee needs. For instance, mutual influence mechanisms allow for changes in work systems, work practices, and worker responsibility. During recessionary times the existence of mutual influence mechanisms seems to have created greater employee acceptance of contract and wage concessions tied to an effort to make the company more competitive.

In innovative nonunion plants mechanisms for employee voice have been installed that support various means by which these plants increase employee involvement and productivity. For example, many innovative plants create open-door policies, use attitude surveys, and install employee committees (sometimes elected) to represent employee views to management. Outside of these efforts at the plant level, however, the use of formal, management-created voice mechanisms does *not* seem to be part of the transformation process we are witnessing. The transforming companies do make extensive use of employee attitude surveys. Numerous task forces allow for some degree of influence over policy recommendations. Even team-building meetings become opportunities to candidly voice thoughts and feelings about the organization and supervisors. But there is an absence of more formal mechanisms like grievance committees and formally structured hearings for white-collar and management employees. In short, at exempt and nonexempt levels mechanisms for employee influence have not been institutionalized as part of the change process we are observing. Is that a reflection of a low level of commitment to employee influence by top management? Does the use of influence mechanisms at new, nonunion plants reflect management's fear of unionization rather than a conviction that employees and the company must have such mechanisms? At this point in our research, we have no firm answers.

HUMAN RESOURCE FLOW

All organizations must manage the flow of people in, through, and out of the firm so as to make available the right mix of talent when it is needed. The organizations we are studying are making changes in a number of policies affecting human resource flow, but attention to this matter is noticeably stronger in firms where technological innovation and growth are greater problems than declining markets or the need to control labor costs.

One of the first important changes is that these companies seem to be encouraging their employees to take more responsibility for their careers. For example, in one large manufacturing company, official company policy stated that the corporation would have sole responsibility for the planning of employee careers. The questioning of assigned career changes by individual employees in the firm reportedly led to an assumption by top management that the employee had little real ambition for advancement. Such an employee was regularly passed over for future opportunities and occasionally even encouraged to seek employment elsewhere. This company has, as part of a larger cultural change toward enhanced participation and involvement, mandated a complete shift in that stated policy. Employees are now to be given more control of their own careers. The role of the corporation, specifically of the employee-relations function, is to provide all the necessary information to allow for an informed choice by the employee. Even if that informed choice means that the individual will seek employment elsewhere, the company is convinced that its own effectiveness is enhanced. This company is too early in the transformation process to allow a good judgment on the extent to which such policy changes have, in fact, trickled down to everyday practice. The change in philosophy as well as the called-for change in practice is, however, consistent with shifts in career control that are taking place in other sample companies.

More attention is being paid to selection as part of the overall change process. Prior to opening an innovative, high-involvement plant, one company created a two-day training program for all potential foremen. The stated purpose of the training was two-fold—to allow the applicants to determine whether they wished to work in such an environment, and to allow plant management to assess the applicants' suitability for the newly defined foreman's role, which would require less traditional top-down supervision and more participation, coaching, and facilitation. In another company, all applicants for a shop-floor position are shown a twenty-minute videotape featuring current employees, who talk with great candor both about the benefits of work in a high-commitment system and the special demands, challenges, and stresses experienced in such a system. Plant management hopes that such exposure will ensure a better fit between employees and the organization. Similar efforts to fit people to a new corporate culture through hiring, assessing, placing, promoting, or terminating people (with the exception of forced early retirement) based on their values and assumptions as well as on more traditionally defined competencies are not, however, widespread among exempt and nonexempt salaried personnel in other parts of the corporation.

All the corporations we have studied are grappling with the matter of employment security. All are committed to performance as a criterion for retaining individual employees, but they are also concerned about the impact of economic cycles on employment stability and employee commitment. Executives at one company also confessed that their recent use of layoffs in reaction to a downturn in the economic cycle had severely damaged their ability to recruit. Still, the only definite trend we have found is the offering of employment security to unionized workers as a quid pro quo for greater flexibility on work rules, sourcing decisions, and wages. It is not clear what these corporations' policies with regard to employment security will be. But it does appear that these policies will fall short of guaranteeing employment security for all employees. Management seems to want to retain the flexibility of reducing the work force in a recession but seems much more willing than in the past to exhaust all other alternatives before laying off (voluntary layoffs, shortened work weeks, transfers to other parts of the organization, out-placement counseling, and reduction through attrition, for example). Moreover, management seems to be more willing, even eager, to communicate to employees about these efforts. In this way they hope to make layoffs more credible and acceptable when they do occur.

REWARD SYSTEMS

There is little question that a shift is taking place toward providing employees with more intrinsic rewards, such as involvement, responsibility, and challenge. This trend is noted in all of the policy areas under discussion here, but most noticeably in work-system changes.

Beyond that, most of the experimentation seems to be taking place at new, high-commitment plants, for example, more skill-based pay systems, relatively less emphasis on status symbols as rewards for hierarchical position, and more openness about the pay systems. At blue-collar levels the ability to experiment is enhanced slightly without the restrictions of a union contract. Even in older unionized plants, where innovations in pay systems have up to now been thought very difficult and even impossible, there is a new willingness on the part of some companies and unions to reconsider the strict, multiple job classifications that have guided pay for decades in favor of broadly based classifications with greater emphasis on individual skill level. In general, piece-rate pay systems are systematically being negotiated out, and efforts are being made to introduce a day rate and in some cases skill-based pay systems.

Experimentation with pay at higher levels of the organization is rarer. In only one company in our study is there a major effort to decentralize pay policies and allow business unit managers and employees more authority in designing and administering pay policies. (This is a highly decentralized company, but pay policies and practices had been centrally set and controlled.) In this case, central control was replaced by a central set of pay principles that had been arrived at by a task force consisting of both line and staff personnel. These principles established, for instance, that pay should be competitive with the local market, wage-survey information should be communicated to all employees, pay ranges should be published, and employees should know both their own pay grade and the pay grades of any position to which they aspired. Divisions would then be free to devise their own pay schemes within these guidelines, as long as the *process* for devising those systems was participative ("diagonal" task forces of divisional line and staff people developing pay plans). One division took its mandate even further by involving people directly in setting not just pay policies but actual pay rates. The corporate manager of compensation and benefits reported that while the resulting systems were "all over the map," the total costs of compensation declined.

We find, however, that such broadly based innovations in pay systems are rare, even among companies purposefully rethinking their basic assumptions about the management of human resources. Despite years of experience with the dysfunctional consequences that inevitably arise from individual-pay-for-performance systems (particularly bonus systems), management seems to be unwilling to shake its long-held belief that pay should be closely tied to individual performance. In the interest of motivating higher performance, pay (merit pay or bonuses) is sometimes coupled too closely with individual performance ratings or goals that have questionable validity or relevance to the long-term welfare of the corporation. At the same time, gain-sharing schemes that might encourage cooperation and economic ownership of corporate performance are not being widely used (although a few plant-level experiments are underway in our sample companies, and profit-sharing has been negotiated by the automobile companies). There seems to be skepticism about such plans on the part of top managers, a skepticism tied partly to doubts about the efficacy of such plans.

There is some evidence that where such plans failed to live up to their potential, they were introduced without the prerequisite pattern of participative management and employee involvement necessary to reshape the organization's culture to one of management-worker and labor-management collaboration. The lack of success of gain-sharing plans may thus be due to their use too early in the transformation process, before changes in management practices have reshaped the culture of the plant or company. With some notable exceptions (the use of the Scanlon Plan at Dana Corporation), pay may be a "lag policy," one that should not be altered until other human resource practices have changed.

While changes in the other HRM policy areas are clearly in the direction of greater openness and enhanced employee influence, there is considerable trepidation about moving in a similar direction in matters of pay. To understand this reluctance, even inconsistency, pay must be viewed as more than an economic matter. Compensation systems are a basic part of the authority structure of an organization. Thus, while moves toward openness in pay-system design, administration, and participation may be consistent with other HRM changes, and may enhance feelings of equity and support motivation enhanced by other means (work design and participation), such moves may still be opposed by both management and compensation experts who hang on to traditional views in this area.

We also wonder whether management's values emphasizing individual performance over plant or unit performance are not partly responsible for its generally skeptical view of gain-sharing plans. But precisely because these organizations are moving to increase openness and employee influence in other areas, we wonder whether employees will eventually expect greater sharing of gains and influence over their pay systems.

Organization structure at the management level and the design of work in the office and plant have substantial impact on delegation of decision making, opportunities for involvement and participation, and accountability. Changes in this policy area are most visible in new plants. Work groups, for instance, are becoming an increasingly popular work design. One new plant created work teams in which members undertake not only the usual task of operating assigned machines but also setup and maintenance. Furthermore, each team does its own administrative housekeeping. Team members keep track of inventory; order and inspect necessary materials; document their team's production costs, attendance, and performance; oversee safety practices; participate in budgeting and forecasting; even hire new team members and evaluate the performance of their peers. Such work groups allow opportunities for job enrichment, delegation of authority, and participation by employees in work-related decisions. Employees in these groups take part in setting specific goals in the context of broad production goals developed by plant management, and they are expected to develop their own skills and competencies with support from trainers and team advisers.

Such work groups are prevalent in start-up situations, and they are an increasingly important part of the new work system model for older organizations involved in HRM transformations. In general, however, they are not a permanent rearrangement of the work systems in the plant. Rather, the groups overlay the traditional work system and are designed to identify and solve problems. A chemical plant in the South, for instance, has moved from a traditional work organization to one where the 450 nonunion workers are divided into cross-functional teams in the plant's four production areas, which meet daily to discuss work-related matters. A small steel plant has created work teams in virtually every plant shop, which discuss work-related problems, and occasional diagonal teams with employees from different hierarchical levels, which focus on problems of coordination and communication. A large industrial company has created over 1,000 problem-solving groups involving unionized workers on the shop floor. While some of these groups focus on work-related problems like reducing scrap and improving equipment maintenance, others deal with issues of plantwide coordination, communications, and interpersonal and intergroup problems.

White-collar, nonexempt work seems to have been noticeably less affected by such innovations. We have not seen, for example, much activity aimed at shaping the application of new technology in the office to take into account the needs of users. And outside of occasional quality circles, we have seen relatively little innovation in work systems at these levels.

At the management level our sample companies seem to be moving toward decentralized structures in which business units are clearly differentiated, with their own identifiable products, strategies, and profit-and-loss results. Managers in business units can now operate with clearly defined goals, much like the shop-level work groups previously described. They now also have the opportunity to transmit those goals downward throughout their organization.

One plant manager described the new process of goal setting within his unit:

> All the plant managers in our company got together with the sales people and the entire top echelon from the head office to talk about how strategic plans are developed. From there, we developed our own strategy within our plant and then made a formal presentation up north. This was worked into a five-year corporate strategy. Now we're working on our yearly business plans to meet that long-range strategy. This is all new, and it feels good. Of course, everyone has always known what we're here for. But now we can see where our plan fits into the total picture. And all our people can participate in determining the plant goals. That ties us all together.

A superintendent, two levels down from that manager, described how the goal-setting process had trickled down to him and to people below him:

> We've never had a business plan before. Now, we're given an outline of what's to be covered in our plant plan. We put our

thoughts together for our bosses, who either accept it or criticize it and ask us for modifications. The whole thing is then folded into the plant plan and sent north again to the head office. Now, we have a whole list of detailed goals that we can work on, and that can be translated into identifiable performance goals, not just for me but also for my general foremen. We've never had this before. It used to be, "Do the best that you can and be sure to keep costs down."

At the same time, levels of management and supervision are being eliminated, moving toward flatter organizational structures with fewer levels between workers and plant managers, and between plant managers and top corporate management. One company opened a new plant without the traditional general foreman's level, for instance. But even in old plants, management levels are being reduced. One company has moved to reduce supervisory levels in the plants from ten to six, eliminating entire levels like assistant superintendent and assistant foreman. At one plant in our study foremen have been eliminated from small (six-person) work crews and so have the industrial engineers assigned to figure incentive pay for the crews. So the crews now supervise themselves in calculating their incentive pay based on established rates. The net impact of such changes is to delegate authority and responsibility downward in the organization. And when such delegation is coupled with an increasing autonomy in a decentralized structure at the unit level, these units become what amounts to large semiautonomous work groups.

It should be noted that despite the important human resource implications of such structural changes, they are often not coordinated with, or even related to, other HRM changes. Restructuring, particularly reduction in supervisory levels, is driven less by the values guiding the overall HRM transformation than by a desire to control or reduce labor costs. The "people" impact is, in some cases, largely an unplanned by-product. In one company, where the shifts in HRM policies and organizational structure seem highly compatible, human resource people were completely left out of the process. "What's the ultimate objective of all our restructuring?" asked a high-ranking human resource executive in one of our companies. "Beats the hell out of me."

Not only can such lack of coordination lead to frustrations on the part of change agents but it can have a dampening impact on the change effort. In this same company, for instance, one of the leading innovative plants was assigned to a manager who was perceived to be unsympathetic to such changes. The result was a complete collapse in the morale of managers and workers at that plant, because they thought corporate headquarters had used this reassignment to signal displeasure with the changes that had taken place. The fact that management had intended no such signal did little to heal the wounds. The costs of inadvertence can be high.

The importance of a value-driven decentralization of planning and decision making to business units is brought home by the case of one corporation. That company is a leader in the transformation of human resource policies and practices at the plant level but has not yet delegated decision making to lower levels. In this corporation functional staff members at the corporate level still involve themselves in detailed decisions several levels down. In contrast with another smokestack company, this company has not reduced corporate staff and pushed it into the business units, in part because the change effort was driven by a pragmatic need to improve productivity and labor relations at the plant level. The result is widespread skepticism about the corporation's efforts to increase participation and employee involvement. That skepticism has not slowed the change process, but it is certainly causing many questions that eventually could affect the speed and thrust of the change. It would appear that work-system restructuring at the plant level must be accompanied by the restructuring of organizational arrangements at the management level, with more emphasis on decentralization and delegation. A commitment to the values of decentralization and delegation can help assure more uniform application of this process to all levels.

ASSUMPTIONS UNDERLYING THE NEW HRM MODEL

We have come to believe that the transformation we are observing amounts to more than a subtle shift in the traditional practices of personnel or the substitution of new terms for unchanging practices. Instead, the transformation amounts to a new model regarding the management of human resources in organizations. Although the model is still emerging, and inconsistencies in its practice are often seen, we believe that a set of basic assumptions can be identified that underlie the policies that we have observed to be part of the HRM transformation. Furthermore, these assumptions differ significantly from the assumptions that formed the foundation of more traditional HRM policies and practices. *Table 9-1* summarizes some of the shifts taking place in assumptions about the management of people in organizations and lists the specific practices that illustrate those new assumptions.

ASSUMPTION 1

Organizations are viewed as systems, with effectiveness defined as achieving a fit between the various components and between the system and the environment.

This approach assumes that organizations are in constant interaction with the external environment, as defined by business strategy, societal values, the marketplace, government regulations, and educational institutions. This system view also looks inside the organization and sees overlapping, interdependent components and subgroups, all of which must work together in a state of congruence, or fit, for maximum effectiveness. At the core of this notion of organizations as systems is the concept of *culture*, which is defined as shared beliefs and assumptions that set informal ground rules about what behavior is expected. The people, structures, and systems that comprise an organization help determine its culture and are in turn affected by that culture. Attempts at significant organizational transformation must then consider its culture. Transformations in HRM seem to incorporate this assumption more than in the past, but inconsistencies in practice suggest it is not yet fully translated into practice.

ASSUMPTION 2

People are capable of growth in terms of skills, values, and commitment if and when the work environment encourages it.

Table 9-1
The Shifting HRM Model

Old Assumptions	New Assumptions and Practices
Reactive, piecemeal interventions in response to specific problems	Proactive, systemwide interventions with emphasis on fit: Linking HRM with strategic planning Cultural change Prescreening, placement, promotions, layoffs based on how individuals will fit with desired new culture Coordinating people and structural changes (semiautonomous work groups and business units)
People as variable cost	People are social capital capable of development: Increasing power of developmental HRM functions Forming work groups, using skill-based pay to broaden employees' competencies Heavy emphasis on training More open communication, greater participation to develop people's commitment More concern about employment security
Self-interest dominates; conflict of interests between stakeholders	Coincidence of interests between stakeholders can be developed: Joint union-management efforts based on improving quality of work life and organizational effectiveness Emphasis on employee self-esteem, with positive human and business outcomes
Seeks power advantages for bargaining and confrontation	Seeks power equalization for trust and collaboration: Joint union-management committees Deemphasis of status symbols All salaried work force

(continued)

Table 9-1 *(continued)*

Old Assumptions	New Assumptions and Practices
Control of information flow to enhance efficiency, power	Open channels of communication to build trust, commitment: Greater sharing of information on business with unions, work groups, organizational units Greater communication about design and administration of pay system
Relationship orientation	Goal orientation: Setting broad goals for work groups Involving organizational subunits in establishing specific goals
Control from top	Participation and informed choice: Participative management style Labor-management participation teams Employee-involvement programs Greater employee control over career choices Diagonal task forces, problem-solving teams

A work environment that allows people increased autonomy and influence can, in this view, lead to increased motivation, commitment, and achievement. This assumption leads to the view of human resources not as a variable cost to be taken on or reduced to meet specific business needs but as social capital. The development of work-force talents and attitudes can thus be seen in terms of long-range investments capable of yielding a stream of benefits over time.

ASSUMPTION 3

There is a long-run coincidence of interests between all the various stakeholders of the organization.

In the long run the aims of the various stakeholders can be largely, if not entirely, compatible, as improved human outcomes will ultimately have a positive impact on economic outcomes. It is up to the organization generally, and its management of human resources in particular, to enlarge that coincidence of interests by creating an environment conducive to the development of collaboration, trust, and mutuality.

Power equalization is a key to encouraging openness and collaboration among stakeholders.

Power inequities undermine trust, inhibit candid and open communication, and reduce the likelihood of collaboration. Organizations can be moved toward greater power parity through adjustments in systems and structures. Equally important is the training and development of supervisors in how to delegate, communicate openly, and involve employees in decisions.

Open communication builds trust and commitment.

Power within an organization rests, in part, on the ability to control the flow of important information. Open communication can then be used to reduce power inequities. But openness can also aid collaboration and mutuality by keeping information from being seriously distorted, by illuminating areas where joint problem solving can occur, and by allowing accurate information about the state of the external environment to be available to all individuals and organizational units and not just to top management.

Employees will be motivated and the organization more effective if they work toward organizational goals that they accept as legitimate.

Having understandable, acceptable goals can lead to enhanced commitment to those goals and improved effectiveness. The way to achieve such understandable, acceptable, and legitimate goals is to communicate not only the broad goals of the particular unit in which employees are working but also how the accomplishment of those goals contributes to the achievement of the larger strategic goals of the organization. Direct participation in setting specific goals further helps achieve understandable, acceptable, and legitimate goals.

People who participate in defining problems and solutions will become committed to the new directions that result from the process of participation.

Organizational effectiveness is enhanced by participation in decisions at all levels, and changes in organizations are best managed by involving employees. Participation implies allowing people free and informed choice, which will enhance their commitment to that choice. Informed choice means giving individuals an opportunity to explore as many alternatives as they think significant and informing them of the consequences of their choices and the realistic steps that must accompany the achievement of their choices. Once such an informed choice is made, individuals will feel ownership over that choice; that is, they will feel committed to that choice and responsible for implementing it.

THE PROCESS OF TRANSFORMATION

Advocates of the HRM transformation, whether line managers, human resource staff specialists, or top executives of companies, must increasingly concern themselves with the management of large-scale organizational change. These key leaders become change agents, bringing in new ideas about the management of human resources and stimulating a process of change throughout their organizations. While organizations involved in that process experience different problems and rely on somewhat different approaches—depending on the competitive environment of the companies, their past histories, their structures, and the talents, assumptions, values, and philosophies of key leaders—we have identified a number of common approaches among the companies we are studying.

THE ROLE OF LEADERSHIP

The ideas and talents of key leaders and their willingness to support innovative HRM policies, together with the help and support of innovative human resource specialists, innovative managers at other companies, and leading academics and con-

sultants, has helped propel the HRM transformation process
in the companies we have studied. Such key leadership can also
come from the union side, especially in companies with a large
unionized work force. Officers at or near the top of the union
can either share top management's concern with the current
employment relationship or take a leadership role in articulating their own concerns. Irving Bluestone of the United Auto
Workers, for instance, started calling in the early 1970s for a
new vision of the labor-management relationship that would go
beyond the traditional concerns of collective bargaining. He
began to question exclusive management prerogatives in the
planning and controlling of work. In another major industrial
union an assistant to the president challenged both management and his own union to consider the need for change. "I
don't know for sure just where we should be headed, but I'll
tell you one thing. The whole concept of working like individuals is *wrong*. In the future, whole plants will have to work
together as a crew, problem solving by consensus. People are
going to have to be given new skills they never had before."

Much of the impetus for change on the part of the unions
will undoubtedly come as a pragmatic response to environmental changes and management initiatives. But like some of
the managers in our study, union leaders will occasionally attempt to push for change based on their personal values and
assumptions.

The views, assumptions, and attitudes of top leaders are critical. Some leaders support change because of poor corporate
performance, pragmatically believing that HRM changes will
"work." In a very few instances, top managers push for change
because of strongly held, nontraditional beliefs about what mo-
tivates people and how they should be managed. The personal
values of these leaders allow them to conclude, and to articulate
their conclusions throughout the organization, that changes
should be made both because they are "right" in some moral
or humanist sense and because they represent good business.
"We are proving to ourselves," said one corporate executive,
"that policies which help employees realize their objectives of
self-fulfillment and self-esteem help the company realize its
objectives of productivity."

One of the more interesting questions, for which we do not have a conclusive answer, is whether HRM transformations propelled by pragmatism encounter different problems than transformations propelled by idealism. Pragmatism ("the changes will work") is likely to result in more relevant human resource practices and policies. Will such transformations lose their thrust, however, as inconsistencies in policies and practices arise because a consistent set of assumptions does not guide the effort? Idealism ("the changes are right") will provide a guiding philosophy that will promote consistency in policies and practices. But will it promote changes that are not relevant, or even detrimental, to business outcomes? We believe some mix of pragmatism and idealism is probably important and that erring at either extreme will create problems in the transformation process.

Whatever the impetus toward change, there is little question that top support is critical at some point in the change process. In some organizations the desire for change has been fermenting for years, often within human resource functions and among organization development people. But only when pressures from the competitive environment or from the work force mesh with top leadership support for change will HRM transformations accelerate and begin to encompass the whole organization. A confluence of these various forces creates a *window of opportunity* that allows HRM transformations to be initiated and sustained throughout the organization and its subunits. Thus, top managers who seek such an HRM transformation must fuse the opportunity created by environmental pressures and work force changes with a guiding set of beliefs concerning the extent to which an organization's management of human resources can contribute to enhance organizational effectiveness and employee well-being.

USE OF SHADOW OR PARALLEL ORGANIZATIONS

In one company they are called special assistants; in another, facilitators; in a third, coordinators. In each case they are individuals from either line management or the shop floor who are given extensive and special training in methods of organizational development and change. They become well-trained, highly qualified change agents who are given a specially created place in the organizational structure with an explicit mission of helping to move the change process along. As organizational insiders, these "shadow" change agents possess intimate knowledge of the company, plant, or shop. But their special training and explicit change mission provide them with new competencies and with a new and different set of norms. They seek new ways of looking at old approaches and ideas; pursue and facilitate change based on a combination of new norms and a deeply rooted understanding of the workings of their organization; and then link back to the formal organization.

At one plant in our study a plant superintendent with a reputation as an innovator in participative management approaches was appointed head of the change effort. That appointment was resented by people in the management development department who felt it was a mistake putting an operations person with no human resource development skills or experience in charge of an effort that would place a great deal of emphasis on development and training. A year later, the human resource manager admitted that it was this superintendent's awareness of whom to involve in the change process and when to involve them, his sensitivity to the pecking order of the plant and to the feelings and needs of each department, that had allowed the change effort to achieve "mind-boggling" success.

In addition to bringing a special expertise to the job, these shadow agents can bypass the traditional hierarchy in the pursuit of change because of their extraorganizational standing. Their mandate allows them to go anywhere and address problems and roadblocks to change regardless of formal hierarchical position or reporting relationships. Their designation provides them with a top-down endorsement, which allows them freedom to operate while also sending a clear signal throughout the organization that change is underway. And as these shadow agents work closely with human resource specialists in training and development, a new alliance is created between the personnel specialists and line managers.

The need for specialists in organization development, employee involvement, or quality of work life to help line management change its management of human resources will undoubtedly be continuous. The designation of line managers to push for change against a reluctant hierarchy may be temporary as acceptance of the changes by line managers grows.

TASK FORCES

All the companies being studied have made extensive use of task forces to manage the process of change. In one company the task forces are composed almost entirely of representatives of the various functions within the human resource department. In this company the task forces are meant to create temporary mechanisms for coordinating the overall change effort. In another company the task forces are composed of a blend of human resource staff and line managers, focused on developing content solutions to specific human resource problems such as redefining management style or redesigning the organization's pay systems. In either case, the task forces allow for some participation in the process of change, help strengthen cross-functional relationships, and create mechanisms for coordination and integration between units. Task forces peopled equally by management and union representatives seem mandatory in instances where one target of the change is union-management relations. Representative membership in these cases adds substance to the claim that the change is truly a joint effort.

EDUCATION AND TRAINING

The companies in our study are making extensive use of education and training. But instead of using training to reinforce the status quo by teaching traditional technically oriented skills, it has become a way of introducing new ideas about HRM as well as signaling the intent of the corporation to change. "Trainers are the most sought-after people in our organization," said the president of a company attempting an HRM transformation, "and they can get whatever resources they need." Another company spends a full year training its managers and supervisory people prior to introducing any joint union-management efforts. A manager in another company has attempted to move quality-of-work-life efforts into the white-collar ranks by attending sensitivity-training courses at the National Training Laboratory. But these kinds of efforts are not well coordinated or integrated with the overall change effort. All the companies that have unions rely on extensive special training to reshape attitudes and behaviors to allow for greater sharing of power, enhanced communication and trust, and problem solving rather than confrontational bargaining. In order to remove the stigma of "management control" from these training efforts, they are almost always conducted by outside professionals, with management and union participating equally in selection of trainers.

CREATING MODELS

Consistent with the notion that new models must exist before change from the old model can occur, change agents are using numerous and varied resources to present new models to their organizations. Managers are taken to visit innovative plants, either within the company or at other companies. Frequent trips to Japanese companies are also made, and where a union exists, these trips usually include representatives of both management and the union. We have seen change agents distribute widely through their organizations popular books like *Theory Z*, which presents a Japanese management model, or *In Search of Excellence*, which gives an American model.

One of the main ways in which corporations are transforming their human resource practices is to develop innovative new plants. These plants usually incorporate participative management practices that are quite radical when compared to older plants and that would be difficult to install in older plants. But the very existence of these new plants challenges the traditional plants to change their management approaches toward the new model. The visits to innovative plants and the transfer of managers from these plants to older plants are means for diffusing newer HRM models to other parts of the company. This strategy of starting with new plants and diffusing change to older plants through personnel transfers, visits, and communication seems to be an almost universal phenomenon in companies transforming their HRM practices.

In many situations, we found that introducing new key managers or union leaders was a prerequisite for significant change. One corporate president in our study acknowledged some general shift in the criteria for placement at the highest executive levels. "Fifteen years ago," he said, "we may have talked about human relations. But our real marching orders were productivity, and productivity and human relations just didn't seem to mix. Now we recognize that the prime function of the manager in any position is his ability to work with people."

It is not clear to us, however, that management decisions about whom to promote are always consistent with the direction of the change effort. Often, effective bottom-line results or technical competence makes it difficult to reach a decision to replace a manager on issues of style. Unwillingness to adopt new criteria for promotion consistent with the hoped-for new culture of the company sends mixed signals down through management ranks that can be discouraging to those supportive of the change. One plant manager in our study noted:

> In the last couple of years the corporation has said a lot about participative management and how it *is* going to happen. But frankly, they've done a lot of floundering. There's a certain amount of frustration for me in the slow pace of change. We have a lot of "autocrats" in this company, and I expect we will for some time to come. But we still have instances where very autocratic people are getting put into important, sensitive jobs. That causes a good deal of questioning on the part of people at my plant. They wonder whether the people at the top are really serious.

A challenge that faces companies transforming their HRM practices is to become more consistent in their selection of key managers while managing inconsistencies more effectively where this is not possible.

CORPORATE ORGANIZATION

Our evidence seems to indicate that decentralized corporations have some advantages in managing the HRM transformation process under certain circumstances. Under decentralization, division managers have considerable freedom to act. When top management is not leading the change efforts, or when its own style of managing is inconsistent with the thrust of HRM changes, this freedom of divisional managers allows the change process to unfold within their relatively autonomous operating units. Moreover, corporate staff groups within a centrally run organization can restrain, even block significant change. On the other hand, when top managers are ahead of their organizations in both a desire to change and in a vision of what the new HRM model should be, a decentralized structure may inhibit their more direct involvement in stimulating that change. Thus, centralized functional structures present a different set of change problems to general managers than do decentralized structures.

ARTICULATING UNDERLYING ASSUMPTIONS

Rarely have American companies attempted an explicit statement of the assumptions that underlie their HRM policies and practices. This seems to be as true of the new model as it was of the traditional model. Earlier in this chapter we identified those key assumptions in the two models. But in only one company have we seen an attempt to pull together a coherent statement of the set of assumptions on which the transformation process (already well underway) rests. What does seem to be taking place more regularly is a limited attempt to deal with business principles and values. One highly autonomous division in our study, for instance, went off-site with the entire top management team, together with an outside facilitator. They spent two days asking, "What is the ideal organization?" and "What do *we* believe in?" and then established a set of principles consistent with those beliefs to guide the division. This articulation of principles was only the first stage of a larger cultural change effort that involved forming participative teams to make implementation recommendations around each principle and a steering committee to help ensure coordination and integration between those teams. Similar efforts to articulate a governing set of assumptions and principles have also been an important step in the development of new innovative plants.

The process of these discussions seems to be as important as the product that results from them. Managers have a chance to educate each other and to develop a consensus around a set of guiding assumptions. A newly articulated set of assumptions, especially to the extent that they elevate the positive role of human resources in the organization, are taken as a signal of transformation down through the organization. Moreover, the philosophy, if accepted and internalized by management, can serve to guide a myriad of HRM decisions.

It might be argued that there are some negative consequences of articulating assumptions. Explicit statements of the underlying assumptions and values toward which the transformation process is heading may, for instance, highlight inconsistencies in the process of change. Explicitness may also serve to raise the level of opposition and resistance to the change effort. But there are also costs to inexplicitness or a lack of complete understanding of the direction in which transformation is headed; those costs are inconsistency and inadvertence.

TEAM BUILDING

Team-building meetings are more than a mechanism for allowing employee influence. They are a way—and in the companies we are studying, an increasingly popular way—of pushing the change process along. The president of one company described what he referred to as a "dynamic planning session" which he had just gone through with his thirteen top executives. "The first thing that we did," he said, "was to get an outside facilitator. He came in and asked us to talk about our problems: production problems, communication problems, whatever was on our chests. And we put all those problems up on the board and for the next day and a half talked about how to solve them." A similar process, he told us, was taking place up and down the management ranks in his organization. An even more elaborate team-building process was taking place in the division of another large industrial company. The divisional vice president, after deciding on what he called a "full-scale systems intervention," brought together each of the top managers of his ten divisions (about eighty top managers per division) for a five-day team-building session during which roles were defined, goals set (including the goal of spreading participative management down through the organization), and channels of communications opened. In yet another company, a top executive noted simply, "Since I've come here, team building has become a way of life, a regular part of the process."

Team building is a method that allows for the assessment of norms, leadership style, and decision-making processes as well as a way to confront roadblocks to cooperation, team work, communication, and change. The team-building sessions that we have encountered, however, are far less likely to concentrate on interpersonal issues than on defining roles and setting goals. The third-party consultants, often facilitators trained from within the company, occasionally lack the skills necessary for the optimum team-building process to occur. And rarely are the individual team-building efforts integrated into the overall change process. But team building does represent a major vehicle for increasing the influence of employees, particularly management employees, on the management of their immediate organization. It is, however, as indicated earlier, dependent on the bosses' willingness to discuss problems.

THE CHANGING ROLE OF THE HUMAN RESOURCE FUNCTION

In most, but not all, of the companies studied, dramatic changes can be observed in the role, structure, and power of the human resource function. There is, for instance, a noticeable shift in power within many human resource functions away from labor relations and toward human resource development. Typically, human resource development includes such functions as training, education, career development, organization development, personnel planning, and succession planning. Executives who head these functions within human resource departments are gaining power and appear to be succeeding more regularly to top jobs within the function. This shift reflects the emerging view that people are an asset rather than a cost, a view reflected by human resource development functions. This shift also signals a change in the competencies required of the human resource function, as collective bargaining, labor relations, and labor law are quickly being joined, or even surpassed, by developmental and change competencies and orientations.

In some instances, the newly empowered developmental people not only rise to the top of the human resource function but also become members of policy or executive committees where they can influence corporate policies and practices in ways that are consistent with the HRM transformation. Access to top management, in fact, appears to be critical. In one company the vice president for human resources was recently placed on the executive committee, reporting directly to the chairman. In addition, the vice president now attends all strategic planning meetings. That vice president sees a threefold advantage to his newly found access. First, he can play devil's advocate with the chairman. Second, his participation in strategic planning meetings broadens his own perspective and that of the entire human resource function, allowing them to better serve the needs of the rest of the organization. Finally, he can now make sure that top managers are making the necessary and appropriate linkages between strategic and human resource decisions.

PROBLEMS AND DIFFICULTIES IN SUSTAINING TRANSFORMATION

Just as we have observed some similar change tools being applied in the various companies undergoing an HRM transformation, so too have we spotted similar problems or hurdles that face these companies as part of the process of change.

Confronting Personal Style and Philosophy. Managers within these companies are facing, with some difficulty and personal costs, the necessity of confronting their own personal management styles and philosophies. Interwoven into many of the changes taking place is a growing awareness that a new style and philosophy of management is necessary and appropriate. That style—more facilitative and less directive, more concerned with achieving involvement and commitment than with contracting for specific actions and contributions, for instance—is often at odds with the personal style and individual philosophies of managers in these companies. Their styles are rooted in both historical traditions and in older systems of training, rewards, and promotions. Expressions of discomfort at the gap between what people believe their style/values are and what they believe their companies want are frequent.

An assistant vice president in a human resource function:

I very much favor more open dialogue, more direct communication with people throughout the department. At the same time, I also have been characterized as something of an intimidator, and I'm trying to alter that view. I've been a pretty strong character over the years. But I think I've improved. And that's beneficial to me from a personal standpoint in terms of being able to work with people.

An assistant plant manager:

Each of us here has some difficulty adapting to a new participative style. Part of that problem is identifying exactly what it is that being a participative manager means. But you can't spend twenty years in a highly structured, conservative organization like ours was and then suddenly make that adjustment without some personal pain.

A plant superintendent:

I'm struggling with this. I just met for two hours with my general foreman. They're asking me to form a steering committee for our division. I didn't give them an answer, but I'll tell you what it's going to be. I'm not ready for it yet. Now, the company has done a lot to help me with the process. We've had training, exercises, and brainstorming sessions. And I'm yelling at my people to share their power. But I've still got a lot of growing up to do. It's an extremely difficult thing to surrender control of the decision-making process.

A common theme that emerges along with this unease is that organizations do have some tools available to help facilitate this personal transformation in ways that will complement the organizational transformation. Articulating the underlying assumptions of the HRM transformation may help, especially to the extent that such an articulation gets translated into specific performance and behavioral definitions of what the new management model should be. The extent to which the implications of this model are transferred to actual promotion and placement decisions may help reinforce and crystalize for managers both the necessity for changing and the direction of the desired change. Actual participation in the change process seems to be the most powerful tool in producing results or at least in producing a willingness to confront the gap between current and ideal philosophies and values. One of the ways one of the organizations in our sample is attempting to address systematically this matter of personal styles is through team-building meetings pushed down through the organization. As noted earlier, participation in such meetings allows for an assessment of leadership styles and values. Finally, some organizations have elected not to rely on individual changes. The plant superintendent who spoke of his need to do a lot of growing up was pressured by the company into early retirement. Strategies like early (often pressured) retirement and lateral moves are used to remove managers, particularly older managers, who are perceived to be roadblocks to the transformation process.

Pressures to Go Top-Down. As stated earlier, at least some of the transformations we are looking at received an important boost from managers at the very top of the organization. But even when the change process starts from some lower level in the organization, there is still a question of when it might be appropriate to insist upon change, even though that change is in the direction of cooperation, openness, and shared power.

We are constantly hearing stories, often told in a joking manner, about a chairman, president, or divisional head pointing at subordinates and saying, "You people are going to be participative, and that's an order!" But the frustration of balancing the need to allow people to participate in the change process with the imperative of achieving rapid progress is real to many managers. One manager articulated his frustration this way:

> I have to keep telling myself, "Trust the process." But sometimes it's *slow*. I have to kick myself at least twice a day to keep my mouth shut. I'm just as authoritarian as anybody else around here. So, I'm dealing with a personal frustration, of thinking it could move faster but knowing damn well that if you force it, you can't do it.

This manager's faith that you can never "force" the process is not universally shared. Managers involved in the transformation will almost inevitably face a choice forced upon them at some point in the process by the relative slowness of a participative, bottom-up process, coupled with the competitive necessity of making rapid changes. Companies in our study have found ways, short of ordering change, of exerting considerable pressure from the top. Formal reporting forums, for instance, where managers gather before the top executive committee to report on the progress of their change efforts serve to spotlight in an unfavorable way those with little of substance to report. Forceful and repeated endorsement by those at the very top, of course, also sends an unmistakably strong signal. The use of retrenchment and early retirements to remove roadblocks comes even closer to a formal mandate of change from the top. Although we have yet to see it, the tying of merit pay in some specific way to progress in the change effort might also be a powerful inducement. Finally, in some of the organizations undergoing a transformation, that point *has* been reached where the person at the top will say, "Change, or else."

The inconsistency inherent in ordering participative management and employee involvement has been creatively solved by one top manager in a large manufacturing company. He set extremely ambitious quality standards for the corporation's product and ordered all products that didn't meet this standard to be scrapped. To achieve this very difficult goal and to reduce the immediate losses due to scrap, he encouraged managers to go for help to the corporate organizational development department. He saw his role as "creating a market" for organization development and employee involvement. By tying the HRM transformation to a valued business goal this executive was creating a context that demanded innovation in all areas, including human resource management. The evidence seems to be that a top-down directive to adopt participative management can become bogged down as managers adopt the form of participation (meetings, task forces, and so on) without clear purpose or objectives. The form unconnected to a business purpose for instance, meetings to air problems is quickly seen as a waste of time by managers. Frustrations with the extra burden of unproductive meetings leads to a reaction against the human resource transformation. Ultimately, the result is that innovations in human resource management are dropped as unproductive. In short, the process of change must be connected to valued and relevant business goals if the credibility of the desired HRM transformation is to be maintained.

Inconsistencies in the Change Process. The dilemma inherent in the question of when or if to go top-down creates one of the inconsistencies we have observed. In all the corporations we are studying, there are some inconsistencies between the statements of top management about the desired direction of the changes and their own styles. One middle-level manager, for instance, expressed his resentment over top management's inclination, despite their advocacy of participative leadership, to occasionally mandate solutions to problems rather than to seek solutions from those affected. "When they really get their asses in a crack," he said, "they revert. It's like, they'll ask me where to put a parking lot. But when it comes to something I really care about, that's important to me and my organization, they don't even ask my opinion." Matters of pay, promotions, retrenchment and reorganization, and layoffs are often mandated from the top at the very time that the organization is attempting to change its culture to allow greater participation in decision making. There are, in addition, the inconsistencies between the practices of innovative plants or business units and more traditional corporate staff groups that demand conformity to corporate policies or direct adherence to policies that do not fit the innovative unit. Finally, there are perceived inconsistencies of sacrifice in smokestack companies when concessions to labor have been made. The granting of large executive bonuses in the auto industry reduced the credibility of management's intention to increase trust and collaboration.

What are the costs of these inconsistencies? Our research has not yet produced any real evidence that such lapses into inconsistency do any permanent damage to the change process. They do create considerable cynicism and skepticism. Most of the leaders we have observed, in fact, combine forceful prodding and occasional reliance on rather traditional top-down approaches with the setting of broad normative goals for the organization and its transformation. Phrases like "quality of work life," "employee involvement," and "self-esteem," or a somewhat more elaborate set of "Ten Commandments" (move from turf protection to team building, from autocracy to participation) clearly establish a general direction for the change. The reliance on such normative goals allows managers to place troubling, frustrating inconsistencies and perceived setbacks in a broader frame. Indeed, many of the managers we have talked with tempered their complaints about perceived inconsistencies in style with an awareness that the general culture of their organization *is* moving, perhaps slowly but nonetheless clearly, in the direction implied in those broader goals. Nevertheless, the task of managing human resource transformations must include active attention to, and management of, inconsistencies to reduce cynicism and sustain energy for change.

Insufficient Change Planning and Strategizing. The HRM transformations we have observed amount to major cultural change with high stakes for corporations that are trying to maintain their competitive edge. In all of the companies studied, many consultants are used, a large number of training programs are developed, internal organization development specialists are hired and trained, efforts in several locations are initiated, managers are replaced and transferred, many different types of meetings are held, and a variety of slogans and programs are launched in the interest of moving change along. Despite this rather large undertaking, relatively little formal strategic thinking and planning is going on among the key executives who are leading and supporting the change. Though there are many informal discussions, no targets for change are formally identified, few corporations have included change objectives in their year-to-year planning process, and even fewer companies systematically monitor progress and plan accordingly.

In short, culture change is not managed as systematically as programs of equal magnitude normally would be. We are not certain about the reasons for this or about the desirability of more systematic planning. It may be that more formal planning is difficult as long as all the top managers are not in full agreement about the direction of change and the assumptions underlying it. Or formal planning may simply serve to strengthen resistance to a well-defined change plan. But it is probably also true that top executives are not yet skilled or comfortable with managing a cultural change as compared to planning a new product introduction. Cultural change is ambiguous, requires higher levels of abstract thinking, and requires attention to process rather than results, the traditional concern of management. In our observation, American managers seem somewhat uncomfortable with planning and managing process. Final conclusions on this question await further investigation.

CONCLUSION

The HRM transformations we are observing amount to major change with high stakes for corporations trying to maintain their competitive edge. As a pragmatic response to a shifting external environment—changes in competition, in demographics, and in the labor market—the companies in our study are engaged in a remarkably similar set of activities with respect to both the content and the process of change.

With respect to content, these companies are all engaged in efforts to move away from adversarial union-management relations to more collaboration, to increase employee involvement through changes in work-system design, to increase employee control over careers through granting more information and choice, to increase employee commitment through more concern about employment security and retraining, to experiment with nontraditional pay systems such as skill-based pay systems and gain-sharing plans, and to emphasize a new style of participatory management. When taken in the aggregate, the changes we are observing increase employee influence over the immediate task and the human resource management practices of the firm.

The processes of change in the companies under study also show many similarities. Change may start at the plant level in smokestack companies and at the corporate level in newer growth companies, but many of the companies develop a network of change agents to move change along, develop model plants or units, use task forces extensively, invest in training and education, utilize team-building methods, employ succession planning and early retirement to replace managers who support change, and develop and widely disseminate a philosophy that articulates new assumptions about management. In all the companies the HRM function is taking on a more proactive and change-oriented role. This is accompanied by a shift in power from traditional labor-relations types to new human resource development types.

Despite significant changes in the companies observed, the changes are far from uniform. There are many inconsistencies between innovative plants and traditional corporate staff groups, between top managers' espoused philosophy and their actions, and between the desire to change culture and the capacity of managers to do so. These inconsistencies are not always managed as well as might be expected. There seems to be little explicit strategizing and goal setting concerning the transformation. Key actors in the change—top management, line managers, the human resource function, and external consultants—do not plan together. Instead they are loosely connected through ad hoc encounters. Only in its relation with the union does management create formal agreements and forums for coordinating and planning changes.

The inconsistencies we have obseved are probably inevitable in major cultural transformations. But, they do create skepticism and cynicism. Since most of the changes described in this chapter arise out of pragmatism rather than out of a commitment to a set of ideal human resource practices, one may legitimately wonder about the durability of these changes. Will cynicism and pragmatism overwhelm efforts to transform corporate culture to the new HRM model? Or will the changes we observe be strengthened over time by new top managers and union leaders who have absorbed the new assumptions underlying the transformation and who will therefore reinforce them through their decisions and actions? Only time will tell.

10
Planning for Morale and Culture

D. Quinn Mills
Mary Lou Balbaky

Books and business magazines have long publicized the importance that some well-known companies give to human considerations in their business strategies. IBM, in particular, has often been cited for its emphasis on a philosophy that begins with respect for the individual and ends with excellence in business performance.

Few other examples were publicized until recently, when business journalists began reporting about companies that are now examining their human resources in a long-term perspective and expressing a basic orientation toward, and a conscious philosophy about, human values. A long-term perspective is perhaps best exhibited in the planning that managers do in order to be prepared for eventualities and also to move the organization toward preselected goals.

Perhaps most American companies of good size engage in activities intended to bolster the morale of employees. These are usually traditional activities of various sorts, including company outings, publications and other forms of communication, employee services, and awards. Less traditional forms of morale building include opportunities for education, wellness programs or sports facilities, and even participation by employees in managerial decision making in certain carefully defined and limited areas.

But increasingly in recent years morale-building activities of the traditional sort need to be distinguished from efforts to build a more substantial framework of employee commitment to the company—sometimes referred to as a corporate culture.

This chapter is concerned with what companies are currently doing in the planning area and with the direction of their efforts. In particular, we are interested in planning efforts directed toward enhancing employee commitment and performance through concern for morale or for the larger concept generally referred to as a corporate culture. This chapter addresses the following questions: How common are planning efforts in the human resource area in large business corporations in this country? Of what do they consist? To what degree are they ad hoc, or alternatively, to what degree are they integrated into some overall framework involving a corporate business plan? Finally, are the human resource elements of a plan motivated by an overall corporate philosophy, or are they primarily expedient in purpose?

A SURVEY OF LARGE COMPANIES

To find out how common human resource planning is in American companies, and to what extent top managers are interested in culture and managing morale, we recently interviewed executives in 224 large firms. We found a growing awareness of the importance of planning for the human side of the enterprise, both in terms of the numbers of key personnel and the morale and performance of the company's employees.

In the summer of 1983 a random sample of 291 companies with over 1,000 employees was drawn from Dun's *America's Corporate Families, 1982 Billion Dollar Directory*. The executives, line for the most part, were interviewed by telephone (by LDG Associates, a Gardner, Massachusetts, survey firm) about their companies' long-range human resource planning practices and their interest or involvement in formally managing morale and a company culture. The response rate to the survey was 77 percent (224 companies)—a far higher participation rate than has been obtained in other surveys in this field. The survey was also unusual in its focus on top line executives in contrast to the almost exclusive surveying of personnel or human resource

Table 10-1
Titles of Respondents

Titles	Percent of Respondents
President/General Manager	28.6
Vice President (Senior Executive) Operations	23.6
Vice President of Manufacturing	14.3
Executive/Senior Vice President	10.7
Vice President of Planning/Business Development	9.4
Vice President of Human Resources/Personnel	5.5
Vice President of Administration/Finance	4.0
Vice President of Marketing/Sales	2.2
Other	1.7
	100.0

executives in other studies. (See Table 10-1 for respondents' functions or titles.)

The focus on line executives minimized the bias that can come from asking human resource or personnel professionals about their company's involvement in planning for people. The positions of the executives surveyed in other studies have tended to bias the responses to suggest a higher level of planning activity than may be acutally going on. Other surveys of human resource planning practices and policies have focused on, and been responded to, by personnel or human resource executives exclusively. Even the most diverse survey, done in 1978, used a survey population that was 50 percent vice presidents of personnel, 37 percent corporate planners, and 10 percent line executives.

Our survey may even tend to underrepresent the amount of human resource planning. Our statistics are based on executive line managers' immediate knowledge of resource planning components and programs. The interview was constructed and conducted to encourage responses even from those companies doing a minimal amount of human resource planning.

Because of the high response rate, out survey results are based on a more truly representative sample than other surveys published in major human resource journals over the last decade. This allows more reliable generalizations to be made from the data. Also, the high response rate of 77 percent minimizes the possibility for respondents' skewing the results by responding if they are involved or interested in human resources planning and declining response if they are not. Response rates for published surveys have not been greater than 44 percent, and typically they are in the 25–30 percent range.

The questions in other surveys tended to focus on the activities and position of human resource planners. Typical types of questions have been: What do human resource planners do? To whom do they report? How many of the companies have such a position or a human resource planning unit? Our study focused less on these institutional concerns and more on the content and implementation of human resource plans, goals, and strategies within the context of overall business planning.

It is difficult to compare our responses with those reported from other studies. Some use unavoidably ambiguous terminology at points and sometimes use different terms for ostensibly similar activities. For example, a 1975 survey asked about "succession/replacement planning" without a formal/informal breakdown and without a time frame. We have gathered more specific data. For example, our data show that 55 percent of the companies surveyed do some sort of formal or informal management-succession planning. Forty-nine percent of the companies have a formal written management-succession plan; 8 percent of the companies include a management plan in their long-range planning process.

The survey was designed to investigate the following questions:

1. To what extent do companies have long-range business plans, and how far ahead do they plan?
2. How many companies include human resource components in their long-term business plan?
3. What events or influences led people to plan for human resources?
4. How does the human resource planning function differ by industry, size of company, and business strategy of the firm?

Executives were asked about their companies' efforts in human resource planning. Questions fell into two distinct categories. First, was the company involved in any human resource planning activities? Second, did the company do formal business planning, and which, if any, of the human resource planning activities were integrated into the business-planning cycle?

Respondents described activities including skills inventories, management-succession plans (formal or informal), recruiting projections, hiring in advance of actual needs, executive development, training and development of employees other than executives, plans to meet governmental regulations, projections of wages and benefits, planning for employee morale, and conscious development of a corporate culture.

Respondents were also rated on the extent of their commitment to planning for people. Many of the questions in our survey were open-ended, and a considerable amount of qualitative data was collected.

PLANNING FOR PEOPLE

There is considerable activity in planning for people in American companies: only 14.9 percent of the companies reported doing little or no people planning, and some of these said they were beginning to do so or should do so. Nearly 44 percent of the line executives were rated as being highly interested or fairly interested in people planning on the basis of what their companies do and on their own knowledge, enthusiasm, and opinions. Throughout the interviews there are several themes repeated again and again: (1) the perception of change in employees' attitudes and the need for older managers to change; (2) the need to do more human resource planning; and (3) the importance of people in the organization. The following comments, from respondents whose companies do almost no people planning, are selected as representative of dozens of similar ones:

> Our environment is changing. The whole approach to personnel planning is entirely different from thirty-seven years ago when I started. It requires more compassion for people, doing away with old ideas about authority. It's difficult to digest.

Table 10-2
Companies' Long-Term Business Plans (Total = 224 Companies)

Time in Advance That Plan Covers	*Percent of Companies*
2 years	1.4
3–5 years	86.6
More than 5 years	11.4
Not applicable/No plan	0.6
	100.0

The lack of long-term HRP will be the limiting factor on this company's growth potential. Numbers are not the issue—the quality of people and their development is the issue. Planning for people is as important as planning for capital assets.

This interest in improving the management of, and planning for, people came not just from companies that did the most extensive human resource planning. In general, most respondents expressed interest and involvement in some form of human resource planning. Even more striking, however, a large majority expressed an interest in improving morale and in developing their company cultures.

Human resource planning occurs in most companies in the context of an existing and reasonably well-developed business-planning process. Formal business planning, which became fashionable in the 1960s, is now so widespread in American business that 90 percent of companies report having a long-range business plan that is distinct from the yearly operating plan. By and large, these plans are extended forward three to five years from the time of their preparation, although one-tenth cover more than five years in advance (see Table 10-2).

Planning is done for different human resource activities in different companies. Table 10-3 defines various human resource planning elements. Table 10-4 shows that while 49 percent of companies prepare a management-succession (or backup) plan, only 12 percent of companies reported that they inventory available talent or skills in their own work force. Further, companies which do conduct a certain activity, and plan for it, vary in whether or not the activity plan is included in the long-term

Table 10-3
Elements of Human Resource Planning

HR Element	Description
1. Wages and benefits	Determining future increases or other alterations in pay levels or benefits
2. Recruiting projections	Determining the numbers of new hires with specific skills needed in a given period of time
3. Compliance with federal regulations	Planning for and tracking compliance with government regulations
4. Morale management	Planning to improve the attitudes, enthusiasm, and commitment of employees as a group
5. Training and development	Improving the capabilities and skills of the existing work force through various programs and courses
6. Skills inventory	Assembly of data about the talent of people in the organization
7. Forecasting personnel needs	Estimating the future supply and demand for people of certain skills and capabilities based on business plans
8. Management succession planning	Identification of one or more candidates as successors for key management positions
9. Executive development	Systematic improvement of the capabilities of managers to meet the requirements of possible future higher positions and increased responsibilities
10. Advance hiring	Hiring people into current positions in order to have them available for anticipated project assignments or other positions
11. Planning a culture	Identifying the desired character of an organization with respect to values, norms, and "purpose"

business plan. Table 10-4 provides estimates of the extent of HR planning and the inclusion of such plans in the long-term

Table 10-4
Human Resource Elements Included in Companies' Business
Planning (Total = 224 Companies)

	Percent of Companies With HR Element		
HR Element	*As Part of Long-Term Business Plan*	*Planned More Than a Year in Advance But Not in Long-Term Business Plan*	*Total*
Management succession/ backup plan	8.5	40.6	49.1
Personnel training and development	19.7	28.6	48.3
Forecasting staffing requirements	45.5	2.7	48.2
Building morale other than by traditional methods	9.8	34.4	44.2
Maintaining or creating a culture	3.6	24.6	28.2
Executive/ management development	12.9	8.5	21.4
Recruitment/ projecting supply	8.0	4.5	12.5
Inventorying available talent/skills	7.1	4.9	12.0

Note: Companies having a long-term business plan including any human resource objectives, goals, or strategies were asked what was included in their plan.

business plan. It should be noted that no single human resource activity is planned for by more than half the companies. However, because some companies do one or more activities but not others, the percentage of companies doing planning for at least one human resource activity is greater than 90 percent.

Finally, companies often described themselves as performing a planning activity but in an informal way, not related to other human resource activities or to the business plan. For management succession, 75 percent of companies describe themselves as having some planning activity—though much is informal and ad hoc.

It is not surprising that companies vary tremendously in their approach to human resource planning. Partly, variations reflect the managerial style of different companies and the preference for formality or informality; partly, variations reflect the importance, or lack of it, attached to planning activities of all types at different companies. As one executive put it, "Planning requires discipline. Managers who don't like human resource planning don't like business planning either." Finally, variations reflect the emerging and not yet codified status of planning in the human resource area.

FIVE STAGES IN HUMAN RESOURCE PLANNING

Analysis of the data indicated that the 224 responding companies could be classified into five stages of human resource planning. The classification was based upon the number of human resource planning elements used by the company and whether planning for people was formally integrated with the strategic or long-range business-planning process. The following stages were identified.

STAGE 1

This stage was represented in 14.7 percent of the sample, or 33 companies. About one-third of the stage 1 companies have no longer-term business plan and do little or no planning for people of any kind. Stage 1 companies tend to have traditional modes of building morale—parties, picnics, awards, mottos, and so on. Several are family firms, others are very paternalistically run. Their conception of human resource planning generally tends to be limited to forecasting needed staff. One executive said, "We have no interest in HRP. There are plenty of people in the local labor market." "We go on faith," said another.

STAGE 2

Into this stage were placed 35.8 percent of the sample, or 80 companies. Of the stage 2 companies, 88 percent have a long-term business plan and many have cited one or two human resource planning components (most often forecasting) as part of the business plan or separate from the business plan.

A number of stage 2 companies felt that planning for people was becoming increasingly important and felt the need to do more. Others saw it as not very realistic especially if they were in a declining industry and "managing for survival." Several stage 2 companies also saw human resource or people planning in a very restricted way. "To most companies HRP is basically counting how many heads are needed," said one executive. "It's numbers."

STAGE 3

This stage was found in 27.2 percent of the sample, or 61 companies. Of the stage 3 companies, 83 percent stated that they did staff forecasting three to five years out, and all the stage 3 companies have several people-planning components that are not, for the most part, integrated into a long-range business plan. A large number of stage 3 managers say that human resource planning is necessary for their success and that their companies are in the process of developing people-planning systems. It is however seen as difficult and expensive. "HRP is essential," said one respondent, "but it takes a lot of hard work and we have no models. . . . It will give us a leading edge if we can do it better." Another said: "Long-term HRP is extremely important. Unfortunately, we've given it lip service because of cost pressures." Some respondents in this stage equate planning with the long-term development of people and speak of people as their most valuable asset.

STAGE 4

Representing this stage were 13.8 percent of the sample, or 31 companies. Stage 4 companies generally reported having a number of HRP components that were, however, not necessarily integrated with the long-range business-planning process. One hundred percent of the companies in this category had a long-term planning process, and 87 percent of the companies had at least one human resource component integrated into the long-range plan. Stage 4 companies do a considerable amount of people planning and are generally enthusiastic about the process. "People are our principal asset," said one manager. "Without good people our company can't do a thing." Another said: "A well-managed company *must* put an emphasis on it. We should be doing more. We often fall short of having qualified people ready when we need them."

STAGE 5

This stage was represented in 8.5 percent of the sample, or 19 companies. One hundred percent of the stage 5 companies had a long-term business plan with several human resource components integrated in a meaningful way into the business plan. Ninety-four percent do some sort of forecasting. Almost all do formal management-succession planning. All stage 5 companies were highly enthusiastic about HRP. A stage 5 company executive said, "HRP is our number one priority—the most important thing relative to productivity. To get people involved, HRP has to be alive and credible."

As one studies the classifications, a movement away from the manpower and forecasting model of people planning (often referred to as "head counting") toward an integrated conception of planning is apparent. In the integrated companies, human resource systems or programs fit together, complement and reinforce each other as building blocks of a larger human resource plan that is developed in relation to the overall strategic business plan of the company. The integrated human resource plan is also developed with a clear understanding of the competitive business, labor, and social environment.

Companies in the higher stages are by and large more active in trying to influence employee performance, and they believe in the effectiveness of their efforts.

Table 10-5 provides an example of the greater activity of higher-stage companies. The proportion of companies in each stage that plan for the purpose of improving communications in order to manage morale rises from 32.5 percent in stage 1 to 82.3 percent in stage 5.

There are also differences between the stages in the degree to which managers believe in the economic significance of hu-

Table 10-5
Percentage of Companies at Each Human Resource Planning Stage That Improve Communication to Manage Morale (Total = 224 Companies)

HRP Stage	No. of Companies in Stage	Percent of Companies
1	33	32.5
2	80	59.5
3	61	64.4
4	31	73.3
5	19	82.3

man resource activities. Table 10-6 reports the answers to a question asking respondents if they believed that employee morale made a difference on the bottom line and asking that they cite evidence, not simply an opinion, to support their judgment. While only 37.5 percent of companies in stage 1 answered affirmatively, almost 90 percent of those in stage 5 (and 96.7 percent of those in stage 4) replied affirmatively.

A PATTERN OF DEVELOPMENT

Is there a pattern of sequential development among human resource activities in companies with or without formal planning, and is there a pattern among activities associated with

Table 10-6
Percentage of Companies at Each Human Resource Planning Stage That Cite Evidence for Morale Affecting Profitability (Total = 224 Companies)

HRP Stage	No. of Companies in Stage	Percent of Companies
1	33	37.5
2	80	66.5
3	61	84.7
4	31	96.7
5	19	88.2

Table 10-7
Human Resource Elements Included in a Long-Term Plan by
Companies at Each Human Resource Planning Stage
(Total = 224 Companies)

	Percent of Companies Including HR Element in Long-Term Plan (No. of Companies at Each Stage Shown in Parentheses)				
HR Element	Stage 1 (33)	Stage 2 (80)	Stage 3 (61)	Stage 4 (31)	Stage 5 (19)
Forecasting	—	21	78	77	82
Training and development	—	—	22	53	65
Executive development	—	—	8	37	53
Recruiting/project supply	—	—	12	10	47
Skills inventory	—	—	7	10	47
Nontraditional morale building	—	3	7	23	35
Maagement succession	—	—	5.4	20	41
Culture	—	—		13	12

formal planning? Two sequential patterns suggest themselves from our data. First, companies at the same stage of development progress in a roughly sequential fashion through activities. Second, there is an orderly, sequential progress from stage to stage. Scaling is a way of drawing out a possible sequence of development from a set of ostensibly nonsequential data.

The suggestion that there are stages of human resource planning suggests a sequence through which companies may progress. When the planning components included in the survey are scaled, two sequences are suggested: one for the inclusion or exclusion of human resource elements in a long-term business plan (see Table 10-7); the other for the planning or doing of certain activities that are not necessarily included in a formal plan (see Table 10-8). For example, sample companies report doing at least informal managment-succession planning no matter how little else they do in terms of people planning. However, succession planning is not included in a long-term plan unless the company does a lot of other kinds of integrated human resource planning. Companies seem to start planning management succession on an informal basis, which does not become

Table 10-8
Human Resource Elements Planned for by Companies at Each
Human Resource Planning Stage (Total = 224 Companies)

HR Element	*Percent of Companies Planning HR Element (No. of Companies at Each Stage Shown in Parentheses)*				
	Stage 1 *(33)*	*Stage 2* *(80)*	*Stage 3* *(61)*	*Stage 4* *(31)*	*Stage 5* *(19)*
Management succession (includes informal)	28	71	80	98	100
Training and development	6	32	63	80	82
Nontraditional morale building	3	33	51	80	94
Forecasting	—	22	83	77	94
Culture	3	13	42	56	47
Executive development	—	8	22	40	77
Recruiting/project supply	—	1	20	17	59
Skills inventory	—	1	14	27	53

formalized until they are doing a considerable amount of planning in other areas.

Training and development, managing morale, and forecasting are activities that are performed and planned for even in the early stages of human resource planning. Also, forecasting staffing needs is one of the first and continuously important components in human resource planning.

Tables 10-7 and 10-8, when compared, indicate that the prevalence of human resource planning activities is far greater than their inclusion in a formal plan would suggest, even among stage 5 companies. For example, all stage 5 companies have management-succession plans, but only 41 percent include these plans in a formal business plan. Also, 94 percent of stage 5 companies do head-count forecasting, but only 82 percent include forecasting in the business plan. A similar result, though at different frequencies, exists for all stages. Thus, the conduct of people-planning activities is more common among firms than the integration of components into a formal plan.

The most common activities are management succession and training and development; forecasting is less common. Yet in formal integrated planning processes, forecasting is most frequent, followed by training and development and management succession only at some distance. It would appear that the first formalized activities are not the most frequent ones, but those which best complement the other aspects of business planning—specifically forecasting numbers and types of personnel needed, traditional morale with its direct impact on performance and productivity, and training with its contribution to day-to-day production.

Yet it should be remembered that the idea of a developmental sequence, both among stages and among activities within a stage, is an inference from the data, not conclusively demonstrated by the data. Scaling shows the activities lined up in a relatively orderly fashion—from which it is inferred that there is a pattern of sequential development.

THE NEW ELEMENTS OF PEOPLE PLANNING: CULTURE, MORALE, AND VALUES

To be successful a company needs competence—the right people—and it needs commitment—people who really perform. Today, it needs flexible and innovative people who can respond to and initiate change. This has led to a new element of people planning—planning for the quality of the organization as a way of creating a more committed and involved work force. Companies are moving from simple work-force planning to planning for organizational and cultural development. For an increasing number of companies, the human resource planning process includes plans for organizational revitalization, the creation and maintenance of a specific culture, and morale building and productivity programs.

In addition, for many companies in our survey, revitalizing the corporate culture and defining the corporate philosophy and values are closely connected to managing morale and to improving communications in the company. Companies that are guided by a strong sense of shared values or purpose consciously or implicitly create the kind of climate that promotes high morale.

Seventy-six percent of the 224 respondents in our survey claimed that they were very interested in the culture of their

Table 10-9
Percentage of Companies "Interested in Culture" (Total = 224
Companies)

Level of Interest		Percent of Companies	No. of Companies
Very interested		76.0	170
Cite efforts	8.1		
Wonder how to change culture	8.6		
Want more involved people	19.0		
Want to communicate culture better	8.6		
	44.3		
Not interested		18.7	42
Unable to respond		5.3	12
		100.0	

organizations (see Table 10-9). And 44.3 percent expressed a
strong interest in developing or changing the culture they have.
Twenty-eight percent of the companies in the sample formally
plan the development of the corporate culture, and 3.6 percent
include this concern in their long-range business plans (Table
10-4). These reports confirm what other surveys have suggested: There is a powerful wave of awareness of corporate
culture on the part of American managers. Yet many top managers are confused even about the meaning of the term. They
are unclear about how to manage such an ineffable concept
and question whether it can be managed at all. On the other
hand, a few companies have very clear-cut sets of values and
goals and have sophisticated systems for selecting, indoctrinat-
ing, and socializing their members. They unconsciously work
to maintain the vitality of their beliefs and strengths. For this
handful of firms, the philosophy of the company and its basic
values are core elements in planning for and guiding the organization. One company respondent said: "Management philosophy is not an afterthought for us; it's a principal
preoccupation." For these value-driven companies, the espoused philosophy frequently includes, as a major tenet, a high
valuation of the people in the organization. "The company's
biggest asset is its people. It's greatest resource is its talent and
the level of commitment," is a typical comment of managers in

Table 10-10
Percentage of Companies at Each Human Resource Planning Stage
That Are "Interested in Culture" (Total = 224 Companies)

HRP Stage	No. of Companies in Stage	Percent of Companies
1	33	53
2	80	77
3	61	91
4	31	90
5	19	100

companies whose planning is grounded in a clear philosophy. "Our management is 'human oriented,'" said one line manager. "Planning for people is our number one issue, a number one priority. It is the most important thing relating to productivity."

"Identifying what our culture is and making people aware of it is extremely important," said a stage 4 respondent. "We are primarily concerned with creating a culture that supports quality and doing a quality job." "We're interested in changing from an adversarial relationship to a cooperative one," said another. "We're putting a lot of effort into modifying our corporate culture," said a third, "we're trying to develop a more entrepreneurial spirit."

A number of companies reported establishing top management committees or task forces or hiring consultants to help define the culture and ways of changing it. But many managers are still confused about what a culture is and in particular how to change it. "We need to destroy our old corporate culture," said a stage 2 respondent. "But how do you do it? Unless we make an effort to change, we'll all be working for the Japanese. We're groping with how to create higher productivity and enthusiasm."

All of the companies in stage 5 (those companies that do the greatest amount of human resource planning) expressed an interest in a corporate culture and most often cited efforts to develop or communicate their cultures (see Table 10-10). "We discuss the company image with employees and ask for their input," said one such respondent. "We actively communicate out business strategy and philosophy to our people," said another. Companies at an early stage of people planning were the ones with the most confusion about how to change a culture.

CONSCIOUSNESS OF A CORPORATE CULTURE

What is meant by a culture? To some people it is a complex set of attributes as defined by social psychologists and sociologists. But for managers it is often best described as the answer to a set of questions—the kinds of questions a job applicant might ask in an interview: How do things really get done around here? How do I get resources? How are objectives set for me? By whom? How does one get ahead, in assignments or promotions? What is valued in the company? How do I get rewarded or recognized? How are complaints handled? Is diversity tolerated? Other questions include how formal or informal the organization is, how seriously rules are enforced, how important status and hierarchy are.

Generally, it may be said that every organization has a culture or a group of subcultures. This is to say, there are answers to each of the foregoing questions in all organizations. But sometimes there are multiple answers, or inconsistencies. Sometimes people do not recognize the interdependencies of the answers.

The important differences among organizations not only concern the particular features of the culture itself but also three general characteristics of all corporate cultures:

1. Is the company's way of doing things consciously planned or not? A company's managers may do things in a certain way, knowing they do so; or they may act in a certain fashion without being aware of it at all.

2. Has the company made its culture explicit, or has it been left implicit? That is, when employees ask how things are done and what is valued at a company, are managers able to tell them clearly—making the culture explicit? In many philosophy-based companies employees are given a printed list of the beliefs or values of the business, and training in what they mean and how they've been applied in the past. In the absence of training and a statement of principles, an employee must discover how things are done by

trial and error, which often involves costly and embar-
rassing mistakes. Making a culture explicit in writing and
in training sessions avoids trial and error and learning by
experience. The trouble with learning by experience, the
old saw goes, is that a person gets the test first and the
lesson afterwards. Formal training reverses the procedure.

3. Finally, is the company's culture managed or not? In a
managed culture a company's executives actively seek to
convey the culture to others, and they attempt to reinforce
it at each opportunity by rewarding behavior in accor-
dance with it. Also, they attempt to apply it to important
issues as they arise, reinforcing the culture by leadership
as well as by reward.

The most prominently publicized recent example of a company that illustrates each of these characteristics of corporate
culture is Johnson & Johnson. Conscious of its culture, the
company had published its creed and expected managers to
live by it. The first item in the company's philosophy was to
attach utmost importance to its customers' safety. When the
Tylenol poisonings occurred, the crisis meetings were made far
simpler by the creed's injunction. There was no real disagreement among top managers that the product had to be withdrawn. Acting in conformity with its creed, the company accepted
short-term losses for what turned out to be a major long-term
gain in consumer confidence and reinforced, by example, the
company's culture for all its employees.

How many companies have explicit cultures? Is such a thing
a rarity, or is it common?

Obtaining data is made complicated by imprecision and common misunderstanding of the term *culture*. Yet, given an opportunity, it would be useful to gain some quantitative measurement.

In late June 1984, some 120 managers of research and development facilities of different companies gathered for a management training session. Most of the companies were in
manufacturing, with an especially heavy representation from
the oil and chemicals industries. Virtually all were large or
medium-size companies.

During the program these managers had an opportunity to

discuss at length the cultures of at least two companies widely recognized as having conscious, explicit, and managed corporate cultures, involving all employees.

Following these discussions participants were asked the question: Does your company have an explicit culture among managers? Among all employees? Because of previous discussions each manager understood the term *culture* in the way described previously here.

The result? Thirty-five percent reported that their companies possessed an explicit culture for managers; and 31 percent possessed such a culture for all employees. Fifty-eight percent said their companies lacked an explicit culture for managers (3 percent could not answer); and 68 percent reported that their companies lacked an explicit culture for all employees (1 percent could not answer).

From this survey, although not representative of all American industry, the conclusion can be ventured that about one-third of large industrial companies today have an explicit culture— a stated way they wish those in the company to behave; and that in the majority of these companies the culture is not limited to managers but is expected to apply to all employees.

Discussions with managers also suggest that more is going on than what comes down from the corporate level. In some instances, division managers report attempting to develop a culture for their divisions, either in the absence of a corporatewide culture or even in contrast to it, motivated by dissatisfaction with the company culture.

At the plant level managers have in several cases been permitted to meet among themselves to decide on a philosophy for their plant, independent of the corporation's own modes of behavior, implicit or explicit. In one instance, expecting a hard start-up of a new facility and foreseeing long evenings at the plant, managers committed themselves as a group to late morning arrivals, so that at least some time could be spent with their families. Other commitments included a successful start-up at whatever cost in effort, open communication to employees, and bottom up participation.

While not yet the norm, the concept of an explicit, conscious, managed culture as a guide to behavior is spreading among managers at all levels. Effective managers increasingly become conscious of the culture of the organization by asking others the questions that define culture and by testing the responses against their own interpretations. Where the existing culture is constructive, managers make it explicit and reinforce it. Where it is nonconstructive, they seek its modification or replacement. In either case, effective managers actively manage the culture as an important contribution to the organization's performance.

MORALE

In addition to having an interest in planning for people and in creating a company culture, a majority of companies in the HRP survey were highly concerned with improving or maintaining the morale of employees. Of the 224 companies surveyed, 95.5 percent report having some sort of formal program to build morale. "Morale is a concern at all levels," said one respondent. "We are trying to improve working conditions." "We don't have a well-defined human resource plan," said another, "but we're putting a lot of time and money into improving morale. It's a high-level priority of the CEO. We've hired a consultant to help."

There were no significant differences between companies at various planning stages in terms of whether they formally manage morale or not, because most companies reportedly do manage morale. However, there were differences between stages of planning in terms of the type of programs used to build morale.

Morale-related programs were categorized into eight groups. Of the 224 companies in the survey, 62.1 percent try to build or maintain morale by largely traditional or sometimes paternalistic methods: sponsoring company picnics and clubs, company newsletters and mottos, performance awards, safety measures, and so on. The use of traditional methods of managing morale was fairly widespread across groups. The evenness of the distribution suggests that traditional methods must be basically useful.

Of the 224 companies, 60.3 percent try to improve morale

by increasing communication in the company both by providing more information to employees and by eliciting more input from them. Eighteen percent of the respondents cited specific programs such as bimonthly meetings to keep people informed about the business and various open-door policies. Increasing communication and information flow was a major thrust, according to many of the respondents, and the higher the stage of human resource planning, the greater the tendency to see increased communication as a way of improving employee morale (see Table 10.5).

Of the 224 companies, 29.5 percent cited educational opportunities as morale builders, and 20 percent reported using some form of participatory management or shared decision making. "We're pushing decision making down, so employees have more input," said several managers. Others said: "We try 38 involve employees in running the company," and "We're getting employees more involved in decision making to foster commitment," and "We're emphasizing a participatory management style." The higher the level of human resource planning, the more tendency there is to use participatory methods.

Some companies use attitude surveys to track morale, and one company hired a full-time person to "keep in touch with what employees are feeling." Others try innovative new programs such as flextime, wellness programs and work enrichment, stocks and special financial incentives, or superb facilities.

Of the 224 companies surveyed, including those in all stages of development, a total of 60.1 percent (or 135 companies) reported that morale made a difference to the company's profitability (see Table 10-11). Asked how, the respondents cited increased productivity, reduced turnover, better attitudes, lessened chance of unionization, and happier customers.

A relatively new phenomenon that the survey revealed is that companies are beginning to plan formally for building the morale of their employees and the kind of culture they want to have. As shown in Table 10-4, 44.2 percent of the respondents reported that they formally planned morale building for more than a year in advance, and 28.2 percent said they similarly planned in terms of culture. The integration of morale and culture planning in a long-term business plan is far less com-

Table 10-11

Percentage of Companies Citing Benefits of Morale Building for Profitability (Total = 135 Companies)

Benefit	No. of Companies Citing Benefit	Percent of Companies Citing Benefit
Intangible but relevant	58	25.9
Increased productivity/efficiency	30	13.4
Reduced turnover; less absenteeism	22	9.8
Better employee attitudes	18	8.0
Increased sales, profits, dollar return	8	3.6
Prevents unionization	5	2.2
Happier customers	4	1.8
Cited more than three of above	3	1.3

mon, but it is perhaps significant that it occurs at all. Only 9.8 percent of the companies in our sample integrate their morale planning activities into a business plan, and only 3.6 percent integrate planning for a corporate culture into a business plan.

It should be noted that these data are reasonably consistent with the results of the survey of research and development executives of major firms reported earlier. In that survey 38 percent of managers reported an explicit, conscious, and managed culture for executives in their companies, and 31 percent for all employees. This was a more sophisticated measure of the aspects of a culture than would be used in the human resources planning survey, because of the more limited contact with respondents. A less precise understanding of the term *culture* was necessarily used in the broader survey. The result, that some 28.2 percent of companies are planning for the purpose of maintaining or creating a culture (see Table 10-4) is reasonably consistent with the finding of the other questionnaire, which implies but does not explicitly explore formal planning for culture.

How do companies in various stages of human resource planning differ with respect to planning for building employee morale in nontraditional ways, and with respect to planning for a corporate culture? Table 10-12 indicates that 94 percent of stage 5 companies plan for morale building in nontraditional

Table 10-12
Planning for Nontraditional Morale and Culture Building at Each
Human Resource Stage (Total = 224 Companies)

	Percent of Companies Integrating HR Element into Overall Business Plan (No. of Companies at Each Stage Shown in Parentheses)					Percent of Total Companies
HR Element	Stage 1 (33)	Stage 2 (80)	Stage 3 (61)	Stage 4 (31)	Stage 5 (19)	
Morale	—	3	7	23	35	9.8
Culture	—	—	—	13	12	3.6

	Percent of Companies Planning for HR Element (No. of Companies at Each Stage Shown in Parentheses)					Percent of Total Companies
HR Element	Stage 1 (33)	Stage 2 (80)	Stage 3 (61)	Stage 4 (31)	Stage 5 (19)	
Morale	3	33	51	80	94	44.2
Culture	3	13	42	56	47	28.2

ways, while only 3 percent of stage 1 companies do so. Of the stage 5 companies, 47 percent plan for company culture while only 3 percent of stage 1 companies do so. Higher-stage companies are the only ones that integrate morale and culture planning into the business-planning process.

PLANNING WITH A PHILOSOPHY

Our survey revealed a small number of companies that say they are, and appear to be, "value-driven." We found these companies among those most involved in an integrated form of human resource planning and most committed to it. What stands out in the survey is not *how many* companies do sophisticated people planning, but how committed and enthusiastic the line managers are of those companies that are doing people planning in conjunction with business planning. All stage 5 companies were rated as highly interested in people planning. We found that these companies tended to initiate planning because of a strong top management commitment, which includes a basic philosophic stance about the company and its employees.

In the business community in general there are reports of a growing number of leading-edge companies who "plan with a philosophy." Both business and human resource planning, when they are done, are guided by the philosophy of the company in regards to its basic purposes and its attitude toward employees. The philosophy is consciously communicated to, and reinforced in, members of the organization, so that it becomes second nature to them and implicit in their day-to-day behavior and decisions. "I'm sure that any worker in any of our plants would be able to tell you what our values are, what we stand for," said one respondent. Commonly shared values that employees can take pride in are seen to be a powerful incentive to superior performance.

One company in our sample is a very clear example of the idea of planning with a philosophy. The company has a sophisticated strategic planning process that includes performance planning systems and five-year training and development plans. It reports being a very profitable company, with $200 million in sales currently and anticipating growing much larger. It is the strongly people-oriented culture and the firm basic philosophy of the chief executive officer that are seen as the sources of the company's success.

"The CEO in our company understood the need for basic beliefs in a company around the quality of the people and the quality of the product," said another respondent. "We believe that if we have high-quality caring, involved people and a quality product, profits will follow naturally. We believe in growth of the individual and of the company. We insist that new hires have people skills no matter how much of a technical genius they are."

PLANNING WITHOUT PHILOSOPHY

Only companies in stages 4 and 5 (21.9 percent of the 224 respondents) could be said to be doing substantial planning for people, and only stage 5 companies integrate human resource planning with long-range business planning. These facts, together with a generally technique-oriented approach to people planning, suggest that while a majority of companies are interested and involved in some form of people planning, many are planning without a philosophy—without a strong overall conception of what their companies stand for and especially without any long-term vision of where the company is going regarding people.

Many companies in the survey began to do people planning at the suggestion of a consultant, at the order of an acquiring company, or as a reaction to a crisis involving people. Under these circumstances companies began to do people planning in a fragmented and instrumental way without an understanding of basic principles. There are dangers of implementing people-planning components and activities in an ad hoc manner. One of the dangers is that line managers, without an understanding of the long-term business significance of the effort, will regard such planning activities as nonessential paperwork. The survey reveals that this type of planning is still quite common. A number of companies in the early stages of people planning report that they see some importance to such planning but find it too difficult and too costly. Also, they have no easy models. "Our human resource department seems to be more concerned about numbers and the like instead of more important qualitative things," said one executive. "I'll have to talk to them about it." "HRP is an overworked exercise," said another respondent. "There needs to be a lot less fanfare about it."

THE PARADOX OF PLANNING IN AN
UNCERTAIN ENVIRONMENT

What is the impact of change in the business environment on human resource planning? Initially in our study we had expected that high-growth companies facing rapid changes and competitive challenges would tend to be very involved in planning for people, both formally and informally. Some were, but others were not, often because fast growth puts such strains on management time and energy that it is very difficult to plan. "Keeping up" is the most overwhelming task; the "bodies" must be gotten on board, even though that may mean expensive termination costs further down the line.

A number of respondents whose companies did *not* plan for people stated that their environment was changing so rapidly that it made plans obsolete, especially labor forecasts. "Long-range planning is fine if the business is stable," said one such respondent. "But, our business is rapidly changing due to a rapidly changing technology. The company forced guys to go through the planning process and a year later the plan doesn't bear any resemblance to the one developed a year earlier." Other companies that did plan their people needs claimed that although in a rapidly changing environment forecasts and plans did not always hold up, there was even more need for planning as a guideline. These observations imply a paradox of planning. Although plans may become obsolete and are highly subject to change, the *process* of planning itself and the development of alternative scenarios allow beliefs and assumptions to surface and act as flexible guides for the future.

PROFITS AND HUMAN VALUES

This final section addresses directly the theme of this volume—mutuality. By and large today, companies planning for the specific nature of a corporate culture stress greater identity of interest between company and employee. Cultures that companies seek to alter are those that appear inimical to greater mutuality.

The most articulate spokespersons for the new cultures are found in new entrepreneurial companies. Several of these companies, often highly successful, appeared in the survey. They do not formally plan in conventional ways but exemplify to a high degree the trend to an intrinsic concern with the contribution that human commitment can make in the business environment. Several well-known entrepreneurs have publicly discussed their concern with creating company cultures and company philosophies that enhance and stimulate human potential. They recognize and make use of the importance of symbols, celebrations, and the frequent articulation and communication of the company's values. The culture of the organization is said to be both a means to commercial success and an end in itself—a *community* for those who are its members.

There also appears to be a new legitimacy for business executives and managers to talk openly about basic values in regard to the management of people and how they do business. What was considered "soft" a few years ago is now a major concern of many top line managers. The vice president of human resources at a start-up whose revenues were $12.6 million in the first year of operation said, "My job is to articulate values, to keep values out in front, to remind [the CEO] of our values when necessary and inject values into the daily operations of the business. I worry about whether our effort adds up to something really meaningful for us all."

While these entrepreneurs want to create meaningful organizations and are concerned that their products have social value as well, they also have a strong desire to become financially successful. Does the human culture of the company take a back seat to market success and profitability, and are human values simply instrumental to profits?

This is a very difficult question to answer, although it may be the key question bearing on the ultimate fate of efforts to develop cultures that create a oneness of purpose between management and employees.

There is evidence in the survey that managers in companies that include human resource elements in their business plans see people planning as contributing to profitability. Only 28 percent said they lacked evidence of its contribution to profitability. Twenty-four percent cited increased sales or profits; 20 percent cited tangible but indirect outcomes; 33 percent said results were intangible but real; and 5 percent believed failure to plan would reduce profits.

But what is cause and what is effect? Is planning for people and a concern with values and culture an instrument to create profitability, or is profitability merely a by-product of a people-oriented culture in itself?

A successful culture should lead to profitability, and those who reject the instrumentality notion nonetheless insist that planning for a culture enhances profitability. But it is not for profitability that the culture is developed, they argue; rather, profitability is a by-product. "We do it (people planning) because it's right," said one executive.

A test of management's sincerity would occur if the business were to lose money. Would the culture be changed in an effort to become profitable? Alternatively, if rapid growth threatens essential elements of the culture, will they be modified to favor increased growth and profitability? Or will the tension between the value placed on profitability and the value placed on a people-oriented culture lead to a search for innovative solutions to the dilemma—new work arrangements such as job sharing and early retirement plans—or to new business strategies, products, or markets?

Some executives say that a culture of mutuality cannot be modified for profitability reasons alone. Any other view risks employees' concluding that management's commitment to a culture of mutuality is no more than skin deep. If management is believed to be motivated primarily by profitability, they say, employees will not offer the trust necessary to establish a system of mutuality.

These executives fear that talk by managers in other companies that identifies a new culture as an instrument of profitability will, if publicized, undo their own efforts to build trust with employees. In consequence of their fears, they bitterly attack those who espouse an instrumentalist view. It also seems to be the case that competitive threats and the productivity-enhancing aspects of people-oriented cultures are sometimes used as sticks and carrots by humanistic managers to move their more traditional peers and other stakeholders toward new values.

These are important but subtle issues, unsuited to quantitative exploration. They have to do with the sincerity of executives and the expectations and fears of employees. The answers to these issues can only be played out in the experience of the next several years.

Human resource planning is taking root in many companies. With quantitative aspects of planning is coming the recognition that a philosophy of human behavior and values suited to each company's people and environment can enliven and guide the planning process.

11
Education at Work: Demystifying the Magic of Training

Jeffrey A. Sonnenfeld

Leaders of all types of social institutions—from old and new enterprises to trade unions and political parties—proclaim the value of employer-sponsored education with such passion that it sounds like a magical elixir. Whether the problem to be addressed is potential decline in technological leadership, intensified international competition, the structural upheaval in our economic sectors, or the need for innovative and highly committed work groups, the importance of developing new technological and social skills in the work force is clear.[1] The success of maintaining and regaining our competitive industrial edge depends on the sophistication of our human infrastructure. A better-educated work force is in the interest of both employers and employees. The following are specific employer needs that we can observe:

1. A concern over the comfort and competence of employees who must show a wider array of skills, more requisite knowledge, and increased discretion;
2. An awareness of the total system of production, so that

The author would like to acknowledge the helpful suggestions of Professors Chris Argyris, D. Quinn Mills, Linda Hill, Leonard Schlesinger, Paul Lawrence, George Lodge, Richard Walton, and Ms. Cynthia Ingols of Harvard University; Professors Martin Meyerson and Robert Zemsky of the University of Pennsylvania; Ms. Nevzer Stacy of the National Institute of Education; Dr. Frederick Jacobs of City University of New York; Mr. Robert Beck of Bank of America; Mr. Del Lippert of Digital Equipment Corporation; Mr. Robert Fenn of The Travelers Insurance Company; Dr. Terry Ebert of Morgan Stanley; Mr. Badi Foster of Aetna Life and Casualty; and Mr. Leonard Langer of Morgan Guaranty.

unpredictable and interrelated tasks can be responsive to mishaps and changes in the process;

3. An appreciation of the flow of products and services in the marketplace as changing customer needs, dynamic contractual arrangements with suppliers, and fluid definitions of the competition defy traditional static relationships among such parties;

4. An ability to manage teams of workers who rely on heterogeneous clusters of internal expertise and the ability to communicate internally with speed and clarity;

5. Increasingly vocalized concerns over employment security and career growth that seem to ask employers to absorb large retraining costs.

Given these learning needs, the postindustrial era may well be a time when we must move from a focus on childhood education to a new focus on the education of adults. While the importance of recognizing this shifting spotlight is clear, how to make this shift has become less clear. Consider this comment of a chief executive of a leading chemical firm:

> I have community leaders calling from Silicon Valley, Route 128, Polymer Valley, and other such places almost weekly with plans for company participation in programs for retraining displaced workers in the industrial north central and northeast. I must trash fifteen slick fliers a day that advertise university-sponsored or commerical vendor-sponsored seminar programs. Inside I have turf battles growing between such departments as information systems, human resources, engineering, sales, and line operations. We are riddled with inconsistent educational practices in implementing new technologies and rewarding employee development. Rather than another "guru" to point out the next frontier, I'd prefer a simple map for exploring this frontier.

Traditionally, on-the-job training and the hiring of needed expertise from the outside are common approaches to acquiring a skilled work force. However, the immediate job-task bias of on-the-job learning and the practical limits of outside recruiting, such as hiring large enough numbers of recruits and the time lag before they are contributing, suggest that these approaches alone will not prepare an entire firm for needed future skills. Today training and retraining are ever more important techniques for upgrading the work force to adjust to major shifts in technology, management practices, and new products and markets.

The need for transformation in our industries excites and alarms both management and the general work force. There is a shared worry over how well we will adapt. The mutual fears of obsolescence, dislocation, and burn-out remind us that all parties gain when we wisely replenish our human resource pool. This chapter examines such replenishment efforts with a special focus on management education. In particular, it considers how the allocation of training dollars may favor certain groups over others and inadvertently lead to waste and misuse of educational effort. After looking at a historical perspective of training, it examines five prevailing training troubles and offers three prescriptions for better corporate training.

HUMAN RESOURCE DEVELOPMENT IN PERSPECTIVE

EARLIER EXPERIENCES

Our differential success between people development and product development is not surprising, given the different experiences that we have had with each set of activities. While Americans greeted the twentieth century as the age of invention as well as the age of education, these paths soon parted. The year 1900 was when Thomas Edison established the nation's first research and development laboratory at General Electric. By 1913, Bell Telephone, Du Pont, Eastman Kodak, and over fifty other companies had established laboratories with budgets of hundreds of thousands of dollars per year. In 1899, just prior to the creation of GE's lab, the nation's greatest educator, John Dewey, led America into some difficult educational introspection with the publication of his revolutionary *Schooling and Society*.[2] In this same period the number of public schools nearly doubled and the number of students increased two-and-a-half times. Higher education enrollments more than doubled, and high-caliber graduate university programs started that at last rivaled those of Europe. Dewey championed more applied learning. He called for occupational exploration and greater assimilation of vocational training into other educational activity. To his dismay, however, educators became increasingly child-centered and abstract.

This spirit of invention survived the Progessive era. Even if studies of post-1960s "deindustrialization"—marked by a preference for overconsumption and overproduction—are current, our practices in managing research and development showed greater sustained devotion than was shown in education. Companies have always done some in-house, on-the-job training. Formal training programs were not established until the late nineteenth century—"corporation schools" that enabled industry to meet its need for skilled labor when vocational education programs were too few to meet demand. Rather than enhance the functions of the employer as an educator, however, the technical advances made by the firm's engineers actually served to restrict personnel development. In addition to Dewey and Edison, another champion of the Progressive movement was Frederick Winslow Taylor. Taylor's work ushered in the reign of the industrial engineer, whose primary mission was more rational organization and management control of the production process. The drive for mechanical efficiency led to job simplification and reduced worker discretion.[3] While the American Management Association, the country's largest training organization, traces its origin to 1913 as the National Association of Corporation Schools (renamed the National Association of Corporation Training in 1920), its role was quite limited until the late 1940s and early 1950s. Rather than develop a committed work force, the common priority was to limit management reliance upon skilled craft workers. A study of training in 1935 reported than only 3 percent of 2,500 large firms had executive training programs. By and large, most training activity reflected residual craft training of apprentices.

RESURGENCE OF EDUCATION

Attacks on the presumptions of limited human potential inherent in scientific management gained influence with the 1939 publication of the famed Hawthorne Studies.[4] This research, conducted between the late 1920s and early 1930s, led to the recognition of work norms, worker motivation, morale, leadership, and the general appreciation of the workplace as a social system. Supervisor training based on a sensitivity to the human relations of the workplace spread quickly. Research in the 1950s by James Worthy and by Charles Walker and Robert Guest specifically identified the costs in morale and in productive output of the prevailing repetitive, low-skilled, machine-paced work. Employers began to return higher skills to jobs through job enlargement and through training programs that provided the required skills. Thomas J. Watson, Sr., the founder of IBM, is thought to have spearheaded this movement when he stumbled upon frustrated and inefficient workers in his factories who complained of highly segmented work activities. Since its early days IBM has been a model for employee training and development.

With the increased civilian and military training activity required in World War II, further appreciation for the capacity of workers to learn new skills developed. A national professional association, the American Society for Training and Development, grew with what was initially a bit more of a technical orientation. In 1947 the NTL Institute was organized at the initiative of the National Education Association with the express purpose of applying the emerging knowledge from behavioral science to organization. Following World War II, as business and industry became increasingly large and complex, a shortage of managerial talent made it necessary for companies to establish their own development programs for supervisory, managerial, and executive personnel. Universities began to move more decisively towards management development programs in the 1950s. In 1950 only three existed: MIT's Sloan Fellows Program (1931), Harvard's Advanced Management Program (1943), and Pittsburgh's Management Program for Executives (1947). The Conference Board found that by 1957 there were thirty-two such residence-based university programs.

In addition to these outside programs, several companies offered internal programs committed to employee education in the post-World War II years. General Electric once again provided a pioneering role for American management. By the mid-1950s one out of every eight employees at all organizational levels in GE was involved in company-sponsored courses. The cost of that training, which ranged from factory-skills courses to advanced education for professional managers, was $35 million to $40 million per year. Although engineering courses for GE personnel were introduced in 1892 with the founding of the company, on-the-job training and functional-skills seminars for basics in areas such as accounting comprised much of the educational effort. In 1956 GE opened the doors on its new Management Development Institute at Crotonville, New York. Its main program, the Advanced Management Course, had thirteen-week sessions that looked at company philosophy, company specific practices, and general managerial skills at a cost of $15,000 per person.[5] General Electric's chief executive at that time, Ralph J. Cordiner, articulated a corporate educational philosophy marked by (1) development of managerial talent internally; (2) the cultivation of a "climate of growth" for all employees, which embraced learning as a lifelong process and which provided programs to facilitate an individual's ability to grow; and (3) an emphasis upon work-force planning for future as well as current needs.[6]

THE MAGNITUDE OF EMPLOYER EDUCATION TODAY

The trend towards increased educational efforts has certainly taken hold in those of the nation's large firms with respected reputations for promoting the mutual interest of workers and managers. Training at firms such as GE, IBM, AT&T, Proctor & Gamble, Raytheon, and Johnson & Johnson, to name a few, has virtually earned the respect and status of academic degrees.[7] People frequently choose to begin careers at these firms, which offer such valued resume credentials. The business and trade press generally rate these firms as among the best managed in the United States. These firms themselves point with pride to their very limited reliance on search firms. Instead, they prefer home-grown talent, because the people are familiar, the management skills are better assessed, and the cultural awareness is greater. In the best companies education is most certainly mutually beneficial, for individuals gain desired knowledge and skills and these companies benefit from a more highly skilled work force. (Parenthetically, these highly skilled workers are often sought-after in the marketplace, and companies that spend a great deal on educating their workers may find employees hired away. These firms must assess the trade-offs of being a net supplier of talent.

Let's look at a few of these firms in particular. Returning to General Electric, more recent estimates of its educational expenses approach $100 million, with 10 percent of that amount spent on management development alone. Estimates of participation in GE corporate management education for 1980 suggest that 5,000 executives were involved in centralized internal programs in the United States; 25,000 managers participated in decentralized programs offered domestically; and another 3,000 were involved in programs outside the United States.

To maintain its skilled work force of over 1 million employees, the predivestiture AT&T provided more education than any university in the world. Estimates for its 1981 spending in education approach $1.1 billion a year. The costs covered the development of courses, compensation of instructors, and the provision of facilities. On any given day 30,000, or about 3 percent of the total AT&T work force, attended classes. The approach was characterized by such features as early assessment of talent, technical training, supervisor training, and yearly corporate policy workshops for the top three levels of management. At these larger firms, there is generally a continuum of programs for job entry and followup programs at each level of management.[8]

Looking at the aggregate, the estimated total costs for employer-sponsored education from the past year were about $40 billion. This is about 0.5 percent of the GNP, or almost as much as the annual expenditure on education in all publicly financed colleges and universities.[9] A recent study estimated that $3 billion is spent by private firms alone, strictly on the purchase of materials and programs outside the firm.[10] The most widely discussed of these studies was conducted by the Conference Board in 1975.[11] This study found that 11 percent of the employees in firms took formal courses offered by their companies. In addition, 89 percent of the employees had tuition aid or refund programs available. Furthermore, 75 percent of the firms authorized their more senior and professional employees to take courses on the outside during working hours and at the company's expense.

It is interesting to note, however, that even this presumed level of expenditure may not be sufficient. Harvard labor economist James Medoff recently conducted an anaylsis of time series data from the Adult Education Survey of the Current Population Survey.[12] These data are based on reports of workers rather than employers. His findings suggest that employer-sponsored education has not increased from 1969 to 1978, either in the percentage of workers who participate (1.3 percent) or in the number of hours spent in such formal study (6.6 hours per year). This low participation rate suggests that smaller firms may, in fact, allocate far less effort to worker education than larger ones. Even in the previous Conference Board study, an association between size and amount spent on worker education was evident. Furthermore, in these studies, certain industries, such as financial service firms, consistently appear to have spent more on employee education.

This increase in reported spending with employer size may not be surprising. Perhaps large firms, who need masses of trained workers, cannot take the chance of relying on available labor pools. On the other hand, perhaps small firms cannot risk training talent that might be pirated away in personnel raids by competing firms. It is also possible that large firms either use training dollars less efficiently or account for them in mysterious ways. As a whole, we may well ask whether we are spending enough. If educational spending has not greatly increased in the last decade, but the business environment and the workplace have been radically transformed, how will the work force be realigned to meet the new challenges? Let's review the nature of some of the new educational expectations placed on employers.

TRAINING TROUBLES

Despite an apparent recognition of the importance of human resource development, corporate training efforts are regularly overwhelmed by the expectations placed upon them. As companies around the country build classroom facilities, or "training temples," costing tens of millions of dollars. It is important to address those concerns that transcend the sheer amount of resources allocated to development. These concerns include (1) expanded roles for employers as educators, (2) poor cost accountability, (3) limited coordination of training with other company activities, (4) a dangerous reliance on possibly biased experts, and (5) a confusing kaleidoscope of educational offerings by suppliers.

EXPANDED ROLES FOR EMPLOYERS AS EDUCATORS

Unaccustomed to education as a primary role, firms have struggled to meet ongoing needs to help facilitate organizational changes, guide career transitions, and provide a steady updated pool of skilled and committed labor. Now the firm's traditional learning curriculum has become crowded with a complex social agenda. We will consider just a few as examples.

First, responding to local concerns and federally sponsored Private Industry Councils (PICs) firms have assumed some responsibility for the "hard-core unemployed" and those permanently plagued by low earnings. These PICs were set up to overcome the weaknesses of publicly administered training through the CETA programs run by local government bureaucrats. Some efforts have been quite impressive. In 1981–82 the Ohio State Board of Economic and Community Development and the State Board of Vocational Education cooperated with forty corporations (including AMC Jeep, Conrail, Chrysler, Teledyne, General Motors, and Control Data) to provide training and retraining for over 50,000 persons. Despite the enthusiastic support of the business community and trade groups, along with $3 billion in federal funds, the Committee for Economic Development has concluded that overall results in this area have fallen short of management expectations. Nonetheless, dedicated cooperative efforts continue under this program with $2.4 billion from the 1983 Job Training Partnership Act.

Added to this new role as a provider of education for those

permanently disadvantaged are the pressures to attend to the needs of those who become suddenly displaced from their livelihood. Such concerns as the structural shifts from manufacturing to service sectors, the geographic flow of jobs to other regions, the alleged declines in international competitiveness due to sweeping changes in the technology of work in the factory and the office, and the convergence of market activities prompted by both technological change and deregulation have alerted management to the need to intensify and widen skill-training efforts. Medoff's work suggested a major imbalance in the labor marketplace due to lags in the skills workers have to meet the needs of employers.[13] Responses to date include (1) the controversial and much maligned Trade Adjustment Assistance Act of 1975, which aids workers laid off due to import-caused job loss; (2) the large-scale compensatory education programs to overcome failure of the traditional educational system to teach fundamental verbal and mathematical skills; and (3) corporate commitments to retrain displaced workers, as in the more limited programs at Goodyear Tire and Rubber and at Jones and Laughlin Steel or the massive commitments made by General Motors and Ford in their concession bargaining with the United Auto Workers.

Finally, retraining by employers has figured prominently in the highly publicized battle between the political parties and branches of government to create a jobs bill. The Job Training Partnership Act has already designated $240 million for retraining. Industry and labor leaders, however, are quick to point out that these current efforts are insignificant in the light of the startling Carnegie-Mellon predictions of the elimination of 4 million factory jobs and the restructuring of 40 million others through technological change. A recent study by Data Resources Incorporated projected that high technology will provide only half as many jobs as it eliminates.[14] Given these figures, it is hard to maintain that training will benefit all adult American workers.

Yet another cluster of factors pressuring business leaders to turn to education as an answer has to do with the gap between work-force expectations and workplace opportunity. While the previous cluster of concerns focused on the prevention of unemployment and the prevention of obsolescence, these concerns have more to do with the personal aspirations and growth of workers. A better-educated work force, now part of an enlarged cohort group, is approaching midlife, traditionally a time of increased dissatisfaction with work opportunity. As the postwar baby boom ages, the reality of limited opportunity for advancement in a hierarchical and pyramidic-shaped organization becomes more apparent. College corridors have gotten quieter at the same time that the clamor in the adult education market has become louder. These highly educated postwar baby boomers ask employers to facilitate their midcareer changes in occupation; career planning; lateral changes to overcome plateauing; and even personal enhancement outside of work. If all these expectations are taken into account, will training yield benefits of equal value to employers and employees?

POOR COST ACCOUNTABILITY

Although a tremendous amount of company money is allocated to training, there is great reluctance by company officials, at any level and from every function, to claim publicly that they know what is actually spent on employee education in their units, let alone their firms. Even those companies frequently labeled "best managed" or "excellently managed" are unwilling to assign approximate figures to this important company investment. A recent study by Hay Associates of 1,200 major firms reported that fewer than one in a hundred even purport to assess the millions of dollars they spend on education annually.[15] Is it because these activities are so amorphous that they elude totals? Somehow many firms do provide figures for other intangibles such as product development, social responsibility expenditures, public relations, and advertising. Is this category of expense so highly valued that it transcends the indignity of quantification? If so, this is quite an unusual category of expense. It may be true that any measurement of benefits can only be superficial, but is this true of cost estimates?

In fairness, it must be pointed out that education costs in large firms are elusive for many reasons. The training activities in a company are frequently spread through many different departments and are buried in unrevealing categories of individual budgets. Some firms consider training as an expense. Other, more inventive, firms capitalize it as the cost of a product or part of the cost of major equipment (for example, computers or airplanes) and carry training expenses as a subaccount of major capital accounts. Frequently time off the job, travel, and in-house and out-of-house expenses are handled inconsistently within the same firm. In addition, internal transfer pricing of course-development activities, budgets for employee development, on-the-job training costs, salaries of employees as trainees, the specification of outside plant-level educational purchases from outside vendors, and tuition assistance for out-placement and retirement are handled in inconsistent ways.

LIMITED INTERNAL COORDINATION

The individuals likely to be considered internal producers of education include training managers, human resource development executives, regional general managers, labor relations officials, customer education specialists, technical and engineering trainers, software and systems developers, marketing and sales executives, operations managers, and professional staff specialists such as the corporate counsel, the controller's office, or public relations experts. Consider the following situations, which illustrate the costs of this poor coordination:

The American Instruments Corporation (a $5-billion company) instituted a training program costing $300,000. This slide program, entitled "Positioning for Excellence," was considered by insiders to be a shallow effort created at the command of a division chief executive who wanted to enhance his own image through such identity-strengthening activities as new advertisements, a new logo, and new training programs. This program was forced on the division over the wishes of the division's trainers and was seen as simplistic by the highly skilled technical and professional employees in the division. When this executive moved on to another position, a trainer convinced his successor to invest in a scaled-down training program to combat high turnover of key talent.

A pilot plan was developed for a research facility with 3,000 exempt employees (engineers and physicists). Morale had been low in this plant because of a 10 percent shrinkage based on a hiring freeze and attrition. This was part of an effort to avoid a layoff and hold onto valuable workers for when conditions improved. The program established credibility after a rough start. After spending $75,000 on training manuals, workshops, job descriptions, information systems to circulate knowledge about openings and opportunities, and counseling, the facility received an abrupt jolt. Three months into this program to combat turnover, 10 percent of the work force was laid off and an additional 3 percent took advantage of an attractive early retirement package. The vacated jobs did not create any opportunity either, since these positions were eliminated as the incumbents departed. The program abruptly died. Two months later the entire division was reorganized, further obliterating prior notions of career paths.

A similarly disastrous example of poor company learning was when MetroBank, a large international bank, attempted to implement a new computer-processing system which would allow for real-time processing of transactions (e.g., loans, foreign exchange, letter of credit, etc.) instead of batch processing.[16]

The new system was also intended to introduce an improved accounting system which would eliminate repetitive and inaccurate manual files and indexes on customers. The system was developed for the bank's European operation by systems development engineers. When it was extended to the operations in other countries, crises abounded. The systems engineers provided technical training and a manual on how to operate the machines and how to input data, etc. They did not anticipate the employee resistance and the importance of local modification. Employees, fearful for their job security, suspected future layoffs. They worried about their own competence in handling the new procedures, and they were confused about how the overall system worked. As a result, they greeted the system with hostility and went back to their manual processing and hand calculators despite the new equipment and programs.

These examples at American Instruments and MetroBank point out just a few of the difficulties that result from poor accountability and coordination in training. In each case, better contact between systems development people, company planners, engineers, operations managers, and the human resource development function could have minimized the likelihood of costly failure. Specifically, fragmentary training approaches lead to (1) poor learning and pooling of information in the organization, (2) wasted effort through duplication in program development, (3) poor budgeting patterns of overconsumption and underconsumption, and (4) the increased chance of unfair discrimination by arbitrary supervisors.

The examples particularly well illustrate the first of these difficulties, poor organizational learning. Therefore, we will now describe each of the other three side effects of poor coordination. Duplication and reinvention are well demonstrated by computer makers who succeed in training customers, through their sales arm, in using their own machines better than the computer makers train their own managers to use these machines. Examples of overconsumption and underconsumption often depend on the budgeting process and manager greed. If training is free, departments and individual executives may grab all they can. If it is charged back to their departments, this may introduce a disincentive for short-term-oriented managers to train subordinates. Managers, fearful of new office technologies, may avoid taking advantage of discretionary courses offered in the use of new equipment. At the same time, examples of overconsumption might be situations where employees seek out courses in time management or influence management far beyond what may reflect the firm's priorities. Enrollments in tuition-assisted programs that lead to employment elsewhere is another example. A training director of a large chemical firm recently learned that the company had inadvertently paid for much of a laboratory technician's course work toward a degree in dentistry. Finally, discrimination is aided through poor accountability in that educational opportunities may be secretly denied some and offered others on the basis of supervisor whim and bias.

DANGEROUS RELIANCE ON POSSIBLY BIASED EXPERTS

Similar to this concern over budgets and coordination, we can see departmental and personal bias manifest itself in the definition of training needs. The problem spurring the creation of a training program is often defined quite loosely. In many cases, there is a generalized concern about a business problem and a particular senior executive may suggest education as the answer. Hard-working, committed trainers often acquire reputations as miracle workers and are pressured to step beyond their competence. A training specialist may be called in to conduct a "needs analysis." This frequently consists of surveys of the target population where the senior executive suggests the preferred solution. Either such self-assessed needs, or the background of the trainer who was dispatched for the needs analysis, may determine which program is actually developed. It may seem to be in the trainers' interest to justify their existence. At times, such assessments are akin to asking a dishonest barber if one needs a haircut—a snip here or there certainly can't hurt . . . or can it? One banker complained, "Our trainers see everything as a problem in stress management, but we need to teach new skills to eliminate the stressors." Consider the following illustration:

> International Chemicals Company, a large multinational ($7 billion sales, 80,000 employees), recently decided to unify its global management to improve chronically poor management systems. The African Middle East Division, with 2,500 people ($125 million in sales and 1 percent of corporate total) decided it especially needed to coordinate its management between companies (Egypt, Ghana, Ivory Coast, Nigeria, Saudi Arabia, Sudan, Dubai) with different cultural customs, varied sophistication in managerial practices, local government pressures for increased hiring of nationals over expatriate managers, and training requests for employees. The chief executive believed that more skill training in sales and supervision was needed. Management dispatched the director of training, who surveyed and interviewed twenty-five managers about their work problems. Each tended to blame the other. Unsure of how to read the conflict definitions of the problem, the training director developed a plan which provided just what management had hypothesized was important from the start, supervisory and sales training targeted at locals. Meanwhile employees, often influential in their home nations, were displeased that they were not being sent to prestigious U.S. universities as they had hoped.

Another example is a multimillion-dollar retraining program for displaced workers recently instituted by the Winslow Machine Company. This program was hammered out with the active involvement of company officials, local union officials, and community leaders. Despite the good intentions and massive commitment of funds, this widely hailed program is now running into dangerous snags. While extensive career counseling was put into place and expert technical instruction was provided free to laid-off workers, hard-pressed local employers are reneging on their agreements to hire the new trainees. People with fresh training in welding and machining, who have virtually exhausted their unemployment compensation and their spirit, are now back out on the street. The problem which the company and its community tried to tackle requires branching out to other regions and other industries. The relocation costs and consequences, however, are threatening to all the program designers.

CONFUSING KALEIDOSCOPE OF SUPPLIERS

Just as departmental and personal bias enter into professional judgments over participation and diagnosis, bias enters into professional judgments regarding program delivery. The program developed and taught may have more to do with who the trainer is than with what the organization most needs. The ranks of professional trainers are certainly swelling as new professional specialists, disillusioned school teachers, former social workers, consultants, second-career executives, and moonlighting professors join them. The American Society for Training and Development now lists over 40,000 members and 100 chapters. *Training* magazine claims 42,000 subscribers and a readership of 150,000 monthly. The clusters of trainers include: (1) internal personnel, (2) outside commercial vendors, and (3) university programs.

Internal Trainers Looking first at internal personnel, an astounding array of trainers exists. Internal trainers may be exceptional managers-on-rotation before promotion, weak performers withdrawn from their mainstream line activities, or professional trainers. As staff specialists, trainers often acquire their own jargon and professional network independent of the firm or its industry. Line executives often bring credibility and an appreciation of the need for job applicability. On the other hand, they often suffer from such drawbacks as the biases of their former department, dated versions of the firm's mission, and inconsistent teaching performance. Professional trainers often are charismatic instructors but lack the status, business acumen, or pedagogical versatility to teach senior managers.

They often find themselves frozen out of consideration for lateral movement to other functions and are thus kept in a rut.

When outside educational experts survey corporate training activities, they are regularly struck by the overwhelming emphasis on behavioral concepts such as interpersonal behavior, team work, group dynamics, motivation, leadership, and organizational development.[17] To some extent, this skewed curriculum reflects the realistic pressures of managing in complex organization structures and varied cultures. Futhermore, the heightened sensitivity to behavioral materials reflects increased employee concern with personal fulfillment at work and the social setting of the workplace. It has also been suggested, however, that this behavioral bent of the training curriculum reflects the background and disposition of trainers and the somewhat closed circle they form with their chosen outside consultants. With slick, simplistic mnemonics, fad-ridden jargon, and catch phrases, training can represent the next most trendy area of corporate activity after advertising. A recent cover story of *Training* magazine entitled "Remembrance of Things Passé" provided its readers with a humorous but at times pointed reminder of the short half-life of the training craze in vogue over the past two decades.[18] Professional competence may also lead trainers to biased use of various pedagogical methods. Preferences for case studies, lectures, computer-aided instruction, simulations, workbooks, and so on seem to depend on who the trainer is as much as on the desired learning.

Commercial Vendors The explosion of general corporate education as well as of specific trends has been supported by the swelling number of commercial vendors. The nonprofit American Management Association's annual income from education has jumped from $11 million to $60 million in ten years. Xerox Learning Systems, one of the largest profit-making educational purveyors, claims a 32 percent growth for the past five years. Wilson Learning and the Forum Corporation claim 30 percent and 45 percent annual growth rates, respectively. The Big Eight accounting firms and consulting firms, such as Harbridge House, the Management Analysis Center, Arthur D. Little, and Temple,

Barker, and Sloane, draw increasing amounts of revenue from corporate training.[19]

While these firms each use professionally trained instructors with curriculums backed by substantial in-house research, many smaller vendors are inconsistent in the quality of their offerings. A content analysis of 1,500 of the reported programs of these vendors performed for this article revealed the following:[20]

1. 75 percent offer professional and technical job-specific training (e.g., marketing, finance);
2. 40 percent offer training in managerial social development (e.g., leadership techniques);
3. 24 percent offer training in personal social development (e.g., time management, assertiveness);
4. Only 3 percent offer courses in basic skills (e.g., remedial reading, writing);
5. Only 3 percent offer courses in personal enhancement (e.g., liberal arts, recreation).

In functional terms, most outside programs were targeted towards marketing and sales (30 percent), followed closely by human resources (25 percent), and engineering (24 percent). Finance and line management (with 2 percent and 3 percent, respectively) were given far less emphasis. Hierarchical level was also quite skewed:

1. Only 14 percent claimed to serve hourly and clerical workers;
2. 50 percent claimed to serve first-line supervisors;
3. 90 percent claimed to serve middle management;
4. 86 percent claimed to serve upper management.

One might ask whether these distributions appropriately meet the nation's priorities for retraining. Who receives the training dollars and to develop which skills remain important questions.

Colleges and Universities Offerings by institutions of higher education also vary greatly in mission and quality. The oldest of these offerings are the residence-based management education programs available largely through leading business schools. A second group consists of less well-coordinated individual courses or seminar topics that highlight specialized needs. A third cluster is the collaborative efforts of colleges and corporations that provide training programs specifically catering to various company needs.

Residence-based management education programs have grown substantially from the three that existed in 1950 (MIT, Harvard, and Pittsburgh). Roughly fifty are now available, from programs that run several weeks to those that run thirteen weeks to a year. Despite this growth, these programs have recently been challenged by several large employers, who have decided that their companies have a sufficient internal critical mass of trainees to develop their own senior managers. These employers complain about the high costs (tuitions of $15,000 and many weeks of lost productive senior executive time) and about the dangers (visibility to executive search firms or lost trade secrets through class debates). With regard to these dangers, most schools actively shield their executive students from search firms and avoid the requirement to verbalize any company-specific plans in class. However, participants make many valuable contacts through these programs, and some people certainly use their new networks to find new jobs. In this case, the employer loses and the individual gains. As to the costs, these can only be assessed relative to the benefits. Researchers Edgar Schein and Kenneth Andrews have found that these programs do provide unique benefits. Schein suggested that these longer programs provide a useful experience for midcareer unfreezing of old learned habits of business analysis.[21] Isolated from job titles, work pressures, and ringing phones, executives develop new professional networks and explore new perspectives on their activities. Kenneth Andrews' study of 10,000 executives who attended 39 programs found that the most favorable aspects of these programs were the lack of instructor condescension, a stimulating atmosphere, the immediate relevance of the course content, and the reassurance of seeing other executives with similar difficulties.[22]

Equally strong endorsements are rarely given to university-based offerings. Eager to recapture revenues lost because of a

10–15 percent erosion in undergraduate enrollments, many colleges have vigorously promoted an expanded complex of continuing education offerings. Employers fund these programs indirectly through employee tuition rebates. However, these programs are also riddled with problems: the instructors are often part-time; the curriculum may reflect the knowledge of the faculty rather than the needs of the students; and the materials are often out-of-date. As their marketing sophistication grows, some schools may be tempted to trade on their campus ambience and status rather than on their expertise. A misunderstanding both of the business world and of the needs of adult learners often leads to a technically competent but pedagogically inappropriate curriculum.

The final group of higher-education offerings, the college-corporation collaboratives, seem to be most commonly found at the community college level. These schools, often young and with a mission to serve the community, demonstrate far more flexibility in format, location, and facilities than universities do. Some large firms, such as IBM and General Motors, work with many community colleges around the country. Smaller firms have also found the local community college to be responsive. Impressive joint programs have appeared with Mercedes-Benz and Thomas Nelson Community College in Virginia and Mountain Bell and Pima Junior College in Arizona. In such efforts, the class component of training has been carefully blended with on-the-job training. Universities that have pioneered dramatic new educational ventures with industry include Drexel University in Philadelphia and the University of Minnesota's School of Management. Drexel's lists of company clients includes such firms as Scott Paper, Exxon Research, CIGNA, General Electric, Du Pont, Honeywell, and Manufacturer's Hanover Trust. The University of Minnesota has treated its twenty-two "partner" companies with a good deal of discretion, providing them with priority in course enrollment and in the recruitment of school graduates. Many established educators and community leaders greet such collaborative ventures with mixed enthusiasm, however. While they are eager for the funding and applaud the innovation, the threat of corporate clientism has cooled the gold rush temptations of some educators.

CHARTING A NEW COURSE FOR TRAINING

Companies must navigate their way around these five training problems by stepping beyond a program-to-program mentality. Instead, they must gain a comprehensive view of firm-wide human resource renewal. As noncontroversial as such a recommendation may seem, few firms have mastered their educational challenges. The prevailing practice among managers is to see training as a magical elixir to which one turns intermittently with money, time, humor, and prayers. Such management practices as goal setting, monitoring, and judgment are confined to the office with the business suit. The basic elements of a comprehensive approach to training include (1) a clear educational mission, (2) a coordinated career system of staffing and development activities, and (3) insightful learning profiles of participants in training programs.

EDUCATIONAL MISSION

Since all firms seek a well-trained and productive work force, we often mistakenly assume that firms do not differ significantly in their educational purposes. The statements of educational missions attempted by some firms reflect this deceptive quality of aphoristic thought. Nations all seek "security" and "economic health" but differ violently as to the details of achieving these universally desired goals. Companies all seek profits and survival, but they differ in their precise goals and means for achieving success. Similarly, firms differ in their intended use of education and training to help the firm succeed.

Each firm has a unique constellation of strategic, cultural, and contextual factors that lead to varied educational expectations and needs.

An example of the influence of strategic factors might be the degree of diversification. Single-product firms may rely greatly on training functional specialists, while multidivisional firms may need to train general management talent through cross-functional and cross-business knowledge. Strategic shifts, such as those that have followed in the wake of the changes in the communications marketplace or the financial service industry, have similarly introduced new training directions in an effort to fill new management and professional roles.[23]

The cultural factors might include the degree of (1) concern for employee welfare, (2) commitment to internal development, (3) dedication to community responsibility, and (4) internal political and status artifacts. These cultural factors may, for example, determine a firm's interest in developing talent versus hiring it from the outside. Similarly, the sense of responsibility for displaced workers or the preferences given certain departments or career tracks may reflect cultural imprints upon training efforts.

Contextual factors, such as sectoral changes, competitive threats, economic fluctuations, new technological advances, and work-force expectations for career growth will interact with other educational influences to determine the emphasis placed upon various training efforts.

The joint impact of these strategic, cultural, and contextual factors leads to the creation of a wide range of training activities. These activities include:

1. Teaching entry-level skills;
2. Orienting newcomers;
3. Creating advanced skills hard to locate in the external labor market;
4. Attracting and retaining talent;
5. Retraining dislocated workers;
6. Meeting equal employment opportunity goals;
7. Improving work-group effectiveness;
8. Reinforcing a company culture;
9. Changing a company culture;
10. Changing job responsibilities for given positions;
11. Providing skills to advancing managers;
12. Reinvigorating burned-out workers;
13. Improving job productivity;
14. Rewarding performance or long service;
15. Enriching the work experience of workers;
16. Assisting the exit process (preretirement counseling, outplacement).

These activities may be classified into three general groupings: (1) job/task-skill training, (2) career enhancement, or (3) organizational effectiveness. They represent different time frames for payback as well as different degrees of attention to individual versus group needs. Hence, a program can easily be a smashing success along some dimensions and a disaster along others. Executives often have conflicting implicit education missions, depending on their judgment and biased perspectives.

An explicit educational statement can increase the likelihood of shared criteria on training efforts. Such statements should specify the firm's stand on such dimensions as (1) targeted populations, (2) relative emphasis on job/task-skill improvement versus longer-run career enhancement, (3) links to other career-system variables (e.g., hiring, assignments, exiting), and (4) links to other organizational change efforts. Such statements bring clarity through specificity. Unlike the old "apple-pie" statements, they cannot be framed and forgotten. It is true that explicit statements of educational mission would have to be adapted to a changing corporate agenda; yearly revisions by senior management would ensure continuing relevance.

COORDINATING THE CAREER SYSTEM

As educational missions vary greatly across industries and by company, so too do the training responsibilities. Customarily, training responsibility is widely diffused throughout a company. Sales and marketing departments, line management, human resource development departments, employee relations departments, benefits departments, engineering departments, organizational department units, and communications departments are just a few of the locations where training activity is likely to be found. Conflicts may occur between these groups as well as between groups responsible for recruitment, succession planning, counseling, out-placement, and quality control.

When we look outside the firm, we see a complex and competitive marketplace filled with commercial training vendors as well as colleges and universities angling for a share of the corporate education dollar. For some firms, the jolts brought on by striking changes in office technologies, production processes, regulatory definitions of industries, and sectoral shifts have made the quality of corporate education a fundamental tool for enhancing performance within each department. This confusing mosaic of educational consumers and suppliers has resulted in a good deal of imagination and inventiveness as well as destructive internal competition and vulnerability to hucksterism.

At the nation's leading computer makers, for example, a great deal of the educational innovation has been driven by the priority of selling equipment and software to marginally informed customers. Sales training and customer instruction accordingly have captured the educational imagination in these firms, while other company training continues along very standard lines. Images of the barefoot children of the cobbler are brought to mind as the customers' employees are often more technologically sophisticated in the use of the supplying firm's equipment than are the employees of the supplier themselves. Managers and trainers in many large high-tech firms complain bitterly that they often first learn of training innovations within their firms through the business press. The sales trainers and customer service representatives do not have the time or the incentive to train internally. They stand to lose valuable time and status by directing themselves inward as a staff-service group instead of as a line-oriented group. Their bosses, furthermore, are uninterested in risking a loss of control by joining the internal training effort.

In small high-tech firms managers tend to raid skilled labor from competitor firms, because they feel unable to take the time and the risks of training talent that they themselves may lose to a competitor. Furthermore, these managers are fearful of internal career-development programs that further develop their subordinates, and they struggle to hoard the staff they accumulate.

In many companies, such as financial service firms, where business units are struggling to meet sudden revolutionary corporate announcements of strategic redirection, fierce turf battles have erupted into open warfare. Formerly, decentralized divisions within banks, brokerages, and insurance companies have forcefully tried to resist company efforts to share product information, distribution tips, technological training, and sales training as part of centralized company plans to create integrated financial-service managers. Divisional training units, data-processing departments, sales trainers, and corporate human resource development departments have rarely worked in a concerted fashion. The introduction of personal computers, electronic funds transfers, and the flurry of new overlapping financial products has made close coordination a necessity. Improved internal coordination of training activity also improves the efficiency of outside training purchasing. Through the new economies of scale many firms have learned that they can afford to internalize many programs that they had repeatedly purchased from the outside. They often have more clout in negotiating with the vendor over copyright issues. One large bank learned through its recent corporate centralization that it had paid repeatedly for the same presumed customization of a training package from its prominent vendor.

Some guidelines for bringing about improved coordination include, first, pooling internal training knowledge. Linking training to strategic planning, succession planning, and new technology can be done through a steering committee with representation from sales training, technical training, management development and information systems officials where the autonomy of each unit is preserved. General Electric has found this approach to be a great help in coordinating schedules, travel and accommodation logistics, curriculum design, and discussion of common teaching issues, such as the introduction of technology or the alteration of program admission guidelines. For a firm where the business is less diverse than at General Electric, a centralized education department can coordinate the different training activities and quickly apply good ideas used in one setting to different settings. Digital Equipment Corporation has actually created a separate department of educational services, which is distinct from human resources and which reports directly to the vice president of sales and service. This department is actually a profit center where Digital can sell its educational products, ranging from management-development techniques to interactive video training packages, to external and internal customers.

A second suggestion is to link training to strategic planning,

Table 11-1
Optimum Level of Involvement in Training for Each of the
Shapers of the Educational Process

	Process			
Shapers	*Diagnosis* ⟶	*Design* ⟶	*Delivery* ⟶	*Evaluation*
Individual learner	High	Low	Medium	High
Middle line manager	High	Low	High	Medium high
Top management	High	Low	Medium	Low
Training experts	High	High	Low	High
Outsiders	High	Medium	High	Low

succession planning, and new technology programs. When training is unconnected to major changes in the market, or to operating or human resources goals of the company, it can only fill a dysfunctionally reactive "fire-fighting" role. Earlier involvement of training in large-scale company change efforts will allow the training program to roll out without a problematic time lag or a too hasty design. One-third of the respondents to a survey of 150 vice presidents of human resources of prominent U.S. firms reported a good deal of coordination of training activities. The most commonly used devices for coordinating were (1) periodic task forces, (2) formal human resource management policies, and (3) common departmental membership for those involved in training. Less commonly relied upon were middle management or top management oversight committees and informal contact.

A third suggested way to improve coordination of training is to involve the corporate training center. Its executives are often considered too late in the change process, and they are sometimes resented as meddlesome bureaucrats by rival staff groups and line managers who value their own on-the-job efforts. Despite this difficult situation, they are expected to be miracle workers by senior management. Part of the problem stems from the way that they, or the bold vendors they hire, oversell their skills. A bit more modesty would help, but much of this situation results from a lack of top-level support and of a clear domain of responsibility. The firm's internal education process includes (1) problem diagnosis, (2) program design, (3) program delivery, and (4) program evaluation. Internal trainers need not be directly responsible for each stage of this process. They can contribute by developing expertise in diagnosis, design, and evaluation. Table 11-1 shows the optimum level of involvement in training for each type of worker who takes part in the educational process.

Assuming a diagnostic role will allow training experts to play more of a consulting part—particularly if they can identify which presumed training needs are not training problems at all but rather arise from other troublesome human resource policies and structures. Acting as referral agents will enhance the credibility of training executives, who will not appear to be "empire building." At the same time, it takes confidence and a healthy rapport to send problems to other units. Program design and program evaluation are time-consuming activities that require an expert skill and knowledge base, which professional trainers are likely to have.

Program delivery refers to actual instruction. Many firms, such as IBM historically and Bank of America recently, have found that except in very few cases it is advisable to use respected line managers as trainers rather than internal professionals or outside vendors. At these places, as well as at such firms as Goodyear Tire and Rubber, Procter & Gamble, and People Express, it is not uncommon for line executives to be rotated through training as part of their development. If group leadership and teaching are recognized as valued developmental experiences for rising managers, the firm will win over skeptical line workers and probably enhance the quality of the training. These line managers as trainers have a more ready appreciation of the world of the trainees. They are likely to speak the appropriate language and to be enthusiastic about the new adventure of this task.

Fourth, the training function can be better managed if clear guidelines are established for the use of outside commercial vendors and university-based programs. Table 11-2 indicates some of the strengths and weaknesses of different types of educational suppliers. The survey on which the table is based suggested that internal training staffs have an advantage when

Table 11-2

Sources of Executive Education Rated by Human Resource Vice Presidents

	Internal Trainers	*External Vendors*	*University-Based*
Received Positive Ratings	Sending signals Participant preferences Corporate culture sensitivity Relevance to firm Direct costs Limited exposure to external executive recruiters Confidential company information Length of program Flexibility in location/schedule		Sending signals Escape from work pressures Access to expertise Cross-industry perspective Informal contacts with participants Freedom from company politics Pedagogical variety Consistency of teaching quality
Received Negative Ratings	Escape from work pressures Cross-industry perspective Informal contacts with participants Access to expertise Freedom from company politics Status/credibility Fixed costs Learning climate Pedagogical variety	Sending signals Sensitivity to company culture Confidentiality of company information Coherence of curriculum	Relevance to firm Sensitivity to company culture Length of program Flexibility in location/schedule

Note: Rating based on a survey of 120 senior human resource administrators attending a three-day seminar on executive education held at the Harvard Business School in 1983. The average firm represents reported sales of $2 billion and employs 30,000 workers. The executives scored a list of twenty attributes of providers for each of the three providers: internal, vendors, and universities, along a five-point Likert-type scale ranging from extremely positive to extremely negative. The table indicates those attributes where the average score for a training provider exceeded the other two providers.

company-specific learning, flexibility, direct costs, and confidentiality are germaine. University-based programs have an advantage when access to expertise, escape from work pressures and politics, teaching quality, and cross-industry exposure are valued.[24] Commercial vendors are not favored as a category along any particular dimension. Many executives inverviewed for the survey explained that while they had had excellent experiences with commercial vendors, quality was inconsistent within the same firm and hard to predict across firms. However, it should be noted that commercial vendors do not suffer from several of the drawbacks common to university-based programs (inflexibility, program length, and relevance to the firm) or internal programs (narrow perspective, lack of access to expertise, poor learning climate, limited pedagogical variety).

This checklist of negative and positive features should help managers consider when to devote resources to internal program development and when to go outside. They might consider such points as (1) the degree of internal reuse, (2) the company-specific nature of the material, (3) confidentiality and the dangers of external exposure, (4) the value of outside perspective, (5) fixed versus variable costs, (6) teaching quality, (7) status, (8) escape from the workplace, (9) flexibility in location and schedule, and (10) the learning climate.

These survey results should also prompt some reflection on the terribly underutilized potential of the university campus. A recent Hay Associates report stated: "Our surveys show that while over 90 percent of companies have some form of tuition refund program, currently less than 5 percent of the employees use it. The numbers are going to increase, as will the contractual obligation to retrain displaced workers." Many colleges and universities are now attempting to dissolve the rigidities of campus bureaucracies to use their resources to meet special business needs. The Office of Adult Learning Services of the College Board, a nonprofit membership organization of schools and colleges, recently published a book entitled *Training by Contract: College Employer Profiles*. These degree and nondegree programs tend to offer technical and supervisory examples.[25] Several prestigious schools, such as Dartmouth and Stanford, have added short Aspen Institute-like liberal arts programs for executives as an alternative to the famous advanced management curriculums of schools such as Harvard, MIT, Columbia, Wharton, and Michigan.

A particularly exciting new alliance is demonstrated on college campuses in Massachusetts through the sponsorship of the nonprofit Bay State Skills Corporation. Private employers and schools collaborate to hold skills-training programs desired by companies on college campuses, with 50 percent funding by private employers and 50 percent funding by the state. The state has spent $8 million in the first two years of this program to train 4,000 people, 87 percent of whom have been placed.[26] Illinois, Minnesota, and Washington State have adopted this plan. The joint effort allows large and small employers, particularly in high technology and the skilled crafts, to share the burden of developing the people needed for new technical positions.

LEARNING PROFILES OF PARTICIPANTS

The training literature has suggested that the greatest and most enduring contribution of educational programs is often more closely related to the participants' prior expectations and interpretations of the meaning of the program than to either the actual program design or the delivery of the materials. The ceremonial significance, the social interaction with peers who have comparable work pressures, the chance to talk about your work with someone who is not a rival or an informed party are shown to be as valuable back on the job as the specific course content.[27] These types of learning suggest the need for an educational process that is shaped to the self-perceived needs of the learner rather than to a rigid training design devised abstractly by "experts."

Crossed Signals This internal definition of the learning process by participants is generally overlooked by program planners. We all have a need to explain the events around us. The job pressures on particular individuals, their special career requirements, their levels of education, and their life circumstances will cause different workers to expect different types of training experiences and outcomes. These expectations then color the meaning projected onto the educational event. Participants wonder: "Why me?" "Is it remedial?" "Is it a reward for good performance?" "Are they just getting me out of the way?" "Is it a sop for having been passed over for promotion?" Both employers and employees intend to signal something through their expression of interest in training, but misunderstanding of such signals is common.

Research has suggested, for example, that outside executive programs are commonly thought to signal an upcoming promotion for the participant.[28] When this promotion does not follow, morale plummets. Similarly, training research has found that without some supportive followup and a boss who buys into the training of a subordinate, the new skills will not be transferred well back to the job.

Explicit Objectives These signals can be improved by making the intentions of the company and of the worker more explicit and by making the training effort more mutual in its payoff. This can be accomplished through a career dialogue between employers and employees. This career dialogue can take the form of either formal career planning or informal discussions. Either way, four types of information must be exchanged regarding (1) the company career system, (2) the cultural context, (3) individual life-stage needs and career needs, and (4) the learning-style orientation of the individual.

First, the company career system must be profiled through the sharing of information regarding job openings; requisite skills and credentials for these openings; and possible advancement, given one's present career trajectory. This information exchange would require some pooling of data across strategic planning, succession planning, and training. A thoughtful explanation of the likely impact of mergers and divestitures can calm employee panics. The blocked career paths of ambitious executives can be candidly confronted. Preparation for new markets or new technology will also require new training. This type of information allows the company and the individual to intelligently plan educational paths in a partnership approach to career development. Secrecy and veiled intentions only lead to waste as valued employees leave and less-valued employees soak up large investments.

Second, the company career system must also be appreciated in its more informal or cultural sense. In some company cultures line executives have more credibility as instructors than do professional trainers. If training is intended to introduce wider social networks in the firm or to serve as orientation to companywide operations, why rely on happenstance and accident? Too often it is the chance encounter that provides the main value of a training program. This awareness has led many companies to change their mix of participants and speakers. Company after company has worked to use training programs to help assimilate newly acquired firms or to make senior line and staff executives more accessible to middle managers across divisions. The cultural considerations also should carry over to how much the training program is likely to be perceived as countercultural. The prior attitudes of one's boss are one of the best predictors of the effectiveness of training. If a bank intends to make its middle managers more entrepreneurial, their superiors had better be thinking along the same lines or the training will be a wasted effort. Hence, a cultural awareness will guide the participant mix, the selection of instructors, and the sequence of programs offered.

Third, the life-stage needs and career needs of workers are important in guiding the selection of courses and type of pedagogy. While some workers may be looking for more challenge and advancement, others may be fearful of great disruptions in their present situation. Within certain banks and insurance companies, for instance, some executives find the changing nature of financial services offering a fresh chance to break free of smothering bureaucracy, while others feel they are losing a frame of reference and a secure role in their local communities. Large training programs, such as executive development programs, serve as symbolic career crossroads and as marker events in many lives. Sometimes the types of competitive learning that can energize and excite one sort of worker can exacerbate burnout in another type of worker. Poor performance in a training program should not be equated with less job promise. Old contacts, interpersonal savvy, and good judgment, for example, may make older workers quite valuable for a firm. These workers tend to be anxious to maintain their reputation and sense of contribution. A threatening learning environment involving public competition and possible failure will probably diminish openness to learning. Frequently, workers frustrated by their inability to keep up with changes in their work situation may be the best judges of what training they need.[29] Unfortunately, they are generally the last to be considered in the identification of company training needs.

Finally, learning style is a useful consideration in the design of training programs, since we all tend to assimilate new information in different ways. Some of us learn best through theory or abstract conceptualization, others through observation of practical applications or through actual personal involvement. It has been suggested that we may differ by job function, age, or disposition. Programs that try to estimate these differences through discussion with the participants will be able to tailor the appropriate mix of lectures, cases, films, simulations, computer instruction, and reading.

CLOSING THOUGHTS

As an industry of packaged training material continues to grow, we should recall what Lyndall Urwick cautioned thirty years ago: "One of the greatest dangers threatening the spread of healthy management development is that people will mistake training systems and techniques for the thing itself."[30]

Whether training is compulsory or voluntary, adults need to be involved in the design of their learning. They need to know why they are being trained. How does this effort meet their personal job needs, and how does it meet company objectives? Clarified educational missions and learners' profiles are the fundamental steps firms must take to halt the great training robberies that abound through waste and poor coordination. Enlarged educational expectations only heighten these needs. Good intentions and large sums of money do not translate into good education for companies any more than they do for schools.

12
Ideological Implications of Changes in Human Resource Management

George C. Lodge

By the early 1980s there was little disagreement that U.S. corporate managers, employees, and trade unions would have to change their ways in order to compete successfully for markets in America and abroad. There was even a surprising degree of accord concerning the shape and scope of those changes. What was lacking, though, was an explicit recognition of the radical implications inherent in these changes for managers and unions. As a result, Americans are faced with the dangers of ambivalence and inadvertence: of lingering too long with outmoded forms of relationships, of moving to new ones without a full appreciation of their consequences, of failing to manage the transition efficiently and effectively.

In the face of intensifying global competition, labor and management in the 1980s were seeking to change their relationship. The United Automobile Workers (UAW) agreed to restrain demands for increases in wages and benefits at GM as it already had done at Ford and Chrysler. Of special interest was the entirely new form of "dialogue." In return for the workers' restraint, management agreed to limit its right to close plants and buy from abroad, to introduce profit sharing, and to move toward some kind of lifetime employment. Symbolically, Chrysler in May of 1980 placed Douglas Fraser, president of the United Automobile Workers, on its board of directors.[1]

This chapter is drawn from Chapters 2, 3, and 9 of the author's book, *The American Disease* (New York: Knopf, 1984).

319

Agreements similar to those reached in the auto industry in the early 1980s were also common in other industries, such as rubber and transportation, where workers demonstrated their willingness to freeze wages and sacrifice cherished work rules in return for the preservation of jobs and a voice in management. Indeed, in the new consensus, a major factor in future competitiveness was recognized to be the ability of management and labor to restrain costs through worker involvement in decisions that had previously been management's alone.

But as the auto, steel, and other industries contracted and innovated to achieve a competitive position, there remained the problem of hundreds of thousands of unemployed workers. An embarrassment for both unions and government, they constituted a mounting pressure for trade protection. If that pressure were to be resisted, many recognized, there would have to be some sort of government policy regarding retraining, relocation, and job creation.

FROM ADVERSARIALISM TO CONSENSUALISM

How long will it take to overcome the bitter legacy of adversarialism? Can the sense of participation and control become a reality? The answers to these questions depend on how well management, labor, and government understand and manage the implications of what is happening.

Phrased differently, the crucial questions seem to be: Can the union be strong if the contract becomes less important? Can the union find strength in consensualism? If we posit that the needs of workers, companies, and the country lie increasingly in the realm of consensus making, then it may prove that the unions that stick to their contractual traditions will die. It may prove that the strong union will be the one that learns best how to define a role for itself within the new consensual approach. If this supposition is true, and the preponderance of evidence suggests it is, there is no time to waste on ambivalence; the unions must face squarely the new relationships and redesign their roles accordingly.

But how can workers with pressing and legitimate short-term needs be expected to take a long-term view of the enterprise?

It will take a considerable broadening of perspective, which must emerge from a widespread sharing of information, a common understanding, and a spirit of partnership.

The role of government cannot be separated from such questions. A clear public policy for trade and investment is essential, and a major responsibility at least for funding the retraining and relocation of displaced workers must fall upon government. It may well prove necessary for the United States to have a national labor plan, whereby skill shortages and surpluses are identified, and appropriate educational efforts are made to promote the skills that are needed.

Predictably managers are anxious about the loss of authority and control that they perceive as inherent in the transition to consensualism. Even though considerable evidence suggests that the power of managers actually increases as they learn to derive authority from those whom they manage, managers who have never done it are understandably anxious. Middle managers and supervisors are especially uneasy; they are literally in the middle. Further, with the greater efficiency of participative systems, it is often feasible to operate with fewer managers, and a legitimate fear of being laid off must be added to their list of apprehensions.

In the broader context, the problem facing managers is identical to the one facing unions: If they do not understand the full implications of their pragmatic actions, they will certainly fail to anticipate the full range of consequences, and they may indeed induce some of the worst possible outcomes of the transition. How can the two converging camps grasp the full implications of their activities? The concept of ideology is most helpful. Only after managers and union leaders fully understand what old assumptions are being eroded can they see the new choices before them and act upon them.

IDEOLOGY AND ITS IMPLICATIONS

Ideology is the framework of ideas that a community uses to define values and to give them institutional vitality in the real world. The term *values* here is taken to mean timeless universal conceptions, such as survival, justice, fulfillment, and self-respect, which virtually every community anywhere has cherished. *The real world* means the factual context within which the community exists, the collection of events, performance phenomena, and scientific insights that together make up the existential reality. The phenomenon of OPEC, for example, emerged in the real world of the early 1970s; it was a blockbuster, forcing changes in and among every institution in its path—industry, unions, banks, the International Monetary Fund, governments, and more. These changes had ideological consequences; they represented a de facto ideological change. Similarly, that extraordinary combination of institutions that design and implement Japan's national strategy have forced changes upon the institutions of the United States that also have had profound ideological consequences.

Ideology is the bridge between values on the one hand and the real world on the other, but it is not a rigid bridge; ideology is not dogma. It changes inevitably as the real world changes. But inasmuch as ideology often takes on the psychological qualities of religion, it does not change easily. Many communities— the USSR for example—spend much time, money, and blood in an eventually fruitless effort to keep the old ideology in place. A successful community—one that is good at defining its priorities and designing policies to implement them—is one that can manage ideological change effectively with a minimum of waste and inefficiency.

Ideology, however, is not easily inspected or renovated. Americans have a hard time even acknowledging that they have an ideology, regarding it as some foreign conception from which their ancestors gratefully escaped. They prefer to see themselves as pragmatists, doing what needs to be done; if what they do does not work, they can undo it and try again. The fallacy of the pragmatist is that no innovation is without ideological effects; they go unmanaged if ignored.

The traditional ideology of the United States, individualism, has been taken by many to be not an ideology at all but rather revealed truth or the law of nature, if not of God. As it is impossible, unprofitable, or foolish to practice what we preach, it is at the same time difficult to preach what we practice. So

Figure 12-1
The Legitimacy Gap

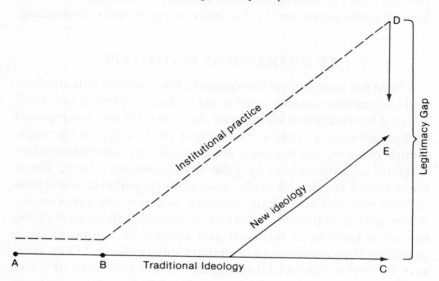

there is a legitimacy gap (see *Figure 12-1*), a separation of action from the traditional ideas through which action was justified. As the legitimacy gap widens, authority erodes, discipline declines, and responsibility decays.

Renovation requires an explicit recognition of the new ideology (line ABE in *Figure 12-1*), which conforms to and justifies effective and desirable practice, and a clear recognition of the goods and bads, or threats and opportunities, among which the new ideology requires us to choose.

For many years the traditional ideology of the United States has been eroding in response to many and varied changes in the real world. A new ideology has been replacing the old, but our affection for the old has prevented us from defining the new or making it explicit. Two sets of problems result. The first has to do with ambivalence: We are slow to move because of our uncertainty about and suspicion of the new, which we feel but do not necessarily see. The second has to do with inadvertence: We change but we are surprised, shocked, or disappointed as the ideological implications of what we are doing dawn upon us. In no field is ideological inspection more important than the management of human resources, where problems of ambivalence and inadvertence are potentially devastating.

TWP IDEOLOGICAL PROTOTYPES

There are two general ideologies in the world—individualism and communitarianism—and many variations of each (see *Table 12-1*). The traditional ideology of the United States is composed of five great ideas that were brought to America in the eighteenth century, having been set down in seventeenth-century England as natural laws by John Locke, among others. These ideas found fertile soil in the vast, underpopulated wilderness of America and served the country well for 100 years or so. Although throughout U.S. history, particularly in times of crisis, the ideas have been buffeted and eroded by communitarian practices, they continue to be remarkably resilient. "They are," says Professor Samuel Huntington, "at the very core of (our) national identity. Americans cannot abandon them without ceasing to be Americans in the most meaningful sense of the word—without, in short, becoming un-American."[2]

THE FIRST PROTOTYPE INDIVIDUALISM

A review of the Lockean five concepts provides a starting point for understanding the transformation now taking place.

Individualism The community is no more than the sum of the individuals in it. The values of self-fulfillment and self-respect are the result of an essentially lonely struggle in which the fit survive. If you do not survive, you are somehow unfit.[3] (1) Individuals are equal in the sense of deserving equal opportunity. (2) Although inherently separated, individuals are tied together by the notion of contract as buyers and sellers, employers and employees, and—in the old days—husbands and wives. Although preferably individualistic, the contract became collectivized with the rise of the trade union movement. (3) Pure individualism was augmented in the real world of American politics by interest-group pluralism. Individuals, unable to

Table 12-1
Ideology: A Bridge between Values and the Real World

Values	Traditional Ideology	New Ideology	Real World
Survival	Individualism	Communitarianism	Geography
Justice	Equality (of opportunity)	Equality (of result) or Hierarchy	Demography
Economy			Economic performance
Fulfillment	Contract	Consensus	Technology
Self-respect	Property rights	Rights and duties of membership	Scientific insights: Newton, Einstein, ecologists et al.
. . .	Competition to satisfy consumer desires	Community need	Traditional institutions vs. New: e.g., OPEC, Japan
	Limited state	Active, planning state	Traditional behavior patterns
	Scientific specialization	Holism	

Interest groups

reach the levers of power, joined into groups, and the direction of the community was determined by the pressure of conflicting groups: sheepherders, ranchers, the railroads, environmentalists, Black Power, Woman Power, and so on.

Property Rights The guarantor of individualism is property rights, *property* meaning one's body and estate. Through this notion the individual was protected against the predatory powers of the sovereign, and from it the corporation derived its right to exist. The authority of managers was rooted in the corporation's owners, that is shareholders.

Marketplace Competition The control of the uses of property is best left to proprietors—preferably small ones—competing in an open marketplace to satisfy individual consumer desires. Adam Smith's "invisible hand" will ensure that the good community results. This idea is explicit in traditional United States antitrust law and practice.

The Limited State Government is a necessary evil; the less of it the better. Its fundamental purpose is the protection of property and the enforcement of contracts. It should be kept separated, checked, and balanced. It should not plan or indeed even be coherent. It thus becomes a fragmented instrument, responsive to crises and interest groups. Says Huntington: "Because of the inherently antigovernment character of the American Creed, government that is strong is illegitimate, government that is legitimate is weak."[4]

Scientific Specialization Knowledge, the justification for education and science, is obtained through specialized analysis. If experts understand the parts, the whole will take care of itself.

Implicit in individualism is the assumption that people have the desire to acquire power—that is, to control external events, property, nature, the economy, politics, or whatever. In combination with the concept of the limited state, this drive serves to guarantee progress through competition. In one sense, this is a corruption of Darwin's theory that the inexorable processes of evolution are constantly working to improve on nature. (Darwin himself might have been made uncomfortable by this extension of his theory.) Scientific specialization has been understood to be a part of this progress.

How can we assess the impact of these five concepts on our history and our contemporary culture? Taking the last idea first, we may fairly say that specialization has produced notable achievements over the past century, including penicillin, computers, and atomic bombs. It is not so simple to label such developments as examples of "progress," however. If "progress" implies change for the general good, we must stop short of that implication. Ballistic missiles are magnificent machines, for example, but they are not necessarily more "progressive" than bows and arrows. We can also perceive other difficulties: to cite a contemporary example, individualistic competition does little to ensure healthy water supplies.

If one takes a longer view and considers the past 5,000 years of human history, one is struck by the extent to which the individualistic ideology is a fundamental aberration. Historically, the norm has been communitarian, not atomistic. Individualism constitutes a revolutionary (and in many ways noble) experiment, which achieved its most extreme manifestation in nineteenth-century America. Bringing our review up to the present, it appears that during this century, pure individualism has been deteriorating in the face of various real-world challenges—wars, depressions, new economic and political systems, the concentration and growth of both population and corporations, ecological degeneration, and a realization of scarcity.

However, the five components of the old ideology retain great resilience. They are in a sense the hymns we sing, the assumed source of legitimacy and authority for our great institutions. The difficulty is twofold: (1) The old ideas perform less and less well as a definer of values in the real world of today, and (2) many of our most important institutions—notably the large, publicly held corporation and the federal government—have either radically departed from the old ideology or are in the process of doing so in response to needs for such things as efficiency, economies of scale, productivity, and global competitiveness.

Although many small enterprises remain comfortably and

acceptably consistent with the five Lockean concepts and probably can remain so, the managers of large institutions in both
the so-called private and public sectors are forced not to practice
what they preach. If the Lockean five are what is meant by "the
free enterprise system," and if that system is regarded as the
basis of legitimacy, we can see why so much of institutional
America lacks legitimacy and thus authority. Public opinion
clings affectionately to the old ideology. Partly as a result of
public demand institutions depart from it, but no new ideology
is explicitly in place and illegitimacy abounds. It is this gap
between the behavior of institutions and the authority they claim
that causes trauma.

If we were to ask, what is the ideology that would legitimize
the actual behavior of our institutions, we would, it would seem,
come up with five counterparts to the Lockean five.

THE SECOND PROTOTYPE COMMUNITARIANISM

Briefly put, (*see Table 12-1*), these are the components of the
ideology that has achieved or is achieving dominance in the
United States: (1) communitarianism with either equality of
result *or* hierarchy, and consensus, (2) rights and duties of membership, (3) community need, (4) the active, planning state, and
(5) holism.

Although this ideology might appear new in the United States,
it is by no means new in the world. If we were to take the notion
of hierarchy instead of equality of result, this ideology resembles
the medieval and neomedieval ideologies of Europe. These were
brought to the United States in different ways at different times
with successive waves of European immigrants and, laced with
a dose of egalitarianism, were made manifest in such institutions
as the New England town meeting and the farmers' cooperative
movements of Wisconsin and Minnesota. But individualism was
always dominant. Today, however, it is the extent of the de
facto dominance of communitarianism that is significant and
that makes explicit recognition of the ideological implications
of what we are doing useful and necessary. Since communitarianism with heirarchy is and always has been the dominant
ideology of Japan, an understanding of it also helps us to perceive the nature of our competition with that country.

Communitarianism The community is more than the sum of the individuals in it; the community is organic, not atomistic. It has special and urgent needs as a community. The survival and the self-respect of the individuals in it depend on the recognition of those needs.

Individual fulfillment derives from a sense of identity, participation, and utility in a community. In the complex and highly organized America of today, few can live as Locke had in mind.

Both corporations and unions have played leading roles in the creation of the circumstances that eroded the old idea of individualism and created the new. But invariably they have been ideologically unmindful of what they have done. Therefore, they have tended to linger with the old forms and assumptions even after those have been critically altered.

A central component of the old notion of individualism is the so-called protestant ethic: hard work, thrift, delayed gratification, and obedience to authority. Business has extolled these virtues on the production side of things even as it has systematically undercut them on the marketing side. Advertising departments spend millions assuring us that the good life entails immediate gratification of our desires, gratification that we can buy now and pay for later. Leisure and luxury are touted as the hallmark of happiness.[5]

(1) Equality of result or hierarchy. There has also been a shift away from the old notion of equality. It used to be equality of opportunity, an individualistic conception under which each person of any group—blacks, whites, men, and women, for instance—had an equal place at the starting line and each was supposed to be able to go as far as he or she was able without discriminatory obstruction. Around 1970, however, this idea was radically altered. The government lawyers enforcing equal opportunity legislation argued that the starting line was bent. As a consequence, they found AT&T, for example, guilty of systemwide discrimination in view of the existence of all-female telephone operators, all-male vice presidents, and minority groups squashed at the bottom of the pay scale. The company was shocked by the finding and responded, in effect, that women like to be telephone operators, men liked to be vice presidents, and minority groups were happy for the chance to be hired at

all. The government said it was not particularly interested in what individuals might like. It wanted to see what amounted to equality of representation at all levels, with male telephone operators, female vice presidents, and minority groups up and down the pay scale in proportion to their numbers in the surrounding community.

Under pressure from government the company set targets, or quotas, and redesigned itself as a whole, as a community. Thus, AT&T adapted itself to inequalities in the surrounding environment so as to produce something like equality of result. The choices its managers faced did not include returning to the old idea; the issue was how to implement the new idea. This AT&T did with considerable skill, recruiting, training, motivating, and placing so as to make the best of it.

Ideological analysis thus helps to dramatize and clarify choices. It also is useful in clarifying obstacles. The government's action amounted to a consensus imposed on AT&T from the outside. It was clearly a threat to the contract that existed inside between the management and the union, which previously had been the device used to resolve inequities in seniority and promotion policies. The union protests, however, were overridden by government.

As managers of government and business contemplate the implementation of the idea of equality of result, a variety of issues come to mind. How does one avoid mediocrity, placing lead belts on the speedy, as it were? How does one handle the appeals of countless groups for representation? And then: Can the idea really last? Is it viable?

We are reminded that in all other communitarian societies, whether in medieval Europe or modern Japan, this slot in the ideological framework has been occupied by the notion of heirarchy. That is, individual fulfillment and self-respect result from knowing one's place in a social structure. One's place could be fixed in a variety of ways, by God, by the King, or as in modern Japan, meritocratically by a sequence of rigorous examinations, with the elite being the summa cum laudes from the University of Tokyo. The vestiges of medieval communitarianism in the United Kingdom are still plainly evident in the power of class consciousness, the working class pitted in an inexorable struggle against the owning class. The fact that the "owning class" has to a great extent dissolved into government, an anonymous stockmarket, or the banks has not yet removed the old ideological strain between hierarchy and equality.

In the 1980s "affirmative action" is under attack in the United States for several reasons. The idea of "reverse discrimination" offends white males; it is regarded by some as demeaning to those it was designed to help; and in the school system it produced what might be called the "nobody fails" syndrome, which eroded educational standards.

Ideologically, there are three possibilities in the light of these objections: (1) The United States could stay with equality of result and try to make it work. Big institutions like AT&T will have a hard time doing anything else because of their current commitments, existing law, and the expectations of their employees. Managers of such institutions may well miss the forceful hand of government. (2) The United States could return to equality of opportunity, which requires, above all, equality of education for blacks and whites. Is this to be achieved through integration, as the Supreme Court mandated in 1954, or some other way? (3) The United States could move to the idea of hierarchy—meritocracy, for example—wherein one's place is determined by knowledge and skills without regard for either form of equality. If it is hierarchy, the questions become who is at the top, who is at the bottom, and how acceptable will these designations be.

(2) Consensus. If the example of AT&T demonstrates a consensus being imposed on a contractual relationship by government from the outside, there are many examples of the same transition working from the inside as managers and unions seek ways in which to restrain wages, close plants, increase productivity, improve employee motivation, and promise fairness. The idea of consensus, as opposed to contract, was what lay behind the work of Stephen H. Fuller[6] and Irving Bluestone at GM. It depends on labor-management trust instead of arm's-length antagonism.

As Donald Ephlin, UAW leader at Ford, said of the 1982 agreement: "It was a problem-solving exercise, not negotiations in the true sense. We had problems that we wanted solved—

the loss of jobs and the lack of security that our members have. The supplementary unemployment benefit plan had gone broke; payments had stopped." On the company side, Peter Pestillo, Ford's vice president of labor relations, was equally revealing: "We make a great effort in this agreement to work toward greater participation by our work force in the business process. I think that's the wave of the future. We use a word deep in the agreement that's simply called 'governance.' "[7] It seems doubtful that Ford and the UAW could have reached their agreement if the company's employee-involvement program—involving workers directly in management decisions at all sixty-five Ford assembly plants—had not been in place.

Pestillo's use of the word *governance* is significant, because it clarifies the debate about that subject. In the past, worker representation in corporate decision making was considered an aspect of constituent representation, and as such had been denigrated, since it was deemed impractical to involve all constituencies.[8] But today, worker involvement in governance is not occurring either for ideological or legal reasons; it is occurring for reasons of efficiency and effectiveness, fueled by real-world events. Managing the effects of the transition, however, requires recognition of its ideological consequences and implications.

Although some would argue vigorously to the contrary, consensual systems are not all good. There is nothing utopian about communitarianism, as even the briefest review of history surely reminds us. As contemporary forces move us toward consensus, it is worth remembering that the idea of contract was invented to protect the individual against the oppressive hierarchy and imposed consensus of the Middle Ages. Group-think jeopardizes many precious attributes of individualism. But if the trade union continues to derive its purpose and legitimacy from an increasingly irrelevant adversarial notion of contract, the labor movement will be in deep trouble. If it fails to adapt, it will certainly perish, and the individual will in no way be protected against economic tyranny.

In order for labor to adapt, it must appreciate fully its new functions in a consensual setup. Pragmatically speaking, unions are doing exactly that, but pragmatic innovation without ideological renovation is insufficient. In the steel industry cooperation—consensus—at the top of the industry between companies and the United Steelworkers of America has been evolving for more than a decade. But this evolution has taken place in a vacuum; neither companies nor union perceived the ideological implications of what they were doing. The result has been estrangement within the union, between the shop steward on the plant floor, who continues to embrace the old adversarial idea, and the union leadership, which has moved to a new concept. If consensualism is to work, it must be introduced simultaneously from the top down and from the bottom up. The industry is now belatedly introducing worker participation at the bottom, but the legacy of adversarialism dies hard.

Rights and Duties of Membership For some years in America a set of rights has been superseding property rights in political and social importance. These are rights to survival, to income, pensions, health, and other entitlements associated with membership in the American community or in some component of that community, such as a corporation. They are "the safety net" which President Reagan promised to maintain. These rights derive not from any individualistic action or need; they do not emanate from a contract. They are rather communitarian rights that public opinion holds to be consistent with a good community. This is a revolutionary departure from the old conception under which only the fit survived.

The escalating rights of members in society have strained the ability of government to raise the taxes necessary in order to pay the bill. All levels of government have placed a firm budgetary cap on rights, actually reducing some. At the same time—inevitably—came the realization that if the community ensures rights it must require duties. The question is: Who decides a person's duty? In Japan the community imposes a sense of duty—it always has. But in the United States liberals and conservatives alike were inclined to leave the question of duty to the individual—to upbringing, religion, and conscience. The realities of communitarianism, however, are forcing government to define the duty of those who do not seem to be doing it for themselves. It is called "workfare." If everyone has a right to a job, as the Humphrey-Hawkins Act suggests, does not everyone who is able-bodied have a duty to work? If so, how does a nation implement this idea? There would seem to be three ways of coping with the idle: government can pay them, government can employ them, or government can coerce or subsidize business to employ them. Europe and the United States have tended to prefer the first two, Japan the third. The United States, however, appears to be moving toward the third. If so, the implications for the role of government and its relationship to business are important to consider.

If the duties of the poor and the weak are to be made more explicit, does it not follow that those of the rich and powerful must also be clear? As the Regan budget cuts made their way through Congress in the summer of 1981, David Stockman, director of the Office of Management and Budget, was shocked at the failure of government to require sacrifice from the well-organized and powerful economic interest groups. He felt that the moral premise of austerity had been eroded.[9]

Not only have membership rights become more important to many than property rights, but the utility of property as a legitimizing idea has eroded. For example, it is quite obvious that our large public corporations are in fact not private property at all. The shareholders of General Motors do not and cannot control, direct, or in any real sense be responsible for "their" company. Furthermore, the vast majority of them have not the slightest desire for such responsibility. They are investors pure and simple, and if they do not get a good return on their investment, they will put their money elsewhere.

Attempts at shareholder democracy represent heroic but naively conservative strategies to force shareholders to behave like owners and thus to legitimize corporations as property. But such action is fraught with practical difficulties. It is a peculiar irony that James Roche, as GM chairman, in the early 1970s branded such agitation as radical, as the machinations of "an adversary culture . . . antagonistic to our American ideas of private property and individual responsibility." In truth, of course, GM was the radical; Ralph Nader and others were acting as conservatives, trying to bring the corporation back into ideological line.

If GM and the hundreds of other large corporations like it are not property, then what are they? They are collections of people, machinery, and financial and material resources, floating in philosophic limbo, dangerously vulnerable to the charge of illegitimacy and to the charge that they are not amenable to community control. Consider how the management of this non-proprietary institution is selected. The myth is that the stock-holders select the board of directors, which in turn selects the management. This is not often true, however. Management selects the board, and the board, generally speaking, blesses management.

Managers thus get to be managers according to some mystical, hierarchical process of questionable legitimacy. Under such cir-cumstances it is not surprising that "management's rights" are fragile and its authority waning. Alfred Sloan warned us of this trend in 1927:

> There is a point beyond which diffusion of stock ownership must enfeeble the corporation by depriving it of virile interest in management upon the part of some one man or group of men to whom its success is a matter of personal and vital interest. And, conversely, at the same point the public interest becomes involved when the public can no longer locate some tangible personality within the ownership which it may hold responsible for the corporation's conduct.[10]

We have avoided this profound problem because of the un-questioned effectiveness of the corporate form per se. In the past, when economic growth and progress were synonymous, we preferred that managers be as free as possible from stock-holder interference in the name of efficiency. But today the definition of efficiency, the criteria for, and the limitations of, growth, and the general context of the corporation are all much less sure. So the myth of corporate property is becoming vul-nerable.

Implicit in quality-of-work-life (QWL) programs is the idea of duty. Both managers and workers limit their rights, conscious of their interdependency and the interests of the whole firm. The Ford-UAW agreement, for example, says that nonunion salaried employees must accept the same hardships as union workers in an equality-of-sacrifice provision. Local union officials may file a grievance if they think that Ford is keeping too many managers on the rolls while union members are being laid off.[11]

Important questions of corporate governance arise: How are workers to be represented in decision making at various levels of the corporation? Do they want to be? This, after all, takes time and effort. Where does the company turn if there is no organized representation of workers, as is the case in most U.S. companies? (Phrased differently, could the auto industry, for example, have made the progress it has without a union to reflect worker interests adequately in corporate decision making, and to make decisions acceptable to workers?) May not AT&T want Communications Workers of America (CWA) President Glen Watts on its board, that is, his own preferences notwithstanding? If so, can Watts responsibly say no?

The CWA believes that far from being superfluous, a union is as essential in a consensual environment as it is in a contractual one. Its leaders cite two reasons: First, the union forces management to take the new programs seriously. As one GM manager put it, "When you ask a bear to dance, you can't stop just when *you* get tired." Second, the rights of workers—including both those of the contract and those that evolve through QWL programs and the like—are protected.[12]

In Japan, where consensualism has resulted in enormous efficiency, workers at Toyo Kogyo used very similar terms to explain why they need a union: "The union is essential to protect the workers from capricious decisions by management." "There are times when management tries to force higher output rates even when they haven't made their investment contribution." "They sometimes expect workers to do it all." "The union must constantly remind management that the worker deserves his share of economic gains that are reaped by the successful Japanese auto firm."[13]

Community Need The needs of the community for clean air and water, safety, energy, jobs, competitive exports, and the like are becoming increasingly distinct from, and more important than, what individual consumers may desire. As a consequence, the means of determining community need requires greater attention, especially when it is impossible for the community to meet all its needs at once.

It was to the notion of community need that ITT appealed in 1971 when it sought to prevent the Justice Department from divesting it of Hartford Fire Insurance. The company lawyers said, in effect: The public interest requires ITT to be big and strong at home so that it can withstand the blows of Allende in Chile, Castro in Cuba, and the Japanese in general. Before you apply the antitrust laws to us, the Secretary of the Treasury, the Secretary of Commerce, and the Council of Economic Advisers should meet to decide what, in the light of our balance-of-payments problems and domestic economic difficulties, the national interest is.[14]

Although the company's motivation was eminently pragmatic, the effects of its action cannot be fully seen or managed unless the ideological implications are spelled out. The suggestion was that ITT was a partner with the government—indeed with the Cabinet—in defining and fulfilling the community needs of the United States. There might be some doubt about who was the senior partner, but partnership it was. This concept is radically different from the traditional idea underlying the antitrust laws—namely, that the public interest emerges *naturally* from free and vigorous competition among numerous aggressive, individualistic, and preferably small companies attempting to satisfy consumer desires.

In the face of serious pressures from Japanese and European business organizations, which emanate from ideological settings quite different from our own, there will be more and more reason to set aside the old idea of domestic competition in order to organize U.S. business effectively to meet world competition.[15] Managers will probably welcome if not urge such a step; they may, however, be less willing to accept the necessary concomitant: if, in the name of efficiency, of economies of scale, and of the demands of world markets, we allow restraints on the free play of domestic market forces, then other forces will have to be used to define and preserve the public interest. These other forces will amount to clearer control by the political order, in one form or another.

At the same time, the old idea of interest-group pluralism is becoming increasingly suspect as a procedure for defining the goals and priorities of the community. It is time-consuming, wasteful, and occasionally corrupt as the rich and powerful tend to exert their influence, often at the expense of the needs of the poor and the weak or of the community as a whole. As a consequence, ways are sought to insulate government decision-making processes from the pulling and hauling of interest groups.

Active, Planning State The role of the state is changing radically. For better or worse, it has become the arbiter of community needs. Inevitably, it will take on unprecedented tasks of coordination, priority setting, and planning in the largest sense. It will need to become far more efficient and authoritative, capable of making the difficult and subtle trade-offs that now confront us, for example, between environmental purity, energy supply, economic stability and growth, rights of membership, and global competition.

Ironically, President Reagan's breathtaking 1981 economic program to cut taxes, increase defense spending, balance the federal budget, increase productivity, cut inflation, and attain full employment may well turn out to mark the beginning of an explicit recognition that the U.S. economy requires government planning, if not a planned economy. Assessing the error of his ways in 1981, David Stockman said:

> The reason we did it wrong—not wrong, but less than optimum—was that we said, hey, we have to get a program out fast. . . . We didn't add up all the numbers. We didn't make all the thorough, comprehensive calculations about where we really needed to come out and how much to put on the plate the first time, and so forth. In other words, we ended up with a list that I'd been carrying of things to be done, rather than starting the other way and asking, what is the overall fiscal policy required to reach the target?[16]

Our government leaders from time to time have found it necessary to plan. But invariably they have cloaked their departures from the limited state in the language of the old hymns, attempting to make their interventions appear pragmatic, ignoring the ideological implications. This delays the time when we will recognize the planning functions of the state for what they are and must be.

If the role of government were more precisely and consciously defined, the government could be smaller. To a great extent, the plethora of bureaucracies today is the result of a lack of focus and comprehension, an ironic bit of fallout from the old notion of the limited state. With more consciousness we could also consider more fruitfully which issues are best left to local or regional planning and which, in fact, transcend the nation-state and require a more global approach.

Presidents Nixon, Ford, Carter, and Reagan have realized this. All have tried to make the executive branch of government more coherent. President Reagan has moved most radically by giving unprecedented centralized power to the Office of Management and Budget. All have tried to close the separation between the executive branch and the Congress, an obvious necessity for the development of a consensus upon which any form of planning depends.

Great corporations recognize both the urgency of obtaining a reliable definition of community need—what's safe, what's clean, and so on—and also that government sooner or later will be the definer of those needs. We are witnessing increased cooperation between big business and big government for this purpose. The forms of cooperation need careful attention. Industry often has the information and analytical skills—the competence—that government needs in order to make an intelligent definition of community need. It lacks the authority, however. Government has the authority but is short on competence. The procedures for combining private competence with public authority must be legitimate as well as efficient. The ideological implications of any particular procedure, therefore, need to be carefully considered and managed. One can imagine the Lockean concern and anxiety—indeed the cries of fascism—as more and more decisions are made cooperatively by big business and big government.

If the American economy is being beaten by foreign government-business-labor systems that are more effective than our own, as Ford's Philip Caldwell and others have said, it seems that we must either raise tariff walls to protect ourselves from this alien competition, or we must assemble our own tripartite apparatus in order to compete successfully. Since tariff protection cannot be effectively maintained in an increasingly interdependent world, our only choice is a tripartite system assembled in the name of community need. The labor movement has generally favored this since 1980; business and government have been somewhat more ambivalent. A great deal of this ambivalence derives from traditional ideological assumptions about the roles and relationships of government and business; it is these assumptions that need inspection.

In 1979 a so-called national accord was established under the leadership of former Secretary of Labor John T. Dunlop to provide a mechanism for cooperation on important national issues among government, business, and labor. Although the Dunlop group had some fruitful discussions and agreed generally on an incomes policy, there was insufficient time to develop the trust and confidence necessary for such cooperation to be effective. In the interim President Reagan took office and let it be known that he felt that no such cooperation was necessary and that free-market forces would produce economic growth and restore employment. As a result, Dunlop took his consensual efforts outside of government, forming an unofficial labor-management group in March 1981. Lane Kirkland, president of the AFL-CIO, headed the labor representatives in the group, and Clifton C. Garvin, Jr., chairman of Exxon, led the management representatives. Focused mainly on national economic policy, the group's statement of purpose read: "The national interest requires a new spirit of mutual trust and cooperation, even though management and organized labor are, and will remain, adversaries on many issues."[17] The situation was less than ideal. There was obviously a serious question as to whether labor and management without the participation of government, could effect meaningful change. There were, furthermore, legal issues involved.

Unlike labor laws in European countries, American labor law has generally evolved after, rather than before, managers and unions have experimented with new forms. It has come after the fact, serving to recognize and perhaps "neaten up" an established situation. Prior to the 1930s the law generally sustained the traditional ideology: The fundamental task of government was to preserve property rights and to protect the sanctity of the contract. Union organization, conflict with management, the Depression, and the New Deal combined to inspire the Wagner Act of 1935. Based on an adversary model of labor relations, it was designed to foster industrial peace by strengthening collective bargaining and assuring the rights of union. It strengthened unions and helped prevent employer interference in their activities. The underlying assumption, of course, was that employers and employees were inherently separate, with different purposes and objectives and that their relationship was best defined as one of controlled conflict. The Taft-Hartley Act of 1947 and the Landrum Griffin Act of 1959, while they sought to make the conflict fairer and more democratic on the union side, did not alter this basic model.

Today's participative innovations reflect a fundamentally different model. Whereas the old structure tended to assume distrust, antagonism, divergent goals, strict controls, limited responsibility, and limited authority, the new one rests on the opposite premises.[18] The law, however, has not evolved correspondingly. As labor lawyer Thomas Schneider has pointed out: "The purpose of the law is to maintain a strict dichotomy between labor and management . . . to force employers to refrain from any action which will place them on both sides of the bargaining table . . . an employer must leave a union . . . scrupulously alone." Also, it strictly forbids an employer from interfering in any way with the formulation or administration of any labor organization.[19] Although Schneider concludes that legislative changes at this point are unwise, his observations highlight the degree to which current trends diverge from traditional assumptions—and from the existing legal structure— regarding roles and relationships of management and labor.

If we assume that these trends will continue, and are indeed vital for efficiency and competitiveness, what are the choices? First, both management and unions could stick with the old conception of their roles and with the adversarial contract. Management could continue to view its basic task as the maximization of financial returns, and the union could retain the notion that its job is to secure more for the workers. The result is predictable: Labor costs rise faster than productivity, causing inflation and a continued erosion of competitiveness; strikes proliferate; the economy suffers. Market share is eroded. Industry disintegrates or diversifies. Jobs are lost. Union membership declines. Both sides are weakened. The industrial face of the country changes, not by choice but by accident.

A second and preferable alternative is to encourage and strengthen the innovations that have begun and to extend and intensify them. This requires a fundamental change on all sides, a recognition of the radicality of what is happening, and a redefinition of the roles and missions of both management and unions. It is unwise to minimize the implications. They proceed, as I have suggested, from the very top to the bottom of corporations, and they extend to the role of government and the relationships of government, business, and labor. Any attempt to introduce changes unmindful of the full extent of their effects will be frustrated by predictable obstructions, emanating from the old assumptions.

Holism (Interdependence) Finally, and perhaps most fundamentally, the old idea of scientific specialization has given way to a new consciousness of the interrelatedness of all things. Spaceship earth, the limits of growth, the fragility of our life-supporting biosphere have dramatized the ecological and philosophical truth that everything is related to everything else.

During the 1970s the U.S. governmental regulatory response to this new realization was characterized by incoherence and by an ecological bias rather than a holistic balance. In the 1980s government regulation appears to be moving toward more coherence and holism; there is a recognition that jobs, tax revenue, and the trade balance are as much a part of the environment as are air, water, and safety. But there are still serious intellectual as well as political problems in making the trade-offs.

Do we scan the environment in a specialized way, as has been the scientific tradition, or do we seek to grasp wholes, looking for the systemic relations that are there? If we choose holism, we are departing radically from the rational tradition, which has not only informed scientific endeavor but has legitimized our educational establishment. We will, therefore, need quite new scientific, technological, and educational procedures. These, in turn, will undoubtedly cause changes in the political institutions that allocate resources for research and education. Until rational approaches to holistic thought can be created, we will be confronted with nonrational beliefs, mysticism, and a new religiosity. This is not to suggest the superiority of the rational over the nonrational, but rather it is to point out that ideological analysis leads us to a discernment of the inevitable. Nor is it to suggest that specialists will not be necessary, but rather that they will need to be managed by those with a holistic consciousness.

THE BRITISH DISEASE

The frustration of transition, especially in the area of human resources, could lead the United States in a direction that it has thus far avoided, namely, into the rigidities of class conflict. American labor has never been a class movement like its European counterpart. American labor leaders have never regarded themselves as leaders of the working class, pitted against the owning class. They have rather taken the view that through adversarial bargaining, essentially economic in nature, they can gain political and social justice for their followers. But if in the face of a stagnant economy and competitive losses they fail in this approach and find themselves increasingly unsuccessful in moving to a more promising and profitable conception of their work, they may well be forced into the sort of political and social action embodied in the notion of class conflict.

The futility and damage of such a course was revealed to me during the summer of 1975, when I studied labor relations at the Cowley works of British Leyland, just outside Oxford, England.

Nowhere have the costs of ideological ambivalence been higher than in the United Kingdom. The British suffer from an even more acute and complex form of ideological schizophrenia than Americans: Their disease embraces *three* conflicting ideologies: two traditional ones, and a new one that is desperately trying to be born. First, there is traditional communitarianism, with roots deep in Britain's history. In this tradition the observer detects notions of hierarchy: class, status, feudal rights and obligations, deference and noblesse oblige, kings, queens, lords, and commons. Here, too, is the origin of the idea of government that, under God, plans for the good of the kingdom. (It is also the wellspring of the old idea of the university as an institution that teaches gentlemen about the world, and all that therein lies, while steadfastly avoiding the earthy practicalities of specialization.)

In the Glorious Revolution of 1689, this ideology came under attack from Lockeanism, and although it was severely damaged by revolutionary individualism, it was not entirely expunged. The notion of equality gradually displaced hierarchy, but it never did so entirely. A curious dialectic resulted: If there are classes and if there is to be equality, there must also be a class struggle through which the working class seeks its place alongside the owning class. The modern history of Britain can be seen as a struggle between these two sets of ghosts, a painful and costly battle to evolve a third ideology—a new communitarianism—that meets the exigencies of the real world.

In the summer of 1975 the Labor Government had just acquired the shares of British Leyland. The company was broke; the banks could no longer meet its payroll. Anthony Wedgewood Benn, then Minister of Labor, had been forced to act quickly. Without even the pretense of a coherent notion about how best to allocate Britain's dwindling resources, he made a crisis-driven judgment that Britain needed an auto industry. At the very least, close to a million jobs were at stake. An angry debate ensued in Parliament, with the Conservatives expressing strong doubts about the ability of the company to increase its productivity sufficiently to meet the demands of competition. They were concerned about the deplorable labor relations, singling out Cowley, where stoppages, slowdowns, absenteeism, and shoddy work had virtually crippled production.

Benn had the votes necessary for the takeover, but he sought to mute his opposition by requiring British Leyland to introduce "industrial democracy" as a way of achieving efficiency and lowering labor costs. The debate did not make the definition of industrial democracy clear, but Lord Ryder, who presided over the government's National Enterprise Board, which held

BL's shares, said that it meant worker participation in management and that it was a serious matter: "Any manager will be sacked who does not introduce it enthusiastically."

I went to the Cowley works, where some 5,000 laborers were at work making cars. It was clear that work was proceeding relatively slowly. The Transport and General Workers Union (T and G) at the plant had been troubled for many years by a Trotskyite leadership. Conversations with both sides were illuminating.

The senior shop steward—an elderly man named Reg Parsons—was still a committed revolutionary, although an ex-Trot by that time. "The party takes too much of my time," he explained, "but I'm still a believer." I asked him what Trotskyism meant, and he explained that it involved workers' ownership of the means of production, carefully distinguishing it from the more statist brands of Communism.

"It sounds something like 'industrial democracy,'" I said, recalling what I had heard in Parliament.

"Well, you must understand basically I am a leader of the working class, inevitably pitted against the capital-owning bastards."

When I asked him who they were, he pointed to the office where the two young men sat who were trying to manage the Cowley works.

"But," I asked, "who owns British Leyland?"

"The government," he said.

"And who is the government?"

"The Labor Party."

"And what's the most important component of the Labor Party?"

"The Trade Union Congress."

"And what's the biggest union in the TUC?"

"The T and G," he replied.

"But that's your union," I said. "Surely you are nearer the ownership of British Leyland than those fellows up there trying to run this place."

"Look," he said, "I don't know what you're driving at. I'm a leader of the working class inevitably pitted against the capital-owning bastards—have been all my life."

Parsons had only a few years to go before retirement and was understandably reluctant to change his life's mission at that late date, whatever the reality. But he was not alone in conjuring up old ghosts to justify his actions. The managers of the Cowley works shared many of his inclinations. When I asked them what the trouble was with the plant, they said: "These fellows have had too much carrot; they need some stick."

"Who is going to wield the stick?" I asked.

"We are, of course. That's our job."

"Where are you going to get the muscle?" I continued. "Where does your authority come from?"

"The prerogatives of management. The right to manage comes from property rights. Everyone knows that."

"But who owns British Leyland?" I asked.

"Well, now that you mention it, it's the government."

"And what's the government?"

"The Labor Party."

"And the biggest component of the Labor Party?"

"The TUC."

"And the biggest union in the TUC?"

"The Transport and General Workers." They paused. "You mean it's that no good Trot down there?"

Symbolism has an important role in reinforcing structures, both outmoded and contemporary. Among the many symbols of the old ways at Cowley were the several varieties of eating places. The workers' canteen had long, bare tables, sporting only a pair of salt and pepper shakers for every twenty workers. One level up, supervisors enjoyed smaller square tables, on which were plastic water jugs. At the top, senior supervisors had the benefits of waitress service and carpeted floors beneath their mahogany tables. One incident seems particularly telling: Early one morning, as I talked with Parsons in a dirty little office below ground level, we looked up and observed through the high window a shiny black car, driven by a chauffeur, pulling up before the main entrance. Out stepped the plant manager. "There goes the bastard now," said Parsons. In truth, the manager was a perfectly decent young man, paid only modestly by American standards, whose perquisites included a company car. The psychological costs of this perquisite in that context were extreme: It would have been far less expensive for the company to have doubled his pay and encouraged him to ride a bicycle to work.

At the end of the summer, in gratitude for the company's hospitality, I wrote a summary letter—unsolicited—to headquarters. I reprint it here because I think its suggestions pertain to many industrial settings today:

> The old basis of management authority has eroded. Lord Nuffield [the founder of Morris Motors, the Cowley assembly plant] is dead; the old conception of managerial rights deriving from property rights is in the grave with him.
>
> The "Government," for all intents and purposes owns BL, but "Government" is an obscure and fragmented entity which has neither the will nor the capability to impart adequate authority to management.
>
> Management must have authority in order to exert the discipline required to make the organization function with justice and efficiency.
>
> There is only one source—as far as I can see—from which realistically this authority can come at the present moment: from the workers via their shop stewards.
>
> That is where real power lies and it must be recognized. The national trade union organizations are of relatively little use in providing a basis of authority at the moment, because they are abstracted and detached from the workers.
>
> Therefore, the Cowley managers have but one choice: to encourage and to enable shop stewards at Cowley to understand and to use the power which is theirs; to make clear to them that in a real sense the authority of management must spring from their decisions; and to help them make their decisions wisely.
>
> If this reasoning is correct, the workers have the right and the power not only to provide management with its authority but also to decide who management is. I would make this clear to the shop stewards and provoke a discussion of what the characteristics of good and acceptable management are at Cowley, what competence is desirable, etc. I would ask, as it were, for a vote of confidence from the shop stewards.
>
> Happily, it seems to me, many of the shop stewards whom I met seem responsible men who would respond well, if somewhat skeptically at first, to such an approach.
>
> I recognize that this is a radical way to define what "industrial democracy" must mean. But management derives its authority

from all those whom it manages; while at first blush this advice might appear shocking to the Cowley managers, on second thought it should appear as merely realistic.

The shock effect would be useful, it seems to me, in gaining shop stewards' cooperation, trust and confidence. If and when management say, "I am working for you—if you will help me," you will have the beginning of a new relationship.

I did not receive a reply to my letter. I did, however, get a Christmas card from the general secretary of the Labor Party that year. The inscription read: "Unity within, the enemy is without."

It appears that changes are occurring at BL, but they are slow and hard. In July 1982 the *Financial Times* reported that all Cowley employees would henceforth eat in the same dining area. "The canteen will be carpeted, however," the paper reported. " 'Some of our executives just cannot get away from the idea they should always have a carpet under their feet,' said one man from the shop floor."[20]

13
The HRM Futures Colloquium:
The Managerial Perspective

Paul R. Lawrence

From May 9 through May 11, 1984, a group of thirty-five senior executives and Harvard Business School faculty (see Appendix) convened to consider the trends and prospects for human resource management in American industry. This conference was the culmination of eighteen months of preparation on the part of the faculty group. The papers that are now chapters in this book had all been drafted. The company invitation list had been worked and reworked to meet our criteria of involving companies and individuals with the richest experience with innovative HRM practices. Site visits had been made to a number of the selected firms to arrange for their involvement and to learn more about their HRM practices. Executive summaries of the papers by the faculty and descriptions of innovative HRM practices written by the companies had been circulated. Faculty discussions had developed an agenda and a sequence of events for the conference. In spite of all this advance activity, the participants came to the meeting with considerable uncertainty about what would actually happen. And well we might have been uncertain because what transpired did, in many respects, come as a surprise to all of us, executives and faculty alike.

Our biggest surprise was the strength of the agreement among the executive participants about the issues raised by the conference. To judge the significance of this agreement, one must be aware of the characteristics of the companies involved. If we had set out to select firms only for their diversity, it would have

349

been difficult to surpass this group of twelve. Consider the contrast in age and size between People Express on the one hand, and General Motors and AT&T Communications on the other; or the shift from the high technology of Hewlett-Packard and Honeywell to the presumed low technology of Schneider National (trucking); or the preponderance of a blue-collar unionized work force at Goodyear and Cummins to the non-unionized, white-collar and professional work force at Bank of America; or the tight business focus of AT&T Communications to the industry diversification of Harman; or the contrast of Bethlehem Steel as the prototype of smokestack America to Hewlett-Packard as the new industrial wave.

A less apparent but important difference was between the firms with long experience using high-commitment HRM systems, such as Cummins and especially Procter & Gamble, and such comparative newcomers to these methods as Bethlehem and Bank of America. Four of the firms held in common the experience of moving away from a highly regulated environment, while others were experiencing severe new forms of foreign competition. It is in the context of these extreme differences that we were so surprised by the fact that these executives found themselves in agreement on point after point. It seems that the one thing that all these firms had in common was their definition of what it meant to be on the leading edge in HRM practices.

This strong convergence of views appeared without any pressure for consensus. In fact, as moderators of the discussions, the faculty had clear instructions to disclaim any interest in, or need for, finding agreement; we even searched for the spark of contrary views. The agreement among company executives arose from the fact that their experiences had been remarkably similar. They essentially agreed on the nature and magnitude of current HRM change, on its driving forces and scope, on the sources of resistance to and facilitation of the change, on the key levers of change, on the timing of the change, and so on. The full significance of this agreement did not dawn on me until I listened to the tape recordings of both the general and small-group sessions in preparing this summary of the conference. Since reporting on agreements is easier than on disagreements, I did not entirely trust my observations. So this chapter has been circulated to all participants with an invitation to take exception to any point, large or small, and especially to register "minority views." All such rejoinders have now been incorporated, so the strength of the agreement can be judged by the reader.

Clearly, at the level of detail of specific HRM policies, these companies do many different things. One example is in their compensation practices. But, even here, they agreed on the need for tailoring compensation policies to specific business and local conditions within an overarching framework of basic corporate principles and values. All these companies did, by design, share a strong interest in pursuing innovative HRM practices. What the conference served to reveal was the underlying similarity of their HRM experiences. It is because of this agreement that it is especially important to report these experiences carefully to a wider audience.

This summary of the conference will roughly follow the sequence of the meeting itself as it moved through three cycles of inquiry. Each of these three cycles consisted of an initial general session. Three or four faculty members gave brief presentations on the key questions arising from their current HRM research. After an hour of presentations the participants broke into four smaller groups to discuss, for two hours, their own experiences as these pertained to the general questions. Each cycle closed with another general session, in which the companies' views were summarized and further explored.

The first cycle focused on the broad question of whether or not a basically new HRM system was emerging on the American scene.[1] The second cycle focused on two aspects of the emerging HRM practice that the faculty believed were problematic and somewhat neglected—the technological and the ideological.[2] The third cycle focused on the change process itself, its facilitators and inhibitors.[3]

CYCLE ONE

The faculty's question about the nature and scope of current HRM change was by no means rhetorical. We, of course, believed that truly significant changes were underway. But we were also aware that we could be mistaken, perhaps guilty of wishful thinking, and that earlier predictions of such changes had not materialized. We, at the very least, expected some differences of opinion on the subject and some major qualifiers to any predictions. The question was posed to the executives with some attention to detailing its various aspects and to putting it into historical perspective. In summary, we asked: Is the current wave of interest in high-commitment HRM systems a passing fad, or is it fundamental and durable? If the latter, why? For whom is it relevant? What is the characteristic nature of the change? Finally, Is it a radical change with important ramifications, or not?

The answer from the managers to our general question was a clear and unambiguous yes. They did see a major, nonreversible change underway. This was true even though only a modest number of American firms had acquired extensive experience with the newer ways of handling the employment relationship. The reason for their confidence in their conclusion was that they had *personally* seen clear evidence that organizations using the newer HRM practices were significantly more effective than traditional ones and that people who worked in the newer settings did not want to return to the traditional ones. The results were better for the firm and better for the individual. Once this fact becomes clearly established, as they believed it now has been, there can be no turning back. The forces of competition alone will drive the process forward. In fact, as the conference was closing, the question was posed in a more extreme form: Is it an issue of adapt or perish? They responded that for any organization facing significant environmental change and strong competition, the answer was that it must change or perish. Firms experiencing the traditional adversarial split between labor and management would not survive. One person added, "And for those firms not now facing rapid change and strong competition, just wait a little while."

The clearest evidence of the results of HRM change came, quite naturally, from Procter & Gamble, the firm with an extensive experience in using the newer methods. P&G executives cited the fact that their ten or so plants using the new ways have consistently outperformed their more traditionally managed plants with similar products and technology by a margin of 30–40 percent in overall product costs year after year for the past ten years. They reported that, once acclimated to the new methods, managers and nonmanagers alike reported that they would never be content to return to the old way of working. Other companies with somewhat less experience reported similar results. All the executives had personally experienced enough of such results to have a sense of conviction about their affirmative answers to the faculty question. They believe that such positive results are now appearing in enough industries to make further spread of these methods relatively inevitable. Once methods of such significant superiority are discovered and tested, they asked, what force could stop their spread?

Looking back, the executive participants saw three forces that have fostered and even driven HRM change so far: changing values, intensified competition, and advanced information technology. All three forces may have been necessary to bring about change. The companies with the longest history in these approaches cited changing values as the reason for early experimentation in their firms. They spoke of management's desire to search for a better way of working with people, which would be less wasteful and conflictful. These early experiments were sponsored by one or more top-level leaders who sought better ways to manage as an expression of their own values. This was particularly true at Hewlett-Packard, Procter & Gamble, Harman, and Cummins, and later at People Express and Schneider.

More recently, this first factor has been joined and reinforced by the pressures of heightened competition, which came for the product-oriented companies like GM, Bethlehem, Goodyear, and Cummins from foreign competition; and for the service firms like AT&T, Bank of America, Schneider, and People Express in the wake of deregulation. Regardless of its source, intensified competition has propelled these companies toward the new HRM system.

Finally, all the executives saw the availabilty of advanced information technology as an important enabling factor. The new technology has made possible a more complete business information base for all employees in the organization. They saw this technology more as an opportunity than as a problem.

Regardless of which of these three forces triggered change in their firms, they reported that all three are now intermingled in supporting the current HRM effort. They did not feel it mattered where the starting point had been.

The participants see these three forces as having a widespread impact in American industry, and they therefore see a nearly universal need to adopt the new HRM approach. This was not entirely expected by the faculty group, who had heard much in the past of various qualifiers to the applicability of high-commitment systems. We tested to learn their reactions to these conditional issues. Were the newer methods relevant only to greenfield plants and start-up companies? Were they only relevant to high-technology industries? Were they only relevant to boom times? Or to recession times? Were they relevant only to certain types of employees with appropriate personalities and education? Were they relevant only to certain regions, for example the West and South? Were they relevant only to the United States? Or only to industrialized countries? Almost without exception the participants responded that these qualifiers did not apply. They did express uncertainty in regard to the suitability of the new approach to all types of employees. They all engaged in unusually careful employee-selection procedures, searching for people who would respond positively to expanded work responsibilities. Moreover, they cited as one of the costs of the changeover the need to shift aside a few traditional managers who were unable to function effectively in the new system. On the other hand, they were finding, even in their older plants, that the vast majority of people who had worked for years under the traditional system could and did adjust to the new system and became its staunch advocates. So their earlier qualifications about the type of people for whom the new methods were relevant were fading away as they accumulated additional experience. The only persisting qualifier on the question of relevance was the one of rapid environmental change and strong competition. They conceded that firms facing static environments and weak or nonexistent competition might not find the new HRM methods relevant to their needs.

The participants found it more difficult to characterize the nature of the newly emerging HRM system. They were some-what uncomfortable with the faculty's efforts to boil it down to a few universal features. Their ambivalence expressed itself in their reluctance to embrace a single label for the new system. They used the faculty's various terms (*commitment, mutuality, consensus,* and *participative*) more as a convenience than with any conviction of their adequacy. Several expressed a real prefer-ence for the term *it.*

The managers were in agreement that the whole point of the HRM change effort is the unleashing of latent creativity and energies of employees throughout the organization in a way that improves results for the entire organization and for its employees as individual members. They also agreed that even in the more advanced applications they have not fully tapped the potential improvements. They were largely in agreement on what methods are needed to unleash this potential, even though they had often started the process in different ways and in different parts of the organizations. In essence, they believed the methods involved nothing less than a new way of managing, which changes traditional work roles from top to bottom. The starting point for most of these companies and the eventual target for all was the expansion of the job scope and respon-sibility of rank-and-file employees. This took different forms under different circumstances. The most typical method was the semiautonomous work team, but others spoke of enriching individual jobs, using problem-solving groups, and so on. For the new system to take hold, however, they agreed that the reshaping of rank-and-file roles must be associated with cor-responding changes in the role of middle managers and even top managers. As the responsibilities at the bottom expand to encompass many of the traditional middle-management duties in regard to such matters as quality control, short-term planning and monitoring of product flows, equipment maintenance, se-lection and training of new employees, and day-to-day trouble-shooting, so the middle-management role must change and expand with eventual impact on the top-management role. These repercussions up the management line are now being felt in most of the participating companies and are still being worked out. One conspicuous result in several of these companies has been the total elimination of one or more entire levels in the traditional hierarchy to remove redundancies and shorten communication lines. It was clear to all that "it" involves significant role changes from top to bottom. While no other company had gone as far as People Express in stating that every single one of their employees functions as a manager, others believed that this is what is really happening.

An essential feature of "it" that was agreed upon was that the firms must engage in an ongoing process of building mutual commitment and trust between top management, as the traditional powerholders, and the rank and file, as the outsiders in the old we-they dichotomy. The two sides of the labor-management split must engage in more complete and intense communication, with the union as the third party in unionized units. Business facts need to be shared. Acts of good faith have to match the words. True concern for the jobs and careers of all employees must be demonstrated in some way. The initiative must rest with management, but eventually an enriched two-way exchange must develop with ideas and energy directed to the well-being of the enterprise and the well-being of all employees as legitimate stakeholders. Shared values need to be developed. The values most often cited by participants were quality, human development, equity (as distinct from equality), resource conservation, trustworthiness, and innovation.

The participants shared the view that the organization they saw emerging would always need a boss. Strong top leadership would be required, both for making major strategic decisions and for establishing and fostering guiding values and broad operating principles. Middle management would be expected to be more entrepreneurial in initiating new business opportunities, in creating new jobs, in planning for the mid term, and in managing the organization's change process itself. Middle managers would be coaching, supporting, and reinforcing the work of the rank and file in managing day-to-day operations. All employees would be expected to have some voice, some influence in regard to strategic decisions. A hierarchy of final decision making based on expertise and perspective would persist, so the term *democracy* with its voting connotation, seemed inappropriate. The concept of decision sharing was closer to the mark.

CYCLE TWO

The second cycle of the conference opened with three faculty presentations. The entire faculty group had selected topics that were, we believed, potential problem aspects of the HRM change that management was inclined to overlook. The three brief talks were focused on the response of rank-and-file employees to the impact of advanced information technology on their work life, the potential impact of this new technology on the wider organization structure and systems, and the implications of the HRM change for the ideology and governance of corporations. The presentations were intended to be provocative.

The responses of the executives to the presentations on technology were mixed. Most of the participants reported that their firms had already gone a long way toward accommodating to advanced information technology. It was their experience that, after some initial problems, hourly employees in both factories and offices took readily to the new equipment. With continuing use of extensive advance planning and employee training, they felt they could meet the challenge of future technology changes with minimal difficulties.

A minority of the participants had more reservations. They all tended to agree that future problems in this regard were more apt to arise from the reactions of middle management than from nonmanagers. They saw two potential problems. One could stem from the enhanced potential of the new equipment to provide detailed and constant surveillance of rank-and-file work behavior. If this potential were used, it would rapidly undermine a climate of mutual trust. Secondly, they saw that the new equipment's capacity to provide all employees with a broader factual understanding of the linkages between their duties and those of others would continue to increase the ability of nonmanagers to make operating trade-off decisions. This would provide an opportunity for continuing improvements in organization effectiveness but at the same time would tend to crowd and threaten middle management's traditional turf. Resistance in many forms could be expected if middle management's role was not simultaneously extended in other ways. They largely agreed that advanced information technology would continue to open up avenues for creative restructuring of organization procedures and systems. This was a major opportunity that would require imaginative planning and thoughtful implementation if it were to be utilized.

The presentation on the ideology theme did prove provocative. Several felt it overstated the implications of the HRM change, especially the argument that the change tended to undermine the traditional rights of stockholders as corporate property owners. The executives pointed out that top managers of large firms with widespread stock ownership have for some time thought of their role as balancing the legitimate interests of four stakeholder constituent groups. These were the same four groups as in the faculty model: stockholders, customers, employees, and the wider community (partially represented by the government). They reported that the HRM changes were serving to solidify this ideological perspective rather than initiate it. They saw managers as deriving their legitimacy from all four groups—not just stockholders (as in the past) or not just employees.

Some discussions arose as to whether new formal structures of corporate governance would or should emerge from later stages of the HRM change. Did these managers expect to see, for instance, more union officials or other employee representatives on boards of directors to provide more direct expression of employee interests? Most of the executives thought such developments were possible but not necessary to make the new HRM arrangements work. They were, by and large, confident that top management could provide the needed balance between stakeholder interests within the context of present board structures. They were, in general, prepared to postpone addressing these issues.

The raising of the technology and ideology issues served to trigger extensive discussions of other, often related, issues that the executives did see as the major current impediments to further progress in making the HRM changes. There was general agreement that the biggest current restraint on the change was the behavior of middle managers, followed by employee concerns for job security, inconsistencies in top management support, and uncertainties about the changing role of the unions.

The discussion of middle management focused on the issue of power and power sharing. Middle managers were quite understandably finding it difficult to relinquish the traditional power over the lower levels in the organization that they had often worked long and hard to secure. Were people being asked to violate their basic human nature in giving up power over others? Could an individual change from being an authoritarian manager to one who, while carrying fully as much responsibility for results, would behave in a coaching and supportive manner toward subordinates? Instances of both success and failure regarding such middle-management transitions were cited. It was pointed out that aggressive energies were still needed in the new arrangement in order to get the job done. Individual managers would still need a positive identity around which to build their self-esteem and status. Perhaps power over others was simply one means of building self-esteem. Successful change-overs were associated with managers receiving recognition and esteem for behaving in the new coaching, supportive mode and for achieving the superior results that can follow. When this happened, the power issue per se disappeared. The participants, however, cited a few painful experiences with well-regarded traditional managers who chose to retire early or to transfer out of line responsibilities to avoid the need to change. On the positive side, they recalled other situations when even high-seniority managers welcomed the change and went on to increase their effectiveness.

The general experience of the group was that the middle-management issue could not be avoided or ignored. Middle managers in the longer run could profit from the change, but in the shorter run they were threatened. Unless a great deal of imagination was brought to bear on expanding their duties beyond the traditional ones, fewer middle managers would, in fact, be needed to handle a given scale of operation. In addition, middle managers were being asked to give up their customary source of status and find another basis for recognition. Care must be taken to define, model, and train for the new roles.

New career paths must be staked out. University-based research could be especially helpful with these tasks. Top managers should give more of their time to managing this specific aspect of the larger change and especially to reinforcing and rewarding positive examples of the desired middle-management behavior. Working through these issues would take time, patience, and resources—but they agreed it must be done or the entire change effort would not persist.

The second problem area that probably received as much attention as the middle-management issue was the broad issue of job security. Everyone saw a direct linkage between productivity improvements and fewer jobs. The unleashing of ideas and energies at the lower levels was the essential key to improved effectiveness, but all agreed that employees would quickly find hundreds of ways of preventing such gains if the gains might cost them their jobs. All the companies had, in one form or another, guaranteed that no one would lose their employment, as distinct from their current job, as a result of employee-initiated improvements. These guarantees were made even in the companies that faced a need for lasting employment shrinkage to cope with foreign competition, labor-saving technology, or falling primary demand.

Such executives believed strongly that they must separate the various causes of work-force redundancies, even though the accounting was difficult, in order to make "it" work. They reported that employees did accept layoffs based on external factors without slackening in their improvement efforts if, most importantly, management had made a consistent long-term effort to educate about external realities and to build trust and credibility in their concern about jobs and in their honesty with business figures. All the firms had made commitments to use layoffs only as a last response to adverse external conditions. The participants reported various examples of top-management behavior in dealing with excess work force that had dramatically demonstrated the last-resort rule. They talked of plant closings and the care that was taken to out place every single employee; of plant modernizations where a majority of the workers were given extensive retraining to qualify for new roles; of challenging and supporting a work group in cutting enough

costs to beat a competitor's price; of equalized compensation
cuts from top to bottom. They cited their efforts to generate
new jobs in allied new business ventures and of the need for
more of these entrepreneurial efforts. Even though some of
the firms represented had gone to great lengths to avoid ever
having a layoff, none of them favored making an explicit "no
layoff" promise. They saw the world as too uncertain to risk
one's integrity or the firm's solvency with such a promise. They
all expected to devote major continuing efforts to managing
the employment-security issue.

The third problem area that surfaced could be called top
management lapses. These were actions by top management
that were inconsistent with the spirit of mutuality and commitment. A number of examples of such lapses were cited, but
the one that was most conspicuous was the high level of executive bonus payments made in early 1984 in the auto industry.
Other examples mentioned were blatant and arbitrary acts by
top people, promotion of notoriously heavy-handed managers,
and layoffs that appeared not to be last resorts. All the participants, of course, recognized that such lapses undermine the
process of building trust. Such lapses must clearly be minimized,
even though, like safety lapses, they could not be reduced to
zero. It was in regard to the lapse issue that participants realized
how paying attention to the ideological implications of HRM
change could serve to reduce lapses. For instance, it is implicit
in HRM change that executive bonus payments can no longer
be treated as a subject unrelated to rank-and-file commitment.
No one visualized bottom-level employees deciding on executive
payments, but the workers' responses would need to be taken
into account if the new system was to work.

Compensation at all levels was also discussed as an issue with
potential for being a problem as well as an opportunity. The
managers reported that their companies were feeling their way
along in this area, trying different methods of payment, searching for ways to reinforce rather than undermine the desired
employment relationship. Many of the companies were using
some form of gain sharing or performance pay. This varied all
the way from Hewlett-Packard's companywide profit sharing,
which applies uniformly from the chairman to the newest re-

cruit, to Bank of America's plan, which ties an individual's pay directly to his or her own performance. Most firms were linking pay to an intermediate measure of performance at the level of the work group or the plant. The participants found they could account for much of this variability in pay methods by the history and stage of development of the different firms. For example, the fact that HP found its profit sharing effective was explained by its long-standing culture of mutuality, established and sustained by its founders. As one participant put it, "A truly effective profit-sharing plan is the ultimate achievement of mutuality, not a starting point."

The final topic that drew a significant amount of attention as an unresolved issue was the evolving role of unions in the new HRM system. All but three of the firms represented were at least partially unionized. Several had a significant number of units of both kinds, with their older plants unionized and their newer ones not. Since this old-new split also roughly corresponded with the split between units using the traditional as against the new HRM system, the question arose as to whether "it" was designed to keep the union out. This was emphatically denied. In fact, the executives believed, any hidden agenda around blocking unionization would make it impossible to build the needed mutual trust. As one individual put it, "The only person you can fool for more than two weeks is yourself." There was a general view, however, that in a well-managed unit with decision sharing, a union was not needed to represent employee interests. The executives from two companies questioned this view, feeling that union representation made it possible to do a superior job of managing within the new HRM system. These two companies argued that no management group could be objective enough to be the sole means of representing employee interests. Most firms with both union and nonunion units reported that their union relations had evolved to a point where unionization was not a deterrent to making progress toward a high-commitment system. They reported that their union relations improved as they moved away from industrywide master contracts toward contracts that could reflect specific business conditions.

Several of the participants expressed concern about the problems unions are having as their traditional adversarial mission is eroding and a new raison d'être is still uncertain. The importance of unions in the broader social and political scene was cited. It was recognized that management is in no position to guide the strategic choices of unions. However, it was suggested that drawing union officials into mutual problem-solving activities, sometimes in regard to governmental issues, is a way of clarifying some of the alternative roles they can choose to undertake.

CYCLE THREE

The conference's third and final discussion cycle concerned the change process itself. Faculty presentations were made to launch the discussion. These dealt with the role of training in the change process, the changing mission of unions, the linkage between HRM strategy and business strategies, and the nature of the change process in leading-edge firms. The resulting small-group discussions were primarily a sharing of experiences to identify effective ways to facilitate the desired HRM changes.

The general approach to change by these managers was essentially pragmatic. They were willing to wade into a new situation, discover what worked and what did not, and act accordingly. They advocated starting something, seeing what problems emerged, and then going to work to resolve the problems one at a time. They expected change to involve stress and tension. Their slogans were, "No pain, no gain" and "Muscles don't develop unless they are stressed." They believed an organization has to evolve and learn from one stage of development to the next. Time must be provided for working through these stages. To shoot directly for some ultimate stage would be unsuccessful and possibly dangerous. They saw the change process in which they were engaged as having no clear end point. "We're building a dock out into the fog." Some issues were emerging that "will not be resolved in my lifetime." This was said even though they all conveyed a sense of urgency about moving ahead as rapidly as possible.

Their experience had taught them some similar things about effective ways to facilitate change. They emphasized eight points.

1. Go for some early success experiences. Use these examples as models for others. Move people from all levels into these successful units and let them stay long enough to make a full, unfettered inquiry. Let them develop their own enthusiasm for what is possible.

2. Invest heavily in training and management development; it pays large dividends. People can learn and change in terms of skills, knowledge, attitudes, and even values. Use a mix of experienced line people and professional educators as trainers, people who can command respect from their peers and who understand and believe in the newer HRM systems. The preparation for training should start at the same time as the planning for the technology and organization of a new plant. New recruit training should often precede, not follow, the decision to offer and accept employment.

3. Use competitive economic pressure to help accelerate the change process. Keep educating constantly about business conditions in ways that make them tangible. Be a "sight-raiser"—set ambitious goals that reflect competitive realities.

4. Work to provide consistent top-level leadership. Provide time for top managers to have thorough discussions of their business outlook and values in order to forge a basic unity of purpose. Promote to key roles those managers who have a record of success in leading change toward the commitment model, people who will take the risks of making things happen.

5. Treat HRM strategy as an absolutely essential part of the overall business strategy. HRM issues need to be thought through and resolved simultaneously with product-market choices, technology choices, and financial choices. HRM is not the entire answer to the competitive challenge but it is equal in importance to other parts of the puzzle. It cannot be handled as an afterthought.

6. Top managers need to spend significant chunks of their time clarifying key values and guiding organizational principles. These must be articulated over and over again and, most importantly, demonstrated by concrete actions.

7. Top management can best speed the desired change in a decentralized operation by fostering, supporting, and demonstrating the opportunities—not by forcing or ordering the change. The latter only results in lip service, which will waste time. Local units must buy the new approach and ask for corporate help in changing. One knows that local units have really bought into the desired change when they start to improve upon it.

8. Not only tolerate but foster diversity in the specific way "it" is worked out in each local setting. Specific HRM practices need to be tailored to local conditions and the historical context. Many varieties of "it" will work as long as they embody some consistent values and general principles.

One widely shared experience coming from all the companies was that getting the rank-and-file employees to buy into the new way of operating was not a major difficulty. If given a reasonable opportunity to understand the alternatives, they quite consistently opted for the new ways. By and large, workers respond postively to enlarged, multiskilled job assignments, to enlarged decision-making responsibilities in regard to their immediate work situations, to advanced technology, and to the implications of stiff competition. This is not to say that the bottom-level change process is quick or easy—only that it is predictably possible.

As the conference drew to a close, both the faculty and the executives expressed their excitement and gratification in learning from one another's experiences. The group sensed the remarkable degree of agreement about the lessons to be drawn from their experiences. They felt the powerful reinforcement this agreement provided to confirm their past efforts and to strengthen their future actions.

Jim Henderson of Cummins was the last to speak on this point, and he summarized the thoughts of most:

> I think most of us, most of the business people here, have an interest in what we've discussed over three days for one reason: It's going to make for more effective organizations. Most of us feel we will implement change faster, not slower; we will get our

costs down and our quality up at a far faster rate than we can do under the old system. There is a conviction that people in our companies can contribute far more, I mean just far more, than our system has permitted them to do until now—and the fundamentals are simple. Our people need to understand the business the way we do. We need to be prepared to share business facts, not just opinion because they'll be suspicious of opinion. Facts speak to people in a way that has legitimacy. By sharing facts, we begin to develop trust and credibility between the management and the rest of the people in the organization. When you have trust, you can then begin to get to the issues and find solutions.

To work more productively, training is very critical, as is technology. Those of us in management have a responsibility to give people the tools to do things differently, and that's both training and technology.

We have to be willing to let go of some things—to tell the people in the organization they have the responsibility, that it's not reserved for management. I sense some concern about whether we still lead if we give up responsibility. I think the leadership job is bigger and tougher than ever before in this kind of environment. Once your people have an ongoing understanding about the competitive situation, management has a continuous role of sight-raising to meet that competition. It creates tension if you're trying to move forward. That's the nature of the leadership job. You are spending a great deal of your time, not in achieving consensus for the sake of consensus, but in saying, "We can do better and here's why. Turn your creative efforts loose." Leadership is getting people to buy into tougher standards and better performance. Leadership is still very important.

Therefore, what we have spent three days talking about is in no way separable from business objectives. We agreed that values and principles are worth agreeing on, publishing, and teaching. I was impressed yesterday when Don Burr said how much time he spends just teaching his managers about these principles. We should remember they are principles and not set policies and this approach is highly flexible. You can get in trouble if you try to take a policy from one situation and apply it in another, whether it's a pay structure or an employment guarantee. There are situations where another's solution is the wrong thing to do.

I happen to believe you can follow these principles even in plant closures; as tough a situation as we have. You share the business reason, and you get input from those affected. For instance, we shut down a plant not too long ago and we got every single employee placed in jobs before we felt our job was done.

Ultimately, there's no substitute for top management's leading

the change. Only then will it become pervasive in the organization.

Finally, we had a discussion about whether we wanted to say
to the world, as a result of this conference, "Adapt or perish."
Well, we're not out to convert the world or to tell others what to
do. However, I think we looked at each other and said, Hey, we
all really believe that! That's why we're here.

Contributors

MICHAEL BEER is professor of organizational behavior and human resource management at Harvard Business School. He holds a B.A. and a Ph.D. in industrial psychology and business from Ohio State University. He is the author of *Organization Change and Development: A Systems View* (1980) and *Managing Human Assets* (coauthored with Paul R. Lawrence, D. Quinn Mills, Bert A. Spector, and Richard E. Walton), published in 1984.

PAUL R. LAWRENCE is Wallace Brett Donham Professor of Organizational Behavior at Harvard Business School, where he earned his M.B.A. and doctorate of commercial science degrees. He has been involved in the study and teaching of organizational behavior at Harvard since 1947. He has published twenty books and numerous articles. A recent book, *Renewing American Industry* (coauthored with Davis Dyer), incorporates his previous work into a more general theory of how organizations change over time in response to both internal initiatives and external conditions.

GEORGE C. LODGE is professor of business administration at Harvard Business School. He teaches Business, Government, and the International Economy in the Advanced Management Program and Human Resource Management in the M.B.A. program. He was a political reporter and columnist for the *Boston Herald* before entering government service, where he was director of information of the U.S. Department of Labor, and assistant secretary of labor for international affairs. He is the author of numerous articles and books including the volumes *Spearheads of Democracy, Engines of Change: United States Interests and Revolution in Latin America, The New American Ideology*, and *The American Disease*.

JANICE MCCORMICK is assistant professor of organizational behavior and human resource management at Harvard Business School. She holds a Ph.D. in political science from Harvard University. Her research has been in national political economy and industrial relations. As a specialist on France, she has written on both French macroeconomic policy and political economy and French labor-management relations. Her work on the United States has focused on labor-management relations. She is the coauthor (with D. Quinn Mills) of *Industrial Relations in Transition*.

D. QUINN MILLS is Albert J. Weatherhead Professor of Business Administration at Harvard Business School and is a member of the Organizational Behavior/Human Resource Management Area of the school. He has taught Personnel, Labor Relations, and Government Relations in many of the school's programs. He helped administer wage and price controls during the Nixon and Ford administrations in 1971–74. He was the labor arbitrator on the building of the Trans-Alaska pipeline. He is a member of the National Commission on Employment Policy by appointment of the president. He is the coauthor (with Janice McCormick) of *Industrial Relations in Transition*.

CALVIN PAVA is assistant professor of organizational behavior and human resource management at Harvard Business School. He holds a Ph.D. in advanced systems planning design and management from the Wharton School. At New York University, from 1978 to 1981, he helped found a graduate program in the application of advanced telecommunications and computing systems. Pava's 1983 book, *Managing New Office Technology: An Organizational Strategy*, deals with practical steps that managers can take to appraise the organizational alternatives made possible by new information technology.

JEFFREY A. SONNENFELD is assistant professor of organizational behavior and human resource management at Harvard Business School, where he earned his M.B.A. and D.B.A. degrees. He is an editor of the *Academy of Management Journal* and is the author of the volumes *Corporate Views of the Public Interest* (1981) and *Managing Career Systems: Channeling the Flow of Executive Talent* (1984). His research and consulting have been in the areas of corporate social performance and human resource management.

BERT A. SPECTOR is assistant professor of business administration at Northeastern University and research associate at Harvard Business School. He received his Ph.D. in American history from the University of Missouri. He has collaborated on several books on human resource management, including *Managing Human Assets* and the forthcoming *Human Resource Management: A General Manager's Perspective*.

RICHARD E. WALTON is Jesse Isidor Straus Professor of Business Administration at Harvard Business School. He received an M.S. in economics from Purdue University in 1954 and a D.B.A. from Harvard University in 1959. Professor Walton taught at Purdue University before joining the Harvard faculty in 1968. From 1969 until 1976 he served as the director of the Division of Research at Harvard Business School. He writes extensively in the areas of work innovations and conflict resolutions, labor relations and organizational implications of technology.

SHOSHANA ZUBOFF is assistant professsor of organizational behavior and human resource management at Harvard Business School. She received her Ph.D. in social psychology from Harvard University and spent one year as a research associate at the Center for Information Systems Research in the Sloan School of Management at MIT. Her research is in the areas of the psychology of work and workplace problems, and the social psychological consequences of work computerization.

MARY LOU BALBAKY is a research associate at Harvard Business School where she has done case writing and course development in the areas of human resource management and organizational behavior. She received a B.A. in psychology from Stanford University and is currently working on her doctorate in sociology at Brandeis University. She is on the faculty of Radcliffe College Seminars where she teaches human resource management.

Notes

CHAPTER 2

1. My thinking about these systems is indebted to earlier work of William Ouchi's on bureaucratic, market, and clan control systems, "Hierarchies, Clans, and Theory Z: A New Perspective on Organization Development," in *Organizational Dynamics* (Autumn 1978); and to Richard Edward's work on simple, technical, and bureaucratic control systems, *Contested Terrain: The Transformation of the Workplace in the Twentieth Century* (New York: Basic Books, 1979).

2. Joseph G. Rayback, *A History of American Labor* (New York: Macmillan, 1959), 58.

3. Ibid, 59.

4. Ibid, 201–204.

5. Ibid, 247.

6. Ibid, 200.

7. Steven Meyer, *The Five Dollar Day: Labor Management and Social Control in the Ford Motor Company, 1908–1921* (Albany, N.Y.: SUNY Press, 1981).

8. David Brody, *Workers in Industrial America: Essay on the 20th Century Struggle* (New York: Oxford University Press, 1980), 48.

9. Ibid., 50.

10. Ibid., 49.

11. Ibid., 69.

12. Arthur Turner and Paul Lawrence, *Industrial Jobs and the Worker* (Boston: Harvard Business School, 1965).

CHAPTER 3

1. William J. Abernathy, Kim B. Clark, and Alan M. Kantrow, *Industrial Renaissance* (New York: Basic Books, 1983); Paul R. Lawrence and Davis Dyer, *Renewing American Industry* (New York: Free Press, 1983); Rosabeth Moss Kanter, *The Change Masters* (New York: Simon and Schuster, 1983; Michael Maccoby, *The Leader* (New York: Simon & Schuster, 1981); William G. Ouchi, *Theory Z* (Reading, Mass.: Addison-Wesley, 1981); George C. Lodge, *The New American Ideology* (New York: Knopf, 1975).

2. Edward E. Lawler III, "The New Plant Revolution," *Organizational Dynamics*, Winter 1978, 2–12.

3. Robert Guest, "Quality of Work Life—Learning from Tarrytown," *Harvard Business Review*, July–August 1979, 76–87.

4. Thomas A. Kochan, Harry C. Katz, and Nancy R. Mower, "Worker Participation and American Unions: Threat or Opportunity" (Working Paper, MIT Sloan School of Management, 1983).

5. Ibid.

6. Field observation.

7. Eric Trist has distinguished four strategic options for management regarding QWL: rejection, laissez faire, selective development, and corporatewide commitment. The more advanced companies in the United States are pursuing a combination of the last two options. See Eric Trist, "QWL and the 1980s," in *The Quality of Working Life and the 1980s*, ed. Harvey Kolodny and Hans van Beinum (New York: Praeger, 1983), 48.

8. "People Express," Harvard Business School, Case No. 9-483-103.

9. Debra Whitestone and Leonard A. Schlesinger, "People Express" (Case 9-483-103, Harvard Business School, 1983).

10. Michael J. Piori, "Why Unions Don't Work Anymore," *INC Magazine*, March 1982, 16–17.

11. Chris Argyris, *Personality and Organization* (New York: Harper, 1957).

12. Others have drawn attention to the emergence of a new dominant pattern in work organizations. For example, Trist has articulated contrasting "organizational paradigms" that are in much the same spirit as the more detailed distinctions I made here between the control and commitment work force management models. He refers to them as the "Old Paradigm" and the "New Paradigm." See Eric Trist, "QWL and the 1980s," 47.

13. J. Richard Hackman and G. R. Olsen, *Work Redesign* (Reading, Mass.: Addison-Wesley, 1980).

14. Richard E. Walton, "Establishing and Maintaining High Commitment Work Systems," in *Organization Life Cycles*, ed. John R. Kimberly et al. (San Francisco: Jossey-Bass, 1980).

15. Tom Burns and G. Stalker, *The Management of Innovation* (London: Tavistock Publ., 1961).

16. Irving Bluestone, "Labor's Stake in Improving the Quality of Working Life," in *The Quality of Working Life and the 1980s*, 33–41.

17. Raymond A. Katzell and Daniel Yankelovich, *Work, Productivity and Job Satisfaction: An Evaluation of Policy-Related Research* (New York: Harcourt Brace Jovanovich; 1975), Hackman and Olsen, *Work Redesign*; Robert Zager and Michael R. Rosow, eds., *The Innovative Organization: Productivity Programs in Action* (New York: Pergamon Press, 1982).

18. Richard E. Walton and Leonard A. Schlesinger, "Do Supervisors Thrive in Participative Work Systems?" *Organizational Dynamics*, Winter 1979; Leonard A. Schlesinger and Janice A. Klein, "The First Line Supervisor: Past, Present, and Future," in *Handbook of Organizational Behavior*, ed. J. Lorach (Englewood Cliffs, N.J.: Prentice-Hall, 1983).

19. Thomas A. Kochan, Robert B. McKersie, and Peter Cappelli, "Strategic Choice and Industrial Relations Theory and Practice" (Working Paper, MIT Sloan School of Management, 1983).

CHAPTER 4

1. K. Wise, K. Chan, and R. Yorkely, *Microcomputers: A Technology Forecast and Assessment to the Year 2000* (New York: Wiley, 1980).

2. R. N. Noyce, "Microelectronics," *Scientific American* 237 (1977): 62–69; M. Shepard, *Distributed Computing Power: Opportunities and Challenges* (Keynote Address, National Computer Conference, Dallas, 13 June 1977).

3. C. Pava, "Microelectronics and the Design of Organization" (Working Paper 782–67, Harvard Business School, 1982).

4. Ibid.

5. Noyce, "Microelectronics."

6. H. Fayol, *General Industrial Management* (New York: Pitman, 1949).

7. L. Mumford, *The Myth of the Machine* (London: Secker & Warburg, 1967); M. W. Weber, "Some Consequences of Bureaucratization," in *Sociological Theory*, ed. L. A. Coser and B. Rosenberg (New York: Macmillan, 1957).

8. O. Williamson, *Markets and Hierarchies* (New York: Free Press, 1975).

9. H. Mintzberg, *The Structuring of Organizations* (Englewood Cliffs, N.J.: Prentice-Hall, 1979).

10. E. Friedson, *Professional Dominance: The Social Structure of Medical Care* (Chicago: Aldine, 1970).

11. K. L. Kramer and W. H. Dutton, "The Interests Served by Technological Reform: The Case of Computing," *Administration and Society* 11 (1979): 80–106.

12. J. Martin, *Future Developments in Telecommunications* (Englewood Cliffs, N.J.: Prentice-Hall, 1977).

13. C. Pava, *Managing New Office Technology: An Organizational Strategy* (New York: Free Press, 1983); Pava, "The Organizational Interface: Management's Emerging Challenge In Systems Design" (Working Paper 784–053, Harvard Business School, 1984).

14. W. Ouchi, *Theory Z* (Reading, Mass.: Addison-Wesley, 1981); A. Pettigrew, "On Studying Organizational Culture," *Administrative Science Quarterly* 44 (1979):570–581; E. H. Schein, "Coming to a New Awareness of Organizational Culture," *Sloan Management Review* 25 (1984): 3–16.

15. A. Toffler, *The Third Wave* (New York: Morrow, 1980).

16. M. H. Olsen, "Remote Office Work: Changing Patterns in Space and Time," *Communications of the Association for Computing Machinery* 26 (1983): 182–187.

17. U. Weil, *Information Systems in the 80's: Product, Markets, and Vendors* (Englewood Cliffs, N.J.: Prentice-Hall, 1982).

18. F. W. McFarlan, "Information Technology Changes the Way to Compete," *Harvard Business Review*, May-June 1984, 98–103; M. Porter, *Competitive Advantage: Creating and Sustaining Superior Performance* (New York: Free Press, 1985); G. Stigler, *The Organization of Industry* (Chicago: University of Chicago Press, 1968).

19. Porter, *Competitive Strategy*.

20. M. Blumberg and A. Alber, "The Human Element: Its Impact on the Productivity of Advanced Batch Manufacturing Systems," *Journal of Manufacturing Systems 1* (1982): 43–52; L. Hirschhorn, *Beyond Mechanization* (Cambridge, Mass.: MIT Press, 1984); Pava, "Microelectronics and the Design of Organization."

21. P. S. Adler, "New Technologies, New Skills" (Working Paper 784–076, Harvard Business School, 1984); Hirschhorn, *Beyond Mechanization*; A. M. Morham, Jr., and L. Norellie, "Adaptive Research in Office Automation" (Paper read at the Academy of Management Symposium, New York, 1982);

Pava, "Microelectronics and the Design of Organization"; S. Zuboff, "New Worlds of Computer-Mediated Work," *Harvard Business Review*, September–October 1983, 145–152.

22. P. G. Herbst, "The Product of Work is People" in *The Quality of Working Life*, vol. I, ed. L. E. Davis and A. B. Cherns (New York: Free Press, 1975).

23. Adler, "New Technologies, New Skills"; Pava, "Microelectronics and the Design of Organizations"; Pava, *Managing New Office Technology*.

24. Hirschhorn, *Beyond Mechanization*; P. R. Lawrence and J. W. Lorsch, *Organization and Environment* (Cambridge, Mass.: Harvard University Press, 1967); Pava, "The Organizational Interface."

25. W. Skinner, "Factory of the Future—Always in the Future?—A Managerial Viewpoint," in *Towards Factory of the Future: Emergence of the Computerized Factory and Its Impact on Society*, ed. L. Kops (New York: American Society of Mechanical Engineers, 1980); Pava, "Microelectronics and the Design of Organization."

26. S. Beer, *The Brain of the Firm* (New York: Herder and Herder, 1972); F. E. Emery, "The Fifth Wave: Embarking on the Next Forty Years" (Working Document, Centre for Continuing Education, Australian National University, Canberra, 1979); Pava, "Microelectronics and the Design of Organization."

27. E. M. Rogers and J. K. Larsen, *Silicon Valley Fever Growth of High-Technology Culture* (New York: Basic Books, 1984).

28. R. L. Ackoff, "Management Misinformation Systems," *Management Science* 14 (1967): 147–156.

29. F. W. McFarlan and J. L. McKenney, *Corporate Information Systems Management: The Issues Facing Senior Executives* (Homewood, Ill.: Richard D. Irwin, 1982); Pava, "The Organizational Interface"; R. E. Walton, "Social Choice and the Development of Advanced Information Technology," *Technology in Society 2* (1980): 391–412; Zuboff, "New Worlds of Computer-Mediated Work."

30. R. J. Boyle, "Wrestling with Jellyfish," *Harvard Business Review*, January-February 1984, 74–83.

31. Pava, "The Organizational Interface."

32. Pava, *Managing New Office Technology*.

33. E. L. Trist, "The Sociotechnical Perspective" in *Perspectives on Organization Design and Behavior*, ed. A. H. Van de Ven and W. F. Joyce (New York: Wiley, 1982).

34. Pava, *Managing New Office Technology*.

35. J. P. Kotter, *The General Managers* (New York: Free Press, 1982); G. Donaldson and J. W. Lorsch, *Decision Making at the Top* (New York: Basic Books, 1983).

CHAPTER 5

1. John Besant and Keith Dickson, *Issues in the Adoption of Microelectronics* (London: Francis Pinter, 1982).

2. Ibid.; *Computerized Manufacturing Automation: Employment, Education and the Workplace* (Washington, D.C.: Office of Technology Assessment, 1984); A. E. Owen, *Chips in Industry: An Overview of the Interaction and Implications of Microelectronics, Robots, and the Manufacturing Industry* (London: Economist Intelligence Unit, 1982); Robert Reich, *The New American Frontier* (New York: Times Books, 1983).

3. Rene Moreau, *The Computer Comes of Age* (Cambridge, Mass.: MIT Press, 1984). See for example the discussion of algorithmic processing, pp. 1–10. A similar point is made regarding the challenges of algorithmic logic as it applies to industrial computers in "Computer Control Will Make You Think," *Industry Week*, 16 February 1970, 23–28.

4. Besant and Dickson, *Issues in the Adoption of Microelectronics*, 41.

5. *Computerized Manufacturing Automation, 59, 69.*

6. A. E. Owen, *Chips in Industry*, 43.

7. In most organizations, information systems and automation technology (e.g., process control, flexible manufacturing systems) are treated as separate disciplines. My point here is that the new microprocessor-based automating technologies are *also* informating technologies. Their consequences are thus likely to be more complex than earlier generations of technology that have substituted various forms of energy for human muscle power.

8. For a discussion of this general approach to plant organizations, see Edward Lawler, "The New Plant Revolution," *Organizational Dynamics*, Winter 1978, 2–12.

9. Michael Polanyi, *The Tacit Dimension* (New York: Doubleday, 1967), 4.

10. Ibid., 18.

11. For the classic discussion of the effort bargain, see W. Baldemus, *Efficiency and Effort: An Analysis of Industrial Administration* (London: Tavistock Publ., 1959), particularly Chapters 3 and 4.

12. For an insightful rendering of the same issue, see Robert Schrank, "Horse Collar—Blue-Collar Blues," *Harvard Business Review*, May–June 1981, 133.

13. An excellent discussion of these dilemmas as they were faced by NASA information system designers is available in J. G. Wohl, "Information Automation and the Apollo Program: A Retrospective," *IEEE Transactions on Systems, Man, and Cybernetics* 12 (July–August 1982): 469–478.

CHAPTER 6

1. D. Quinn Mills, "When Employees Make Concessions to the Company," *Harvard Business Review*, July–August 1983, 103–113.

2. Robert McKersie and Richard Walton, *A Behavioral Theory of Labor Negotiation* (New York: McGraw-Hill, 1965), 11–13.

3. Jack Stieber, "Steel," in *Collective Bargaining: Contemporary American Experience*, ed. Gerald G. Somers (Madison, Wis.: Industrial Relations Research Association, 1981), 205.

CHAPTER 7

1. See, for instance, T. A. Kochan and R. B. McKersie, "Interpreting Current Developments in Collective Bargaining and Industrial Relations" (Working Paper 1377–82, Sloan School of Management, MIT, 1982); D. Quinn Mills, "Reforming the U.S. System of Collective Bargaining," *Monthly Labor Review* 106 (1983): 11–22; Michael Beer and Bert Spector, "Human Resources Management: The Integration of Industrial Relations and Orga-

nization Development" in *Research in Personnel and Human Resources Management*, vol. 2 (Greenwich, Conn.: JAI Press, 1984).

2. For a more detailed description of how these programs operate, see Bert Spector, *General Motors and the United Auto Workers*, Case 9-481-142, Harvard Business School, 1981; Robert Guest, "The Sharonville Story: Worker Involvement at a Ford Motor Company Plant" in *The Innovative Organization: Productivity Programs in Action* (Elmsford, N.Y.: Pergamon Press, 1982); and J. J. Fisher, "The Labor/Management Participation Team Concept: A Pilot Effort at Lebanon Plant, Bethlehem Steel Corporation" (Unpublished master's thesis, Pennsylvania State University, 1982).

3. See, for instance, P. J. Champagne, "Using Labor/Management Committees to Improve Productivity," *Human Resource Management*, Summer 1982, 67–73; H. C. Katz, T. A. Kochan, and K. R. Gobeille, "Industrial Relations Performance, Economic Performance, and QWL Programs: An Interpretive Analysis," *Industrial and Labor Relations Review* 37 (October 1983): 3–17.

4. This notion of "formally" democratic organizations is derived from J. Hage, "An Axiomatic Theory of Organizations," *Administrative Science Quarterly* 10 (1965): 289–320; Max Weber, *Economy and Society* (New York: Badminister, 1968); and G. L. Cafferate, "The Building of Democratic Organizations: An Embryological Metaphor," *Administrative Science Quarterly* 27 (1982): 280–303.

5. Much of this evidence is summarized in Richard B. Freeman and James L. Medoff, *What Do Unions Do?* (New York: Basic Books, 1984).

6. George Lodge, *The New American Ideology* (New York: Knopf, 1975).

7. This discussion is based, in part, on Thomas Kochan's model for understanding the various internal and external factors that influence the formation of union goals. T. A. Kochan, *Collective Bargaining and Industrial Relations* (Homewood, Ill.: Richard D. Irwin, 1980).

8. See, for instance, W. H. Holley, H. S. Field, and J. C. Crowley, "Negotiating Quality of Work Life, Productivity, and Traditional Issues: Union Members' Preferred Roles of Their Union," *Personnel Psychology* 34 (1981): 309–328; T. A. Kochan, H. C. Katz, and N. R. Mower, "Worker Participation and American Unions: Threat or Opportunity?" (Working Paper 1526–84, Sloan School of Management, MIT, 1984).

9. The United Auto Workers is divided into relatively autonomous departments (Ford, General Motors, and Chrysler, for example) with a union officer, usually a vice president, assigned to head each department.

10. After the 1982 "concession" contracts, a number of local leaders who supported these contracts lost their bids for reelection. Often these leaders were *also* supporters of quality of work life or employee involvement. While their election losses were most likely not tied to their support of QWL or EI, the oft-repeated assurances to local leaders may well have become somewhat clouded.

11. T. A. Kochan and L. Dyer, "A Model of Organizational Change in the Context of Union-Management Relations," *Journal of Applied Behavioral Science* 12 (January 1979): 61–78.

12. "Naumkeag's Story," *The Survey*, 15 January 1930, 466.

13. S. M. Jacoby, "Union-Management Cooperation in the United States: Lessons from the 1920s," *Industrial and Labor Relations Review* 37 (October 1983): 18–33.

14. This description is taken from Otto S. Beyer, "The Technique of Co-operation," *Bulletin of the Taylor Society* 11 (February 1926): 7–21.

15. All collaborative agreements include specific admonitions against involving work teams in the contractually based grievance procedure. Nevertheless, work teams inevitably surface a good many problems that would, if unresolved, lead to the filing of a formal grievance. Thus, work teams offer a kind of preventive grievance procedure, and reports of significantly reduced numbers of unresolved grievances at plants with collaborative efforts point to their relative success in such a role.

CHAPTER 8

1. Richard E. Walton and Wendy Vittori, "New Information Technology: Organizational Problem or Opportunity," *Office: Technology and People* 1 (1983): 249–273.

2. These two contrasting models of human resource management are outlined in Chapter 3.

3. Summer Slichter, James J. Healy, and Robert Livernash, "Union Policies Toward Technological Change" in *The Impact of Collective Bargaining on Management* (Washington, D.C.: The Brookings Institution, 1960).

4. *Automation and the Workplace* (Technical Memorandum, Office of Technology Assessment, Congress of the United States, 1983), Appendix B, 55.

5. Doris B. McLaughlin, *The Impact of Unions on the Rate and Direction of Technological Innovation*, Report to the National Science Foundation, Grant PRA 77-15268 (Detroit: Institute of Labor and Industrial Relations, University of Michigan–Wayne State University, 1979).

6. Markley Roberts, "Technology and Labor," in *Automation and the Workplace* (Technical Memorandum, Office of Technology Assessment, Congress of the United States, 1983), 91.

7. "Union Policies Toward Technological Change."

8. Leslie Schneider and I are studying the early experience with these mechanisms in AT&T and CWA and the factors that determine their effectiveness.

CHAPTER 11

1. See Richard E. Walton, "From Control to Commitment: Transforming Work Force Management in the United States," Harvard Business School 75th Anniversary Colloquium on Technology and Productivity, March 27–29, 1984.

2. John Dewey, *Schooling and Society* (Chicago: University of Chicago Press, 1899).

3. Frederick Winslow Taylor, *The Principles of Scientific Management* (New York: Harper, 1911).

4. Fritz J. Roethlisberger and William Dickson, *Management and The Worker* (Boston: Harvard Business School, 1939).

5. *The Crotonville Story* (Crotonville, N.Y.: Management Development Institute, 1978).

6. Ralph J. Cordiner, *New Frontiers for Professional Managers* (New York: McGraw-Hill, 1956).

7. Jack Porter, "Corporations That Grant Degrees," *Business and Society Review*, Spring 1982, 41–45.

8. Lester A. Digman, "How Well-Managed Organizations Develop Their Organizations," *Organizational Dynamics*, Autumn 1978, 63–80.

9. Thomas F. Gilbert, "Training, the $100 Billion Opportunity," *Training and Development Journal*, November 1976; and Ernest A. Lynton, "The Role of Colleges and Universities in Corporate Education" (Unpublished manuscript sponsored by the Ford Foundation, 1981, available through author, University of Massachusetts, Amherst, Massachusetts).

10. Ron Zemke, "U.S. Training Census and Trends Report, 1983 Training Budgets," *Training* 20 (October 1983): 34–39.

11. Seymour Lusterman, *Education in Industry* (New York: Conference Board Report, #719, 1977).

12. James L. Medoff, *The Importance of Employer-Sponsored Job Related Training* (Working Paper, National Bureau of Economic Research, Cambridge, Mass., 1982). Similar interpretation is offered by extensive analysis of such census data in Robert Zemsky et al., *A Statistical Sketch of Employer-Provided Training and Education, 1969–1981* (Philadelphia: Higher Education Finance Research Institute, University of Pennsylvania, 1983).

13. James L. Medoff, "Labor Markets in Imbalance: Review of Qualitative Evidence" (Working Paper, Harvard University Economics Dept., 1982).

14. "Retraining Displaced Workers: Too Little, Too Late?" *Business Week*, 19 July 1982, 178–179.

15. David McLaughlin, "The Turning Point in Human Resources Management," *The Hay Report* (Philadelphia: Hay Associates, 1984), 6, 8; and Kenneth N. Wexley and Gary P. Latham, *Developing and Training Human Resources in Organizations* (Glenview, Ill.: Scott, Foresman, 1981).

16. Adapted from Gloria Shuck Bronsema, "Education and Technology Change in the Corporate Context" (unpublished analytic paper, Harvard University Graduate School of Education, 1983).

17. Lynton, "The Role of Colleges and Universities in Corporate Education."

18. Jack Gordon, Chris Lee, and Ron Zemke, "Remembrance of Things Passé," *Training* 21 (January 1984): 22–38.

19. Jeremy Main, "The Executives Yearn to Learn," *Fortune*, 3 May 1982, 234–248.

20. Based on a categorization and coding of sources listed in *Training and Developing Organizations Directory*, 3d ed., ed. Paul Wasserman and Janice McLean (Detroit: Gale Research Co., 1983).

21. Edgar H. Schein, "Management Development as a Process of Influence," *Industrial Management Review*, May 1961, 59–77.

22. Kenneth R. Andrews, "Is Management Training Effective? II: Measurement, Objectives, and Policy," *Harvard Business Review*, March–April 1957, 63–72; and Kenneth R. Andrews, "Reaction to University Development Program," *Harvard Business Review*, May–June 1961, 119–121.

23. For more insight linking such human resources practices to business strategy, see Noel M. Tichy, Charles J. Fombrun, Mary Anne Devanna, "Stra-

tegic Human Resource Management," *Sloan Management Review*, Winter 1982, 47–60.

24. For an interesting look at an unconventional university offering, see E. Joan Kemp, "Expanding Management Minds at Dartmouth Institute," *Management World* 9 (July 1980): 8–11.

25. *Training by Contract: College Employer Profiles* (New York: College Board, 1983).

26. *Annual Report 1983* (Boston: Bay State Skill Corp., 1984).

27. P. C. Buchanan, "Laboratory Training and Organization Development," *Administrative Science Quarterly* 14 (1969): 466–489; Robert J. House, *Management Development* (Ann Arbor: Bureau of Industrial Relations, Graduate School of Business Administration, University of Michigan, 1967), 9; A. H. Kuriloff and S. Atkins, "T Group for a Work Team," *Journal of Applied Behavioral Science* 2 (1966): 63–94; Abraham Zaleznik, *Foreman Training in a Growing Enterprise* (Boston, Harvard Business School, 1951), 205–214; W. J. Underwood, "Evolution of Laboratory Method Training," *Training Directors Journal* 19 (1965): 34–40.

28. Pierre E. DuJardin, "Residential General Management Programs and Adult Development: An Exploratory Study" (unpublished doctoral dissertation, Harvard Business School, 1981).

29. M. S. Knowles, *The Modern Practice of Adult Education: Androgogy Versus Pedagogy* (New York: Association Press, 1970); and K. Patricia Cross, *Adults as Learners* (San Francisco: Jossey-Bass, 1981).

30. Lyndall F. Urwick, *Management Education in American Business*. Part I: *Management Education for Itself and Its Employees* (New York: American Management Association, 1954), 30.

CHAPTER 12

1. Dale D. Buss, "UAW Chief in an Awkward Spot," *Wall Street Journal*, 12 August 1982, 21.

2. Samuel Huntington, *American Politics: The Promise of Disharmony* (Cambridge, Mass.: Harvard University Press, 1981), 63.

3. The harsh interpretation of Locke followed and contrasted with that of many of the founding fathers—Thomas Jefferson, for example—for whom individual fulfillment and happiness required a "moral sense" or participation in, and obligation to, a community.

4. Huntington, *American Politics*, 39.

5. See Daniel Bell, "The Cultural Contradictions of Capitalism," *The Public Interest* (Fall 1970): 38–39.

6. Fuller became vice president for personnel administration and development in 1970 and was responsible with Bluestone for the introduction of QWL.

7. The MacNeil-Lehrer Report (transcript), 15 February 1982, 2, 4.

8. See, for example, Bayless Manning, "Thinking Straight about Corporate Law Reform" in *Corporation at the Crossroads: Governance and Reform*, ed. Deborah A. DeMott (New York: McGraw-Hill, 1980), 26–27.

9. William Greider, "The Education of David Stockman," *The Atlantic Monthly*, December 1981, 50–54.

10. Quoted in Herman E. Droos and Charles Gilbert, *American Business History* (Englewood Cliffs, N.J.: Prentice-Hall, 1972), 264.

11. John Joerr, "Smudging the Line Between Boss and Worker," *Business Week*, 1 March 1982, 91.

12. Charles Hecksher, "Unions Play Key Role in Quality of Work Life," *Workplace Democracy* 9 (Winter 1982): 18.

13. William J. Abernathy and Kim B. Clark, "Notes on a Trip to Japan: Concepts and Interpretations" (Working Paper 82-58, Harvard Business School, 1982), 8.

14. See *Hearings Before the Committee on the Judiciary, U.S. Senate, 92d Congress, Second Session on Nomination of Richard G. Kleindienst of Arizona To Be Attorney General* (Washington: Government Printing Office, 1972).

15. The 1981 decision of the Justice Department to drop its antitrust suit against AT&T is a current example.

16. Greider, "The Education of David Stockman," 54.

17. Press Release, 4 March 1981.

18. Thomas J. Schneider, "Quality of Working Life and the Law." Speech given at the Kennedy School of Government, Harvard University, 19 November 1981, 2–5.

19. Ibid., 8–12.

20. 7 July 1982.

CHAPTER 13

1. The faculty presenters were Paul Lawrence, Janice McCormick and Quinn Mills. (See Chapters 2, 6, 10 for their views.)

2. The faculty presenters were Calvin Pava, Shoshana Zuboff, and George Lodge. (See Chapters 4, 5, 12 for their views.)

3. The faculty presenters were Bert Spector, Michael Beer, and Jeffrey Sonnenfeld. (See Chapters 7, 9, 11 for their views.)

Index

This book was set electronically in Baskerville type on a Mergenthaler Linotron. John Baskerville (1706–75) introduced this transitional face, which broke for the first time from a pen-stroke form to one that considered the printing technology of the day. This typeface was a favorite of Benjamin Franklin, who introduced it to the American colonies. The book was printed by offset lithography on acid-free paper.